Looking Inside Out

By Elaine Davis

Elaine Davis

5-15-12

Contents

Acknowledgements

To Jennifer Hansen, for your assistance in writing this book. I couldn't have done it without you! We spent many enjoyable hours together. Your editorial skill, your suggestions and your computer expertise were appreciated more than words can say! I thank God for bringing you into my life.

Thank you, Mom, for your unconditional love for all of your children. For the Godly, caring, and unselfish way you live your life. I am confident that your constant prayers for my salvation and my safety were heard by God. I love you.

To my dear friend, Diana Elting. How very glad I am that I got to know you. It was meant to be! Thank you for encouraging me to open up when writing the manuscript. Your confidence in me moved mountains. You are a very special woman!

To Verla Sylvia. God ordained the moment when our paths crossed. Through your encouragement and constant prayers I have been strengthened in my battles to write and complete this book. Your continuous support and inspiration helped keep me focused. I love you, my precious friend.

May God Bless Each of You

Preface

They that sow in tears shall reap in joy.
Psalms 126:5

How does a person write a book, who hates to write? That was my dilemma…. For years I struggled with that thought. I knew that I could not do it on my own. But God, in His infinite wisdom, gave me the words to say and as I sat at my computer I constantly asked for His help. My story isn't that unusual in that many others have suffered and gone through much more than I have. All have a story to tell. This book has been written because God impressed it upon my heart to tell *my* story. So, I became determined to complete what I felt were His instructions. It was a difficult journey. In the early stages, there were times I went to the floor in shame and agony in recalling past memories. But from the beginning of my life, God had already orchestrated all of the chapters, painful or not. And that makes my story!

Thou hast turned for me my mourning into dancing: thou hast put off my sackcloth, and girded me with gladness; To the end that my glory may sing praise to thee, and not be silent. O LORD my God, I will give thanks unto thee for ever. Psalms 30:11-12

In my early twenties, I mentally fell apart and had to be hospitalized. As a possible result of shock treatments given to me at the time, some of my memory is gone. I have done the best I could in remembering certain events, although a lot of memories are lost forever. I have striven to ensure accuracy, and I hope the reader will forgive me if I have erred, however these are my true recollections. I happen to be a saver of memorabilia and those papers came to my rescue many times. I saved letters, divorce decrees, newspaper articles and journal entries. This book could not have been written without those documents. I have changed the names of some individuals mentioned in the book to protect their privacy.

I grew up in a religious Mennonite home and some of that church doctrine had a negative effect on my life. I speak quite freely about it. I can never escape my heritage, even though I am no longer a practicing Mennonite. Still, the fact that I am also different from the world is something that has never left my soul either. This book shows the conflict that religion had in my life. What I went through is *my experience* and mine only. I had to write my story as I lived it and I had to tell the truth. Yet, it is the religion of some of my loved ones. I am sure there are other church members who cannot comprehend my story, who have lived a whole and satisfying Christian life in the Mennonite faith. This book is not meant to be derogatory toward the church. I ask the reader to understand that.

This book tells the story about my search for love from my father. I tried endlessly to please him. My longing for love continued into adulthood, where I went from person to person trying to win the love that was withheld from me as a child. I didn't understand fully how codependent I had become. In order to earn love I smothered men with attention and control. I finally realized that I needed to break the cycle and become well myself before I could ever have a healthy and loving relationship.

It is my desire that the reader of this book will understand how the cycle of abuse can continue in the life of a person who is not mentally sound. I also hope that I demonstrate how the cycle can, and must be broken.

Running parallel to my life was my father's troubled life. How could I fix both? Only after I gave my heart to Jesus did I find the love of a father, my Heavenly Father. I found out that God's love is sufficient. I am worthy in His eyes. I am good enough—I do not need to, nor can I, fix my father's troubles. I can be complete...without my earthly father's approval.

Only on my father's deathbed, did he realize completely the love *he* received from his Heavenly Father. A love he longed for on this earth. But Heaven was a place he longed for, even more....

Chapter 1

In the Beginning

In the spring of 1945, the sand hills of Kansas were sunny and peaceful. Farm country surrounded the small town of Montezuma.

In the Mennonite (a strict religious sect) community that lived there, a certain young woman, Ruth Toews, (rhymes with Braves) prepared to marry Ben Schmidt, a man she barely knew.

They met through their church. As dating wasn't allowed, their marriage came about almost like an arranged marriage, with each one totally unfamiliar with the other person's traits or heritage.

Ben and Ruth would become my parents.

During World War II, Ben was working for the Federal Government as a conscientious objector (one who for reasons of conscience refuses to take part in warfare). He had signed up for two years, and the Forestry Department had stationed him just outside of Colorado Springs, Colorado.

When his friends started getting married, Ben thought he should do the same. He wrote to the ministers of his church and asked whom they might suggest. They mentioned Ruth, who had admitted having feelings for him to others, though the two of them had never personally met. They had only seen each other a few times through church activities.

After some thought he reasoned to himself, "Why, sure, I want a girl that has feelings for me, and I shouldn't look for another." He asked the ministers to convey his proposal to her.

When Ruth heard of this, at first she was unsure, because he had not paid her any attention. But soon she accepted by letter, through the same ministers, and the young couple began planning their wedding by mail. The first thing that really impressed Ben about her was her fine handwriting!

At the age of twenty-two, Ben was thin and tall, a bit over six feet. He always stood with his back straight and knees slightly bent. He had fair skin; blond hair over a high forehead; a prominent nose and ears that stuck out from his head; a wide mouth; and large green eyes that could gleam in a friendly smile or blaze in sudden anger.

Ruth was twenty years old, petite and slender with well proportioned legs. She had shiny brown hair and hazel eyes in a gentle, refined face. A welcoming smile revealed even white teeth. Her manner was softhearted and shy.

One week before the ceremony, Ben came home by train from Colorado. It was a busy week preparing for the wedding. As he didn't own an automobile, Ruth and her parents, Henry and Anna, took him shopping for his wedding suit in Dodge City. Because Ben worked for free while in the service, he had no money. Ruth gave him some to pay for his suit.

On May 20, 1945, they were married in a country church three miles northwest of Montezuma.

The next day, Ruth's family took them to the depot in Dodge City and they rode the train to Colorado. She writes of their train ride, *"I thought it rather strange that he didn't seem enthused or affectionate. He was downcast and said he had a headache."*

Ben had to report back to work so they didn't have a honeymoon. Conscientious objectors or CO's, as they were called, were required to live in government barracks without their wives. That meant Ruth had to find a job and a place to live.

A wealthy couple in Colorado Springs, the Shearers, hired her as one of their live-in servants. The Shearers' home sat on a tree-lined avenue, and a black wrought iron fence surrounded it. Though their two-story house was not huge, still it must have been intimidating for someone not used to the finer things in life. (After all, Ruth had come from a modest home, with an outhouse equipped with a Sears Roebuck catalog!)

Every working day, Ruth put on a neatly pressed white uniform. Her job was to cook all of their meals. It was quite formal. The Shearers would ring a bell for service and Ruth would respond to whatever they needed. She was a compassionate, caring and service-oriented person. Other servants in the home did the cleaning and laundry.

Ben soon became quite taken with his young, slender, beautiful bride, and the novelty of married love. He could visit her on weekends. Ruth's private living quarters included a bedroom and bath upstairs. Ben would come in through the kitchen door and go up the back stairway. (The front entrance was not to be used by the servants.)

Sunday was Ruth's day off. Sometimes they would go to the government barracks for noon dinner. Then often they would go for a scenic drive to the Garden of the Gods area, a National Park of towering red sandstone formations, or just to the countryside with friends who owned a car.

Very soon, Ruth began to wonder: Whom have I married? What kind of person have I married? Where did he come from?

Both their families had emigrated from areas of Poland and Russia to escape religious persecution and to seek a better life. [For a brief Mennonite history, see Appendix.] But they came from vastly different backgrounds. Ruth's ancestors were a cultured strain, educated and industrious. She had grown up in a clean, honest, good Christian home, and didn't know that Ben was from a line of self-righteous, rough, extremely poor people. At first she thought he just had bad manners, but then he began bursting out verbally in anger. Daily he broke her heart with insults, and she often wept.

Ruth became pregnant right away. Because Mennonites do not believe in wearing jewelry, she didn't wear a wedding band. Whenever she rode the bus to the doctor, alone and looking so young and vulnerable, she could feel other people's icy stares and wondered what they were thinking about her, and her protruding stomach. Did they think she was carrying an illegitimate child?

On March 30th, 1946, I was born and they named me "Gladys Elaine." Ben had wanted a boy. He was disappointed with me from that day forward.

When Dad completed his duty in the service, he moved the family back to Kansas. They were poor and owned nothing but their clothes and wedding gifts. Dad looked for a job, a car and a place for us to live. He accepted work on a farm as a laborer, which included a small apartment over the garage for his family. Mom said it was so cute! She was thrilled to start housekeeping. Finally they were a family on their own!

Happiness was not granted for very long. Dad made meager wages and he was frustrated in trying to make a good living for his wife and new baby.

He would get angry over nothing. When I was about a year old Dad tried to get me to walk. I couldn't, and he became very impatient—then enraged. He grabbed me and threw me down on the bed. Mom witnessed this and she sobbed, heartbroken that her precious child was being abused. It was more than she could stand. Angry, and possibly ashamed, Dad hurried outside, realizing what he had done.

While he was outside, Ruth's parents happened to drive in the yard. Before they could get out of the car, Dad rushed inside to tell Mom to wipe away her tears and stop crying. He didn't want any of his conduct exposed to others! He *ordered* her not to ever go for help, and even threatened, "I might as well kill myself if you do."

Shortly thereafter, Dad acknowledged the fact that there was something wrong with him. He was a tormented soul and he constantly apologized to Mom for his sinful behavior.

He went to the ministers of their church and asked them to pray over him to get rid of his "evil" nature. They would not. The ministers were not educated in dealing with psychiatric issues and they could not realize the severity of his mental illness. In essence, they ignored my father's plea for help.

In 1949, hoping to improve their finances, Dad found work with a company that constructed grain elevators throughout the Midwest. Different job locations required us to move frequently.

Dad built a small wooden trailer to carry our belongings and we towed it behind our car. Mom took it in stride, packing and unpacking. She had a knack for making each place her very own, placing lace doilies around and pretty curtains on the windows.

We were living in Alta, Iowa when Mom became pregnant for the second time. Alta was a small town without a good doctor available, so she made plans to have the baby back home in Kansas. A couple of weeks before the due date, Dad drove her and me to Montezuma. We stayed with his sister Jane and her husband Jake in a nice house on Main Street.

My sister, Pearl Alice, was born June 22, 1950. I was four years old and I became Mom's little helper. When Pearl was two weeks old, Dad came to pick us all up. He showed enthusiasm and a good attitude towards his new baby daughter.

Around 1951, Dad heard that some Mennonite people from Central Kansas were moving to South Dakota because land was cheap. Dad longed to be a farmer and he thought he might be able to afford acreage there. So we became the third Mennonite family to migrate to South Dakota. With very little knowledge about the state, we moved into unknown territory, far away from family and familiar things.

We first rented a house on a farm owned by Joe Arbeiter, about five miles west of Iroquois. It was a decrepit old place. Weeds and sunflowers as tall as the house covered the yard. The outhouse was quite a ways away down a path between the weeds, and for me it was a scary place to go.

It wasn't easy living there. Joe was very hard on Dad, having him milk the cows as early as four-thirty in the morning, work through the day in the fields, and then milk the cows again as late as ten at night.

One of my memories of that place was a shed behind the house that had a lot of books and magazines stored in it. I spent time in that shed, looking through old magazines such as *Life* and *Look*. I loved being surrounded by so many books, even if I couldn't read them and they smelled awfully musty.

On August 11, 1952, my second sister Mary Jane was born in Huron at St. Johns Hospital, twenty miles away and our biggest town in the area.

Our family was growing, but Mom grew sadder as she watched Dad's coldness in not showing love towards his children. He continued to want a son, only now there were three daughters in the family.

I entered first grade in Iroquois. I was the oldest child amongst the families that had migrated and therefore the first Mennonite child to make an appearance in the local school. My new classmates initiated me into the world of school by making fun of my pigtails! That was how little Mennonite girls wore their hair, and it was different from the other girls. The kids liked to sneak up and pull them whether I was sitting in class or climbing the stairs on the slide at recess. I was always saying, "Stop it!" I didn't like being teased.

During lunch I would walk by myself to the store and buy penny candy. It was hard to choose from all of the bins. I would run my fingers over the brightly wrapped pieces as I tried to make my selection. I thought it a real treat to be able to walk down the street from school and go into a store!

Dad would resume his grain elevator work during the winter months. After starting school in Iroquois, South Dakota, we moved and I continued first grade in Ringwood, Oklahoma. We lived in a small apartment alongside three other units that looked like a motel from the outside and were painted a dark brown. I had neighbor friends and we played on the sloping hills behind our apartments.

Our home was within close walking distance of the school. Here, I wasn't made fun of—it was a Mennonite community and my hair and style of clothes were a common sight. My favorite thing at recess was to play on the stainless steel slide. It had curves in it and was real slippery. I thought it to be huge!

Soon it was time to move again, to Fairview, just about ten miles west of Ringwood. I was still in the first grade. Now I had to walk across town to school. And on the way home in the afternoon I would take my time, lingering along the way. Being in "town" always fascinated me; it was so different from the country life. There were lights, and activity in town.

When Dad was finished with his next job, we moved back to South Dakota. I completed the first grade in my fourth school that year, in Osceola, South Dakota.

Chapter 2

Pioneers

In late spring of 1953, when I was seven years old, my parents bought their first home on the South Dakota prairie. The farm was half a mile west of Osceola, and seven miles north of Iroquois. Dad was pleased that he was able to purchase one hundred and sixty acres of land along with the farm buildings. He paid twenty-seven dollars an acre. We moved out of the rental farm, away from the landlord and onto our own piece of property.

Our driveway was just off the main road that led into Osceola. We had all the typical farm structures: A red barn with hayloft, where we often played among the hay bales; granary where we jumped in the stalls of oats or wheat; a tiny one-car garage, a shed, and a combination pig/chicken house. I detested the sloppy pigpen, as I had to go through a portion of it to get to the chicken nests to gather the eggs.

The windmill and a round galvanized horse tank sat a short distance west of the house. The windmill had a ladder attached and I often tried to climb the lower rungs but was never successful; it was just too high! One of my duties was to fill the horse tank. We had no horses, only cows, but have you ever heard of a cow tank? I would attach a long metal chute from the water pump to the tank. Up and down I would go and after a little bit the water would start flowing. The faster I went the faster the water gushed out and the tank would fill up.

In the summertime we kids would get into the tank to cool off. In the winter, it froze solid. Dad would have to chop through the ice on a regular basis so the cattle could have water.

Although it was the fifties, we lived like pioneers in our white wood frame house. On the first floor were the entry room, kitchen, living room and my parents' bedroom, all small rooms. Our only heat source for the whole house was a brown heating stove that stood in the middle of the living room. It burned oil and vented its smoke through a stovepipe that went up through the ceiling. Cold, but always clean, linoleum covered the floors. From the living room, a stairway led up to a hallway with two bedrooms where we kids slept.

Pearl loved to walk on the banister that overlooked the stairway. It was a long way down; had she fallen it could have been a serious injury. She was adventurous and kind of a daredevil!

We didn't have a bathroom or indoor plumbing. We had to haul in water for everything—back and forth, a never-ending task through all kinds of weather.

The outhouse stood east of the house, maybe twenty feet away with a wood-plank walkway and the field just beyond. To a child in the night, it seemed terribly far, especially when wind rustled the corn stalks in the field. Coming back from the outhouse, I always felt sure that *something* was behind me, and I couldn't run fast enough.

Monday was wash day. In the early days it was quite a process to do the laundry. First, Mom heated water in a large copper boiler on a two-burner hot plate in the utility room. She pulled the Maytag washing machine out of the corner to the middle of the floor and plugged it in. Then she pulled over two washtubs on legs and set them adjacent to the washing machine. The machine had an agitator to wash the clothes. I would stand there, intrigued with the clean smell and motion as the clothes twisted back and forth in the soapy suds. To rinse, Mom pulled out the soaking wet items with a stick and ran them through a wringer that she cranked with a handle. They dropped into the first washtub of clean rinse water. I would watch as she twirled them around with her hands and then repeated the wringer process into the other tub of rinse water. Then they were ready to hang outside on the clothesline.

It was my job to wash the line by walking along wiping a wet rag the length of it. I didn't like it when clothespins had been left on the line and I would have to take them off first. After the washing was complete and all the clothes hung out in the fresh air to dry, Mom would take a long hose and hook it up to the machine. She then pulled the hose through the open door and outside a long way. When she unplugged the holes in the tubs, the water drained out.

Once she discovered the convenience of a Laundromat, we piled our dirty clothes in laundry baskets and drove to Huron. I thought that was big time! I loved the sound of so many machines swishing. I would frolic, happy and content when we were at the Laundromat. There was noise and activity and we got treats. *I felt secure in places such as this.*

Saturday night we got our bath by the kitchen cook stove. In winter, Mom would turn on the oven and the gas burners to heat both the kitchen and the water kettles. We bathed in a small, galvanized tub that Mom put as close to the stove as possible. I huddled up and basked in the heat from the open oven and the warmth of the water.

Since we moved into the house, our utility room had been the place for laundry, washing our hands and getting a drink of water. Upon a washbasin sat a bucket of water with a long-handled dipper. When I got thirsty, I would take a drink right out of the dipper. We all used the same one and what water we didn't drink went right back in the bucket! On the washbasin was a white aluminum round bowl to wash our hands. To the side sat a white chipped aluminum soap dish with lye soap.

We kept a milk separator in one corner of the utility room. Our dairy cows blessed us with sweet milk every day. Using the separator, we would crank the handle with milk going one way while the wonderful, rich, thick cream went into another container. Mom cooked using a lot of cream.

Eventually water was plumbed into the house to three faucets, the kitchen, the utility room washbasin and the bathtub. And we got a hot water heater! Dad partitioned off one end of our utility room, just large enough for a small claw-foot bathtub. Now we had a bathroom…minus the toilet.

Mom would often kill a fresh chicken for our dinner. I watched from afar as she caught it and cut its head off. That chicken would flop all over the yard for quite some time! After it was dead, we took it to the windmill where we had access to water. I would bring out some boiling water from the house and Mom took the chicken by the legs and dipped it in the hot water, to make it easier to pluck the feathers. Pearl and I helped, but what a stink and a mess! The feathers stuck to our hands, and we needed lots of water to rinse off.

We had a mean rooster with big spurs. He was determined to chase us kids and frequently tried to jump on us. Mom was afraid that he would hurt us with his spurs. One day, the rooster actually followed me all of the way into the house. I screamed; one of the girls held the screen door open and I "shooed" him out.

Mom had had enough of his meanness! She thought, "I am going to punish that rooster so he won't do that again." She got her broomstick and chased him all over the yard. But when she gave him a good whack with the broom he keeled over right way. She hadn't meant to kill him, just teach him a good lesson! I can't remember if we ate him or not. Mom says he would have been a tough old rooster.

As I was not the boy Dad dreamed of having and I was the first child, he focused his personal anger and frustration on me. Dad couldn't stand that I was left-handed. He did everything he could to change my eating habit, determined that he would not have an "imperfect" child. At mealtime, as we sat at the kitchen table, he would slap my hands, once with a table knife while my family watched.

While doing my homework, I would write with my left wrist curled around the pencil and the paper nearly upside-down. Dad would become agitated if he happened to walk by and caught me writing that way. In anger, he would change the position of my hands and the paper.

I was corrected in whatever I attempted to do, criticized and faulted in how I looked. I was hurt, as I always attempted to do my best in everything I did.

My father was not affectionate. He never told me he loved me. He never held me or had me sit on his lap. Never was there a word of encouragement or praise. My dad didn't talk to me or acknowledge me except to say something that would lower my self-esteem.

I worried about this as I wandered around in our yard. It made me sad and bewildered, and I thought, "Why can't I make my dad happy?"

Pearl seemed to flow into everything and didn't cause problems of any sort. She, like all of us girls, was deprived of our father's love, but Dad wasn't unkind to her. She reports a happy childhood of her own.

When Mary Jane came along, Dad ignored her. She went to Mom for comfort. She has said she survived her first five years by being rocked in Mom's arms.

For the next few years, my father continued to do grain elevator construction work in the winter months in states to the south, and then return to work on our farm in the summer. I remember living in Texas, Missouri, Minnesota, Oklahoma, Nebraska, and Iowa. We usually had some of Dad's brothers and their families and other coworkers around us as we traveled from place to place.

On our frequent car trips going back and forth, we were often traveling on the road after dark. Sitting in the back seat, I watched excitedly as the lights of a town got closer and closer. I would go from one window to the other to take in all the sights and lights I possibly could. That was in the time before seat belts, and we could move around in the seat freely. As we passed through and beyond a town, I peered out the window, wanting the lights to last forever. I was sorely disappointed as the darkness crept back and surrounded us once again while we drove into the night.

Two Christmases stand out from the early years. In 1953, in Stromsburg, Nebraska, we lived directly across the street from the schoolhouse where I attended second grade. Although we did not believe in Christmas trees, decorations or Santa Claus, that year Mom allowed me to have a part in the Christmas program as a singing tree. She dressed me up in a green sheet with a hole cut out in the middle for my head to stick through. Then she wrapped silver garland around me. I had never worn such glitter. I shined and sparkled! I felt special. *For once, I looked like everybody else!*

In 1954, during my third grade year in Lincoln, Nebraska, we had a Christmas like no other. Our presents were few, but I got a doll, and best of all, two new books. I believe they were *Little Women* and *Hans Christian Anderson and the Silver Skates*. Really, the contents didn't matter so much as the fact that they were *my own books*, shiny and new.

Aside from Dad's ever-present criticism towards Mom and me, and always the abuse that he had towards me, for the most part the "elevator days" were pleasant for Mom. She didn't have to work like she did on the farm, and so her daily responsibilities were less.

My parents socialized quite a bit with coworkers and family members. And she made many "worldly" friends. Anybody that does not belong to the Mennonite church is considered "worldly." The term is used frequently and widely.

Dad was making better wages that were constant, and that would keep down his level of anxiety and worry concerning finances. At one point, Dad got promoted to foreman on his job. Because this gave him the authority and leadership that he craved, it also helped Mom's home life—he seemed to ease up on her.

Dad built a wooden tool box to store all of his tools. He painted it gray. That box went everywhere we went. We still have it in the family. When Dad got home from work each day, I would watch from a distance as he knelt down on the floor in front of the chest to put his tools in order.

There were always things to be done in the summer on the farm in South Dakota. And Dad insisted that I help. I worked as hard as a son would have when I was moving hay bales around or any other chore he would assign me. He also used teenaged hired hands on occasion. They wouldn't stay long. After being the target of one of Dad's tyrannical screaming fits, they'd walk away, never to come back.

I had such an unfulfilled longing for love and approval from my Dad. Every day I put great effort into my work to try and make him happy, but the outcome was always the same.

Usually I drove the tractor to plow or disk the fields. But I wouldn't do it the proper way and he would yell at me because I turned the corners wrong, didn't go straight enough or ruined equipment in some way. As I drove the tractor, he'd be running along behind it, waving his arms and hollering, "You just don't know how to do it right! Why can't you understand?" When he shouted, I couldn't think. That added to my frustration and confusion.

I did better at cutting and raking the alfalfa. That was my favorite because it was quite easy after Dad bought a big shiny new John Deere tractor. With the mower attached, I drove around the field, fascinated in watching the green alfalfa fall fast to the ground. I loved the sweet smell that permeated the air.

There were some mishaps when I drove the truck, like the time we had just filled it with bales of hay. I was sitting behind the wheel, poised to go, and I thought I heard Dad tell me to go, so I did. Well, I heard wrong, and he had not yet secured the load. I was right at an incline at the end of the field, and as I drove up it the hay bales tumbled off. I kept driving, not knowing how to stop a stick shift while going uphill. I was sure my dad was under those bales, but he appeared, running beside me, waving and yelling "Stop the truck!"

Another time, during harvest, Dad was on the combine loading grain into the truck bed while I sat waiting in the truck. I heard a shout and thought Dad wanted me to go, so I drove away, letting our hard-earned grain fall to the ground. That brought a really loud yell. It wasn't funny then, but it is now.

I wanted a bicycle and I begged Dad for one for a long time. One day he came home with a used bike. I wasn't real excited, as it was quite beat up. Dad found some leftover cans of orange and black paint and painted it. Then I thought it really hideous! I was devastated that he gave me something so ugly. I did not know he couldn't afford a better one.

I rode that bike around a little. Dad had told me sternly to stay off the main road; I could ride in the yard only. We had a good size driveway and I would ride to the edge of it, right next to the main road. One time Dad saw me do this. From his perspective, it appeared I had turned around on the road. He came running and yelled at me. I ran into the house with Dad following.

I have forgotten what happened next, but my sister Pearl had witnessed the incident and said Dad started beating me with a stick. Around and around we went. Cries of terror came from me, and dishes fell from the cabinet to the floor. Finally it was over, and I went to cry on the couch.

Pearl has written in her notes:

As a young child I knew there was a problem in our home…Dad had an extreme temper. His wrath and anger didn't come down on me, but I witnessed it often, on Mom and Gladys. I have many memories of Dad coming in with eyes "of fire" and yelling at Mom. Mom would be silent, the tears falling…falling on the floor, as she was peeling the potatoes or whatever. At times it would be mealtime, Mom would see to it that the food was all on the table, we were taken care of, even pouring the coffee for Dad, and then she would leave to cry…alone in their bedroom. I would feel so bad; I couldn't eat either…so upstairs to my bedroom I would go.

Chapter 3

Looking at the World

At a young age I began withdrawing into myself; trying not to let the darts of criticism and abuse penetrate too deeply within my soul. I changed my personality to fit the circumstances, and swayed my behavior to try and please whomever I was with. I did not develop my own character, but started pretending to be something I was not, for I felt certain…that I couldn't be me.

I didn't play with my sisters much. Pearl loved the cats on the farm, and she would dress them up in baby clothes and carry them around cradled in her arms. Mary Jane followed her everywhere.

Caught up in my own world, I spent a lot of time in my bedroom reading *True Story* romance magazines that my school friends gave me. Sometimes I played "schoolteacher" with a row of chairs in my make-believe classroom, or typed with my make-believe typewriter in my make-believe office.

Every morning before school we had a routine. Nervously, I would dress for the day, come downstairs and slip into my place at the breakfast table, hoping Dad wouldn't notice what I was wearing. I was afraid he would scold, or worse yet, make me change. It made no difference how I dressed or did my hair—he always found something wrong.

Next he'd read from the Bible for our daily devotions, then we would all kneel at our chairs for what seemed like an eternal prayer. Sometimes the school bus arrived and had to wait while we finished devotions. I didn't hear what Dad said then; all I could hear was my own mind saying, "Hurry up, hurry up so I can get on that bus!" I didn't like it if the bus had to wait for me.

My hair and dress were very unconventional from the other girls, and the older I got the more people noticed the contrast. I could not wear jeans, shorts, sleeveless dresses or white shoes. Mennonite girls had to wear plain dresses with sleeves (long or short), pleated or gathered skirts, and no lace or bright colors. Every dress was supposed to have a waist-line with a belt. Because of the cold winters, I also had to wear thick brown stockings while other children wore long pants. I hated all these things that made me feel *different*. I can't think of any reason for the ugly shoes. I really begged not to have to wear them.

Every once in a while I would get a box of hand-me-downs from a "worldly" friend, the daughter of one of my folks elevator coworkers. My mother was more lenient in her religious thinking, and she didn't mind if I wore these "fancy" but still modest clothes. Of course, she would never make or buy any such thing, but because we were poor, these clothes were needed. I loved to wear the ready-made blouses, dresses and skirts with cancans, but they were included in that early morning ritual at the breakfast table. And it all depended on Dad's mood whether I would be permitted to wear them or not.

While the "worldly" girls wore their hair short and curly, I was not allowed to cut my hair except when it became too long and hard to manage, and then we only trimmed the length.

As a young girl, I wore the required pigtails; then as a teen I wore it pulled up in a French twist. Most of the other Mennonite girls wore their hair parted in the middle. I rebelled by wearing mine parted to the side with maybe a little "spit curl" tucked in close. If Dad objected to my hair on a day that I dared to wear the little curl, maybe he would let the dress issue go and vice versa.

We couldn't wear makeup of any kind. I do remember sneaking (at school) a little lipstick on occasion when a friend would share.

Most of my elementary school years were spent at Osceola. In warm weather I could walk to school. Walking back and forth to town, with the sun overhead, I would look at my shadow as I walked on the gravel road, swaying my hips back and forth, intrigued by the movement of the shadow.

I was teased quite a bit. My first name, "Gladys," gave me nothing but trouble. The other kids would call me "Glad Ass" or "Happy Bottom." How I hated that! I did have a big bottom, big ears, big lips and too large a head for my body. I was as skinny as they come, and to top it off, bow-legged! And the children let me know it. I am double jointed at my elbows and while standing at the teacher's desk with my hands resting on her desk, my elbows would just stick out. The others thought that looked really freakish and they would point and laugh.

Always made fun of. *I was just not normal.*

For entertainment at recess we would carry a bucket of water and search for a gopher hole. A brave kid would pour the water into the hole while the rest of us watched. Then the gopher scrambled out, soaking wet. With all its fur slicked down, it looked like a drowned rat, and we thought it was hysterically funny.

Our classroom had all eight grades in one room. The building itself had four good-sized rooms, but only one was utilized for a classroom. Another room was a lunchroom, one was for play and big enough for a basketball net, and the fourth was used for storage. In this room were the stairs to the basement, which held the furnace area and coal room with the coal chute. Near the ceiling of this basement room was an opening into the crawl space under the rest of the building.

For a long time we kept hearing thumping and banging noises coming from under the floor of our classroom. It was exciting *and* scary, especially for any unlucky student who had to go alone to the storage room to get anything. None of the adults took us kids seriously when we told them about the strange noises.

One day during recess, some of the boys ran to our teacher, Ms. Claassen, speaking animatedly and out of breath, saying they had found something in the basement and she should come and see! So we all followed her, as she went down to peek into the crawl space. We saw a straw bed and empty pork-and-bean cans. Someone was living in there!

It was time to get our parents involved: maybe now they would believe us. They came to the school to figure out what was going on, but they were all too afraid to go to the basement! The men started banging on the metal door of the coal chute, and yelling, "Get out!"

I guess they scared the hobo away because the strange noises stopped after that. Our childish thoughts went wild as we imagined what he might look like. We assumed it was a hobo, anyway, and that he probably hopped on the train that went through town.

The local people called the train "the doodle-bug." I was fascinated by it, and relentlessly begged Mom to take us on a ride.

One day Mom gave in and gathered us kids and we got on the train for a trip to Huron. It wasn't even a passenger train. We sat in the caboose on wooden seats. Actually, the ride was quite rough! But I loved it. The desire to travel was quickly burning within me, and the whistle and the rhythm of the "clickety-clack" were soothing to my soul. Someone picked us up from the station and drove us back home.

On our farm, my favorite place was my upstairs bedroom. I would sit on the floor with my back against the bed and the open window just at my feet. It was a narrow space and I had to curl my knees in to fit. There I would read with the cool breeze wafting over me, the plastic curtains billowing gently. I could hear the birds singing. Mockingbirds, robins, and song sparrows filled the air with their melodies. This was my place of refuge, my escape from everyday life. I could dream of a better world.

I sneaked magazines into the house and cut out a collection of movie stars from them. If Mom had known about these magazines, she sure wouldn't have allowed them around the house!

I also cut pictures out of the Sears catalog, and those were my paper dolls. I kept those precious paper belongings stashed in a box underneath my bed. Natalie Wood was my favorite. I didn't really know anything about her, as I had never seen a movie, but she had big beautiful eyes and she was pictured in so many magazines.

Every once in a while Mom would decide to clean my bedroom. When she made up her mind to do something, she went after it. If she was in a "cleaning mood," watch out!

One day Mom took to my room with a broom to sweep the floor. She found my box under the bed and into the trash it went. Sitting on the floor just inside the bedroom door, I cried and *begged* her not to throw my things away. I was devastated. I sat there, watching what I loved being destroyed. My *possessions!* I don't really know why she did things like that. Maybe it was the contents, or maybe it was her general frustration. She was a busy person and didn't want anything extra that she would have to clean around.

In the summertime our house got so hot that Mom would take her dress off and do the ironing in her slip. She had a lot of ironing, with all of our cotton dresses! She kept a wet washcloth close by to wipe her brow as she perspired. We did not even have a fan in our house to cool down with.

When the temperature became unbearable, we would go to Huron and visit Newberry's, the one store that had air conditioning! We would hang out as long as possible meandering through the aisles. In the middle of the store was a lunch counter with stools, and Mom would treat us to a cherry Coke. I sat dangling my feet, sipping the cool iced drink, while observing the people all around me.

Some years we had frequent tornado activity. Because we couldn't have a radio or television, (and before weather radios) Dad's only way of determining the weather was to watch the clouds.

Often late at night, he would stand by the stairwell and call up to us, "Wake up, wake up! There's a storm coming! Hurry!" Having no storm cellar, we needed to go to the church basement, a mile away, as that was the only tornado shelter in the area. In our nightgowns we stumbled downstairs, half asleep and confused. While Dad herded us to the car, we clung to our blankets against a ferocious wind. It tried to rip off our clothes, and oftentimes it hailed or the rain poured. By the time we got settled on the hard benches in the church basement, the storm would be over. Gathering our blankets, we went home and back to bed.

We went from hot, windy, summers to bitter cold winters! As I have said before, we had a heating stove in the living room, and one time we set a glass of water six feet from it. The water froze. I doubt there was any insulation in our old two-story house. I presume the wind must have blown right through the cracks.

At night, we girls would take a flannel "sheet" blanket and spread it over the heating stove. When the blanket was hot, we folded it and ran upstairs as fast as we could, laid it between the open covers of the bed and jumped in. Often we used a hot water bottle for our feet. We piled on the blankets so thickly that we could hardly turn over, as we lay listening to the wind wailing like an animal. Some nights the wind whistled as it blew. I burrowed in deeper when the house creaked as though it would fall apart in the buffeting.

When we awoke one winter morning on the farm, the world had vanished into a blizzard. But Dad was determined to meet an appointment in DeSmet. He loaded us all into the car and we struck out in the weather. Snow was falling heavily, and the wind was quickly blowing it into big drifts on the road.

At the same time that Dad realized we couldn't continue the way we were going, we spotted a road grader on another road, and the folks decided if we could follow him, we would be OK. Turning around we went in the road grader's direction. Even after following his path, we didn't drive very far before getting stuck in a snowdrift. Now what?

Dad knew there were some neighbors not too far away, he would go for help. But Mom was afraid to stay in the car because she thought it would get covered up with snow. If another road grader came by, he might not see our car, and then he would plow right into us.

We all took out walking, in what seemed a long distance, but actually only a half a mile or less. It was just so terribly cold. My sisters and I had only our thin dresses on under our coats. Surely we had long stockings on, but I don't remember. When we found the farmhouse, our legs were already frostbitten.

The five of us huddled at the front door, knocking and knocking and hoping for someone to answer. I remember looking up at my Dad. He seemed so tall. All around us was white blowing snow. I shivered, in desperation for relief from the cold. It seemed like an eternity before a friendly face opened the door and welcomed us in.

Two old maids, three bachelors and their mother lived there, whom we had all met before. It was so warm in their house; I didn't mind staying there at all. We spent three days huddled around the fire stove, all of us in one room. At night Mom and we three girls all slept in one bed in an upstairs bedroom. I thought that quite an adventure!

The weather cleared up, but our car was still totally covered over with snow. The people that lived in the house took us by horse and wagon to our friends that lived two miles away. The snow banks were steep and it was scary…we were afraid the wagon would tip over. So whenever the wagon leaned too much we would get out and walk alongside.

We stayed with our friends for another day, before being able to retrieve our vehicle and wind our way home.

In its other moods, snow couldn't be more beautiful! On a bright sunny day, the very top layer would melt and in the evening, when it froze again, it just glistened and sparkled.

Under a full moon, there wasn't a prettier sight. The whole earth shone with brightness from the reflection off the snow. Pure white snowdrifts and wind-swept valleys. Raw splendor.

I have very emotional ties to the snow as the snowy prairie could also bestow upon the recipient a very lonesome feeling, with nothing but silence to listen to. When I walked through the deep stillness, my footsteps made a crisp sound, almost echoing. Amazed, I could stand in absolute quiet, hearing the distant neighbor's voices traveling across the plains. It seemed so empty and barren and I had a real sense of aloneness and what it meant. I was a solitary being.

During the Christmas season in South Dakota, we would go shopping in Huron. Usually on a Thursday evening, as that was the only night the stores were open. It was always a picturesque scene. Streetlights revealed the glimmering snow as it fell to the ground. I walked on the sidewalk, taking in the lights and sounds of Christmas. Music played on loudspeakers outside the stores on the street. I loved hearing *Pretty Paper* and *Silver Bells*. Once in a while we would be treated to caramel apples or caramel corn from the candy store. I was happy there, almost in a fantasyland.

When I was about in seventh grade, the school in Osceola closed and we had to take the bus seven miles to Bancroft. Grade school and high school were in the same building, with freshmen through seniors in one room.

Here I liked school much better. There were more students in my age group and so I could hide behind the others. At the same time, I didn't get as much negative attention. Friends were easier to come by and I seemed to be accepted better.

I volunteered to work in the kitchen during lunch hour where I helped ladle out meal portions. Behind me was a refrigerator with a radio on top, and I could listen to all the forbidden Fifties music that I so loved.

I wanted to be involved in the school activities. One year the drama teacher offered me the lead role in a play, and I had to decline. Remember, this is a very small school with an average class size of four to ten students! I think I really got asked because my pigtails and my southern accent fit the part. I was often teased about my accent, which I had acquired because of our many moves back and forth from the south. To me, it was slight, but the northerners noticed it!

Later, I was nominated for homecoming queen and had to say no. Again, a very small class, with only a few girls eligible and different rules. Nevertheless, it was difficult. To achieve some recognition, then to go through the humiliation of saying no, when I didn't want to say no.

My classmates did not understand why I couldn't participate. I didn't understand either. I knew only that Mennonites considered all such activities "too worldly." It was a constant reminder of the fact that I did not fit in. I didn't fit anywhere.

I especially yearned to go to the dances! I craved the feeling of celebration, *the joy that I imagined dancing to be.* One time I peeked into the auditorium when it was decorated and ready for the prom. Blue and silver streamers and stars hung from the ceiling. Everything seemed to glitter. I envisioned myself twirling in the middle of it all and thought, "I just *have* to find a way to attend." But I knew I could only stand outside and look in with longing.

While riding on the school bus one day, a classmate, Nick, asked me to be his date. There was no point in asking my parents, and I told him that I could not go.

The one activity I was allowed was singing in our music class. I participated in every school group I had time for, whether it was in the chorus, solo or girl's glee. Plus, I had a big crush on my music teacher!

I learned the songs *Bless This House, May the Good Lord Bless and Keep You,* and *He* at school. I would practice singing at home and Mom told me later, "You did the best you could! I don't how you could sing with such feeling and so good, when everything was bad all around you at home." After rehearsing, I then soloed in church each of those songs at different times.

Each year our school would go to other towns to compete in school contests, and this was always a highlight for me.

We had a State Blind School in the area and one year their students sang *Somewhere Over the Rainbow.* They walked to the stage in a line, each one touching the shoulder of the person ahead of them. I could not comprehend how these young people could sing this song with such conviction. After all, they could not see the beauty of a rainbow or the blue skies. How could they be so happy? I was miserable and I could see!

Dad did not attend my school events. (I do think when I was in Osceola he came to a couple of Christmas programs when I was quite young, but they were casual and more social events). I had a very difficult time accepting that. He was a sociable person in other areas of his life, how could he not take any interest in me? Not even to go to my eighth grade graduation! Crushed, I wanted him to acknowledge my achievements.

There was no place to find acceptance or comfort, other than my bedroom, where I was alone. In my room I wasn't reminded of my inferiority, or my differences. I was safe from criticism. My discovery: *The only time I am happy is when I am by myself.*

That caused me to be in constant turmoil. The conflict between being isolated and happy, where no one could attack me, but not wanting to be alone, because of the gut-wrenching loneliness.

We often went to St. John's Hospital (which was owned by the Catholics) in Huron to visit sick friends and acquaintances. We kids had to stay in the lobby, as children were not allowed into the patients' rooms.

While I waited, I would notice the nuns in their flowing black habits. Back and forth they scurried, past us and down the hall. Their headdresses seemed so tight on their faces, and their rosary beads dangled in the folds of their long robes. They were *different*, as I was different. Fascinated, I sat there thinking, *"But I am different even from them. How do they feel? Do they take pride in their dress, or is it just more rules to follow?"* We were both bound by the customs of religion, and we were not ordinary. They appeared to embrace their faith, as I fought mine.

Chapter 4

Family Ties

S everal times a year, we would travel to Kansas to visit both sets of grandparents, where they both lived during my youth.

Dad was the oldest of fourteen boys and girls, five of which had died in infancy or at a young age. He often talked about his brother Eddie, who was born in the truck and died three months later in the same truck, for the family was constantly traveling, like Gypsies.

Growing up, all he could see and feel was poverty, sickness and sorrow. He said they never had enough food to eat, nor clothes enough to wear. His family lived in shacks with dirt floors. This acute poverty and feeling of inferiority was something that he spoke of so often to our family.

Dad wrote in his notes:

When I was a very little boy I used to stand by the telephone pole and listen to the hum of the lines and I would be very, very sad of other sounds of distance.

As a teenager, a lot of responsibility was put on him to help earn money for food and gasoline. During a time they lived in San Antonio, Texas, he and his younger sister Mabel made broom holders by twisting wire and sold them door-to-door for ten cents. He also spent a lot of time picking cotton, cutting his fingers on the bolls, which are the tough, sharp seed pods containing the cotton.

Sometimes he picked watermelon. When he got hungry he would find a good melon and drop it on the ground. It would split open to expose the center, the sweetest part, and he would eat it. Then on to the next melon he would go, until he was full.

Eventually his family settled in Oklahoma where they were from originally. Going to school was extremely difficult for Dad because he was teased for wearing shabby clothes and having bare feet. He really did have to walk five miles to school. One of his schoolteachers told him he could be a great teacher or leader, and that is truly what he wanted to become. He often reminded us of her words.

When he was about eighteen, he and his parents became members of the Mennonite church. For his dad, Louis, it was short lived. Louis thought he knew everything better than anybody else; self-righteousness is what they call it. He even knew better than the church; he was always right and would listen to no one else's viewpoints. Soon after joining, he was excommunicated.

In my Dad's memoirs he wrote:

We lived a very simple life because of lack of money. Sometimes dad would take the songbook and sing such songs as "At Calvary" and "Rest over Jordan." I would stand behind him as he sat on a chair and try to sing along with him. Those songs taught me something about Jesus. Mother would often sing "Hallelujah, Thine the Glory, Revive Us Again." Through these songs I learned something about our Lord. I never went to church except for funerals for

*my brothers and sisters. It was a sad life for me, and
I often cried.*

Eventually, his parents moved to Montezuma, Kansas.
My paternal grandmother Cora died when I was about ten
years old. I remember seeing my father sobbing, grief-
stricken at her funeral. I hardly knew her.

After my grandmother's death, my grandfather eventually went to live with his children, staying with one, and then
traveling on to stay for a while with the next one.

I was always frightened whenever Grandpa Schmidt
came to spend time with us in South Dakota. It didn't matter
if he came to our house or if we were at a relative's home.
He would come after me and attempt to greet me with a bear
hug. If he did catch me, he would attack from behind, his
arms reaching around to grab at my small tender breasts. He
would laugh and giggle as if making fun of his playfulness!
I would squirm out of his arm hold and break away, saying
over and over, "Don't touch me, *don't touch me!*" I would
run and hide behind my mom for protection.

My Grandpa gave me the creeps. I wanted nothing to
do with him. I didn't like to see the look in his eyes. I knew
I could not trust him. To me, he was a dirty old man with a
scraggly white beard. Yet, on occasion he would give my
cousins and me shiny silver dollars as a gift, and we thought
that was special. It was like, "grab it and run."

As I tried to escape being around him, I did not realize he
was also fondling my female cousins. Talking in later years,
we realized we had all gone through this molestation and
terrible fear of him.

We wondered why our parents never confronted him.
Maybe it was just too difficult to deal with. In those days,
where would they have gone for help?

Mom's maiden name was Toews. She grew up in Montezuma, Kansas. Even with two brothers and eight sisters in her family, she said she had a happy childhood. Although her family was poor, they had a stable family life. They seldom moved, and always stayed in the same area.

Grandpa Henry was a serious, quiet man, not very ambitious. To help make ends meet, Grandma sold goods in town—home-baked cookies, pies, and bread, eggs and fresh butchered chickens. She always sang or laughed with the children as they did their chores. Sometimes Grandpa would say, "Is it *that* funny?"

Mom's family heritage was Mennonite, and she grew up in a strict Christian home. She has written in her journal:

Dad gave us instructions from the Bible, and Mother taught us to be submissive to our husbands. We all got hugs and kisses and love. Quarreling and anger were not allowed in the children.

Once when we were traveling through the Kansas sand hills on our way to Grandpa Toew's home, my parents got into a loud argument over her driving. Mom pulled over and stopped the car on the side of the road. Dad jumped out, hollering and waving his hands. I sat in the back seat, terrified. There was no place to run to; I had to sit there and watch and listen. I started wringing my hands excessively. After a while Dad got back in the car and we continued on our way. When we arrived at my grandparents' house and got out of the car, it was as if nothing had happened.

The emotions of that day have stayed with me. For years, if I heard any kind of argument or simply recalled painful memories, my hands would begin to tingle strongly, itch and break out in red with white speckles, like they had on that frightful day. I still cannot tolerate listening to any kind of debate or strong discussion.

I liked to play with my cousins, and there were usually some around whenever we visited. We would walk down the drive and onto the road. It was very sandy, so we would take our shoes off and trudge our way through the automobile tracks. I thought it a lot of fun. The sand was deep enough that a car could get stuck.

For one of our pastimes, we kids would sit and watch Grandma Anna working at the kitchen table, spreading it with lots of flour and making thick noodles. Sometimes she would cut out donuts and then fry them in the skillet until they were the biggest and plumpest I have ever seen. We could hardly wait until we could eat them. Ah, that wonderful taste and aroma that filled the kitchen.

With such a large family, they had a big table so everyone could fit around it. On the backside along the wall was a long bench to sit on. And at mealtime, with Grandpa sitting at the head of the table, we bowed our heads while he prayed. They were long slow prayers and he seemed to mumble. I never could discern a word he said! I wonder if the others understood.

Top: My father (in back row second from left) and his siblings. Bottom: Dad demonstrating how to make broom handles. (used by permission Fairview Republican)

Chapter 5

Pluma Mousse

I grew up in a very religious home. Sunday was a full day. We would scramble to get ready to go to Sunday school, then morning church service. Afterward, almost every family had dinner with others somewhere, or had company at their own home. It was tradition. Perhaps the adults would take a nap in the afternoon.

The day finished with an evening church service—and then my anxiety would rise. When I was quite young, the ministers started pressuring me to "join church." Sometimes after the evening service, when I sat in the back seat of the car waiting for my parents, I'd spy a minister walking towards me in the night. *Oh no.* My heart raced as he tapped his fingers on the window and asked to talk. I'd be thinking; if I wanted to talk, I would still be in the building. But nevertheless he would get in the front seat. He'd turn around and point his finger in my face, saying: "Aren't you concerned about your salvation? Don't you feel convicted? Don't you know you'll go to hell if you don't join?" I felt helpless. My body tensed up with fear and anxiety. Of course, I wanted to be a good girl, but I didn't want the ministers telling me what to do. I was tired of their threats and I rejected their insistence. I would know when I wanted to accept Jesus as my Savior!

Revival meetings were held once or twice a year. Prior to revivals, the local church membership would vote to request guest ministers from other Mennonite congregations. The meetings would last for about two weeks, with church every night.

During the day, the ministers would go around and visit members at home to make sure they were ready for the upcoming Council meetings. Suppose you wanted to join church. A person could go forward and accept Jesus when the invitation was given in church. Or you would tell the ministers when they met with you and then later, in church, you would need to publicly make your confession of when you experienced God coming into your life.

Any new converts would be baptized in regular church services. Baptism is done through the sprinkling of water.

During Council meetings (in which only members could attend) each church member was expected to stand and give a personal testimony of what was happening in their life spiritually. The ministers would determine whether the congregation was ready to have communion, if they felt satisfied with the unity and humbleness of the members.

The Revival ended with a special Council meeting when the ministers held communion and foot-washing with the members.

Finally I gave in, and to appease the ministers, I was baptized into the Mennonite Church in October of 1957 at the tender age of eleven.

When a girl or woman was baptized into the church, she was then expected to wear a head covering everywhere, even at home. For everyday, the covering was a triangular piece of solid-colored cloth that we tied on the back of our head, securing it with bobby pins and tucking in the ends at the nape until it was round and smooth. As young girls, some of us would try and pin the covering as far back as possible so our hair in the front would show.

For church we wore what we called our "Sunday" head covering. This was shaped like a regular square scarf but was made of a special material. Some were fancier than others in fabric, either light or sheer, or thick, or hemmed with a scalloped stitch. It was folded in a triangular half before putting on. This went over our basic head covering.

Upon first entering the church building, girls would head for the restroom and spend quite some time adjusting their coverings, centering the point in back, and making sure the tails under the chin were tucked in. After a final glance in the mirror we walked out of the restroom and into the sanctuary for the service. There I would sit with my precious cloth handkerchief folded neatly in my lap. I had quite a collection, as I would always try to match the color of my handkerchief to my dress.

Whenever we went visiting to another congregation, which was often, we would have to bring our Sunday covering. To keep it from getting wrinkled, we would wrap our covering in newspaper, roll it up, and put it behind the back seat of the car, the safest place. It was unthinkable to enter a church service without the Sunday head covering.

When I was young, I wore my covering to church, but rebelled and would not wear it at home or to school, and continued to put my hair in a French twist. Funny, Dad didn't comment about the missing head covering, as much as he did about my hairstyle. My hair was either too wavy in the front or parted too far to one side. According to the "doctrine" or rules, it was supposed to be parted in the middle.

Conversely, if a woman chose to leave the church, she would shed her head covering and cut her hair, maybe even take to wearing makeup and fashionable clothes.

Sometimes such an (expelled) person would come to a wedding or a funeral. I would stare at her, wondering, *"How could someone just throw away her Mennonite heritage?"* It was inconceivable for me to imagine doing such a thing. Even in questioning many facets of the religion, I didn't think it possible. Until years later, *until it happened to me.*

Somewhere around this time my little brother, Earl Monroe was born. Dad finally got his son. I remember that Mom wore such pretty dresses during her pregnancy. In those days, pregnant women always wore two-piece outfits. For whatever reason, she bought ready-made dresses. One in particular was navy blue with white accents. The top had pressed in pleats. That was one time I realized how very beautiful my Mom was! Earl was born on the ninth day of February, 1958, in Huron at St. Johns Hospital. I am the oldest and my brother is the youngest of the family. With an age span of twelve years between us, we didn't share many things growing up. He was very cute and a good child. As he grew, of course, Dad couldn't help but spoil him a little bit. But I was gone from home by then.

Shortly after my parents moved to South Dakota, the Miller family moved and they had children around my age, Lyle, his brother Stewart, and their sister Marilyn (they also had older and younger siblings). Also, a distant cousin, Corrine and her family came. The membership was growing, and I now had a small circle of church friends.

We would hang out together almost every Sunday after-noon. Lyle, being the oldest of our group, would drive us around. Gas was cheap back then!

If we felt really brave, the guys would let air out of the tires. Then we would line the car up onto the "doodle-bug" train track that ran through our farm property and away we would go. Or maybe we would put a penny on the track and wait for the train to come by and run over it. We would retrieve the smashed coin, feeling proud of ourselves.

The church had many rules. We couldn't have a television, radio, or any musical instrument in our home. We were not allowed any "worldly" activities such as dancing, playing cards, watching or playing in baseball or basketball games, swimming in public pools, going bowling or attending movies. I was drawn toward photography, but owning a camera and taking pictures were not permitted. Sometimes on the sly I would use my Uncle Fred's camera (he was not a Mennonite). Other church people seemed to just accept the rules, but I hated them.

Our most usual entertainment was getting together with other young people, to spend an afternoon or evening singing. Often others would join in, younger and older. Once in a while one of the guys might have a pitch pipe in his shirt pocket and that helped get us started in the proper key.

Our songbooks had shaped notes to help us sing *a cappella* in a beautiful four-part harmony, soprano, alto, tenor and bass. Many of us just sang by ear. I will never forget the day we discovered a new song—*How Great Thou Art*.

Marilyn and I grew up together as girlfriends. I liked being with Marilyn for the fun times we had. Her personality was carefree, outgoing, and never at a loss for words. Many a Sunday afternoon we would gather in her kitchen, us girls sitting on the counter with our feet dangling, while Marilyn made fudge or unbaked chocolate cookies. Lyle loved to tease. He would get a kitchen towel, twist it up and swing at us with it. The towel made a scary popping sound and we would jump away, much to his delight.

Lyle liked me and we started "going together." We just kidded around. He had a great sense of humor, and I needed laughter to forget the sadness in my life. We spent a lot of time with each other.

I guess we knew we would get married someday. I don't think we dated alone until I was about sixteen and he was nineteen. We were not supposed to "date," but we broke the rule.

As we were not allowed to do the usual teenage activities, he and I would drive around. Lyle would park in a deserted field just off a main road, then get the antenna out of its hiding place in the trunk, attach it to the car, and turn on the radio. There in the dark with the moon shining in through the car windows, sitting close in the front seat we would listen to music and smooch. Before leaving, the radio process would have to be reversed to be sure the telltale sign of the antenna was put away. Most of the members of the church ripped the radio itself out of the car so this sneaky trick couldn't be used.

Driving us home from Huron on hot summer days, Dad often stopped by the produce stand. The watermelons were kept chilled in a cold water aluminum tank. Telling us to listen, he would tap each one to find the right sound. "When a melon is ripe, it has just the right echo."

After making our purchase we would either take the melon home to eat, or better yet, go to the city park that was nearby.

Sitting at a picnic table under a large shade tree, with the soft green grass beneath our feet, we would indulge in the wonderful coolness of the sweet melon, savoring any respite from the heat.

I loved the park. It sat next to a winding river. There was a special flower garden with beds of flowers arranged in beautiful colors. In another area a lily pond resided. A stone wall with an archway separated the flowers from the playground. This place was another haven for me. I could be swept away in its beauty. With its lush grass and immense trees it was different from the dry dusty dirt and mostly weeds on the farm.

I looked forward to rainy days, which meant we couldn't do any farm work. We would go to town or have company. That is when we had time to make ice-cream, and it was the best as we would use our fresh cream from the farm. The men would cover the ice-cream freezer with a stack of towels and rugs, and then we children took turns sitting on it while the adults cranked away. It was fun and we laughed, especially when my folks' good friends, Ernest and Viola came over. We would not do this as a *family* activity, only when we had company.

On Sunday, almost always we either were invited out or we had company for the noon meal. Mom fixed fried chicken, mashed potatoes with cream gravy, corn, tossed salad, sliced tomatoes, creamed sliced cucumbers and homemade bread or rolls, or pot roast with brown gravy. Most of it was home grown and home canned.

We grew up enjoying to the utmost her special German/ Dutch cooking. Things like *pluma mousse*, a plum pudding, or *vereniki*, a sweet dough that she stuffed with a dry cottage cheese mixture or Concord grapes, and then deep-fat fried. We poured syrup over the fritters. She also made New Year's Cookies (a sweet dough filled with raisins) deep fried and then rolled in granulated sugar. They were best eaten hot out of the frying pan! Yummy!

Mom worked outside the home to earn money to pay the bills and especially the groceries. She believed that the man should provide for the home, but came to realize quite early in their marriage that she would have to contribute financially. Mom accepted it, albeit reluctantly.

With us kids in tow, Mom cleaned house and did the ironing for a number of different households in Huron. A wonderful couple, Bob and Betty Snyder, had a collection of hundreds of record albums. While Mom worked in their home, I operated the record player. This was an opportunity for me to listen to "worldly songs." Mom enjoyed them as much as I did; in fact she'd sing them later. I would go through the albums and make my selections of songs, hoping there would be enough time to listen to all of them.

My father was a hard worker. He put in long hours when the seasons called for it. I remember when he would be out in the field working by the tractor headlights late at night. There wasn't a lazy bone in him.

Dad loved to go out visiting in the evening, and insisted that Mom go along. She had no choice, and tired of it quickly as she was not a sociable person like he was. Dad was such a talker and they generally returned home late.

That was very hard on Mom, as Dad did not help her with anything. It was her responsibility to dress all of us kids, including braiding our hair when we were young, prepare the meals, keep the house clean, do laundry, help milk the cows and slop the pigs, in addition to her house-cleaning jobs. I saw her take frequent naps. She said it was to keep herself going mentally and physically.

Summertime meant taking lunches out to the field. Dad's farm machinery seemed to frequently break down, and too often Mom had to drop everything when Dad needed her to run an errand for repairs. To Dad, only what he needed done was important.

In addition, Mom was enduring judgment from the church. Dad's constant complaints to the ministers brought visits to her from them on a regular basis. They would go sit in the car to keep us kids from overhearing the conversation, where the minister would shake his finger at her in disapproval, of who knows what.

In Dad's illness, he couldn't see that he was the cause of his own misery. Quite possibly Dad had inherited some of the mental problems that were manifested in his family background.

I remember when we used to go visit relatives in Oklahoma. There, I always heard about the "crazy aunts." They kept ferocious dogs on the yard, and the aunts walked around with long sticks. I sat in bewilderment at the scene and listened as the adults argued. I couldn't wait until it was time to leave.

In moments of desperation Dad admitted to himself that all was not right in his mind. He tried to change over and over, but there seemed to be another force in control that he could not overcome. He *must* have evil in him, what else could it be?

Mostly, he believed *everyone else* was the reason for his unhappiness. And *they* needed to be fixed! *And then, everything would be OK.* Of course, Mom was his main target.

One cool autumn day his rage towards Mom got too loud and I ran away, out into the cornfield. I walked between the rows of the brown droopy cornstalks, until I came upon a wagon out in the field where I sat until I felt it was safe to go back to the house.

Other times when Dad started raising his voice inside the house, I would go sit on the front porch steps to get away. Then Dad would come outside and head towards any of the buildings on the farm. After a while, Mom would follow and fearfully ask, "Where's Dad?" He would frequently threaten her that he was going to kill himself. If I told her he went to the barn, she'd whisper, "Oh Gladys, I don't want to go look for him. What if I find him dead, hanging from a rafter?" As a child, that was almost more than I could take.

Yet, another day would dawn, and I would find Mom working and singing in her beautiful soprano voice, *Love Lifted Me, Cruising Down the River,* or even better, *Mocking Bird Hill.*

Mom told me, "One time I'd had all I could take and I decided to leave. You were probably in your teens then. I packed the car and headed out of the driveway. I stopped to pick up the mail, and there was a letter announcing that company was coming. So I went back, unpacked the car and got ready for the visitors."

Chapter 6

Desperate to Please

We kids were frequently left to ourselves whenever Mom and Dad were out visiting. I would stay by myself as though in my own little world. Home alone, the yard always seemed bigger and scarier. Nevertheless, I spent a great deal of time just outside the front door. If I felt brave enough, I would walk a little distance from the house and look towards the northern lights, or maybe see just how far the Milky Way went across the sky.

There was something fascinating about the moon. In the country there were no lights to interfere, nothing to detract from its glowing presence. As the evening darkness fell, I would sit on the front steps of the house and feel the warm breeze, while staring at the immense sky with the moon and all the stars shining brightly. It was comforting and yet haunting, because I was alone, and the space around me was so vast, as if it went on forever. I felt like such a tiny, insignificant creature, unprotected, naked and surrounded by a frightening solitude.

If folks were gone, sometimes in the evening I would sit at the kitchen table, my head resting on my folded arms, while listening to a small beige transistor radio that Lyle had loaned me. I was drawn to real country tunes with their steel guitar twang.

The popular song *Harbor Lights* was a favorite of mine, a song about loneliness in love. But hearing it only made me sadder. I would listen to this music and sob from the depths of my heart, a gut-wrenching ache of despair, with no hope of better things to come.

I wanted to be hugged by my dad. I wanted him to approve of something that I had done. I wanted to be praised by him. I wanted to be acknowledged. But in my heart I could only see another sad day ahead, just like the one I was living.

I was very aware, and in tune with Nature. When the wind blew through the wheat fields, I was transfixed by the way the golden stalks bent and glistened in the gusts. And, in our difficult dry soil, I planted pink, red and yellow zinnias in front of the house, and pink petunias along the path to the outhouse. There was comfort in watching the colorful blooms as they struggled to survive. Even in their sparseness, I thought they were just beautiful. They were the color in my world, those bright pink petunias....

I strained to hear every chirp from a mockingbird or song sparrow. Their music consoled my spirit. It drowned out the silence of my strict life and the echoes of reproving words. It was perfection, and I wanted to stop time so as not to lose the sound.

We lived only a little over a mile from Osceola Lake, so it didn't take much of an excuse to go there. From the main road, a narrow lane led down to the lake. Whereas we didn't have shade trees on our farm, the lake had plenty. In the spring, we had to squeeze our car down this path between rows of overhanging lilac trees. A purple fragrance filled the air. Cattails bloomed in swampy areas and from a small dam the occasional spilling water chuckled.

The park's east area had a grove of tall shade trees and a stone fireplace. Before our new church building was completed, weather permitting, we would hold our church service under the trees, sitting in a circle on log benches with the breeze wafting about, keeping us cool.

Often we would bring our picnic baskets and share a meal together. Afterward I could run freely and play with Marilyn and other friends. This lake became a sort of sanctuary for me; most of the memories are happy.

A few times Dad went fishing at the lake, and he would bring us girls. It would be a big decision for him to take the time off. We grew anxious as we watched him get bait and tackle ready.

When we arrived at the lake, he didn't engage us in the activity, didn't show us how to bait a hook or use the pole. We sat on the bank and watched while he threw his line in again and again. Soon, as the sun sank to the west, Dad still wouldn't have a fish. I hunched over as if to call one up for him: *Please, please, I want Dad to get a fish so he will be happy.* Usually we went home empty-handed, with sad faces and mosquito bites. My sister Pearl, on the other hand, thought the outing was fun.

Occasionally Dad would take us out in a small rowboat. I think the old boat just resided at the lake, as Dad didn't own one.

One particular day, Dad announced, "You kids need to know how to swim. Maybe I'll just throw you all out of the boat." He didn't, but to appease him, I waded out in the muddy water for a short while. I was in an "everyday" dress, as we were not allowed to wear swimsuits. Upon arriving home I took my wet clothes off in the utility room. Then I screamed in horror, and jumped around terrified: My legs were covered with black leaches. Mom came to my rescue and pulled them off one by one. It was a dreadful incident....

With friends and family, we would also have picnics at Spirit Lake, about fifteen miles east of our farm. The water was clean, with a small sandy beach. This is the lake made famous by the Laura Ingalls Wilder books.

One time my family took an overnight "vacation" to Lake Poinsett, about forty miles away. We were *so* excited about going. Dad rented a cabin right close to the water. We were thrilled with our little cottage with a screened-in porch.

That evening, before I went to bed, I walked to a small store nearby and bought a candy bar. As I returned, a radio somewhere filled the air with Patsy Cline's song *Walking After Midnight*.

I was in awe of everything…the music, the bright cabin lights shimmering through the trees in the darkness, the summer sounds of frogs by the water and the waves splashing onto shore…. As I skipped along, my mind was filled with the realization of a bigger world out there that I was not a part of. Yet, for a brief moment, I *felt* like I belonged. I was content. I felt secure.

The next morning Dad rented a motor boat. We had never ridden in one before, and we couldn't stop grinning as we sped across the lake. All too soon, it was over and we had to go home.

Even though some of Dad's siblings didn't really get along, where one moved another eventually followed. When I was around the age of thirteen or so one of Dad's younger brothers, Uncle Dean, worked for Dad and for a time lived with us.

We spent time together in the evening when my parents were out visiting. He spoke kindly to me, with lots of flattering words and attentiveness. It wasn't long before his attention became sexually motivated, in how I could make him "so happy" if I would consent to "be with him."

In silence, without letting anyone know, I endured that presence and pressure from him, struggling to reason it out. Even when I was visiting at a relative's house, if Dean was there, he would motion to me, signaling that he wanted to get together with me later whenever we could be alone.

At home, he would call me into his upstairs bedroom to listen to his radio. As it was a small room with no chairs, we sat on the bed. Soon he would get me to lie down beside him. He tried to kiss me. As we lay on the bed he told me, "You could really make me happy if you would take your panties off." I knew it was wrong, but I was *desperate* to please somebody, and he was very convincing in his bribes. He whispered, "I will buy you what you want!"

He then attempted to take my virginity away. I was scared, naïve and too young to understand the implications of what was happening. Shaking with fear I would protest, "It hurts too much," and he would stop before penetration. I didn't want to do this, yet his disappointment was too much to bear.

One particular evening Mom and Dad were gone and some other young people were at our house visiting, including Lyle. Uncle Dean drove up in the driveway. By the time we realized someone was in the yard, we were hearing gunshots. Uncle Dean had a gun and was shooting at the house. Not wasting any time he quickly drove off, and we came outside to see what had happened.

We were standing around in shock and panic stricken, discussing among ourselves, "what was his purpose and what were we going to tell my parents!" when friends of my folks happened to stop by. They wondered what all of our commotion was about. Naturally, our scare was told to them with frightening excitement. The friends stayed until my parents came home. Had they not shown up we still couldn't have kept it a secret as the east side of the house had bullet holes in it.

Someone asked Uncle Dean why he shot at the house, and he replied "he was jealous of the guys that were there."

Rumors of the molestation and the shooting traveled fast, and soon the minister paid us a visit. Sitting in our living room with my parents and myself, I was told by the minister that the church would have to "excommunicate me, as I was a church member and I had committed a sin."

There was no counseling done with me on my behalf, neither was there an understanding of what I had been going through.

I accepted the fact that the molestation was totally my fault.

The next Sunday morning, we went to church as usual. It was announced that the church needed to have a Council meeting that afternoon. (Councils are handled during the year the same as at revival time, only members could attend.) The reason for the meeting wasn't mentioned, but my family knew what it was regarding.

We had a quiet dinner, then Mom and I stayed home while Dad went back to church for the meeting. During Council, the minister declared, "One of our members has committed a sin that has to be dealt with."

He brought my name before the congregation and said that I had been involved with Uncle Dean, and incest had taken place. The minister called for a vote, and by a majority it was declared that I had to be excommunicated from the church.

Now everyone whom I knew found out what I had done. It was surreal. Just like that, one minute I was a fellow Christian, and the next minute I was ex-communicated.

If I wanted to be re-accepted back into the church, I would need to confess and repent of my "sin."

Because Uncle Dean was not a member, *he was not held accountable*. The church could take no action against him. Neither was the molestation of an underage child reported to the police. I was the one who had to pay the price.

When a person is excommunicated, the other members are supposed to avoid him or her. This denotes that there is to be none of the usual greetings where we acknowledge each other by shaking hands, kissing or hugging.

It also means not eating together at the same table, unless the food is served buffet and not family style. Therefore, anyone that belonged to the church couldn't eat with me. During this time, my own family shunned me. I ate at the kitchen counter where I sat on a white step stool in the corner, while my family sat at the kitchen table.

My father repeatedly threatened me, "If you don't come back to the church, you will have to quit school." Perhaps he knew that was what meant the most to me. I was very sorry for what had happened, though I felt that something about it was unfair. Now, for the second time in my young age, I was being *told* what to do in regards to membership in the church. I resented being unable to make my own choice.

Well, I didn't want to quit school. It was too important to me. I was singing in music classes and learning how to type! I got to do volunteer work in the principal's office. Those were the only things that gave me any value. I couldn't give that up!

One day Dad came up to my bedroom, and we sat on the bed while he asked me what I intended to do. I told him I would come back to the church. We stood, and for the first time in my youth (that I can recall), we hugged.

We were preparing to leave for church the day I was to be re-accepted, and when I walked into the living room Dad told me, "Gladys, you really look nice today. I am happy that you're coming back to the church."

He extended his arms towards me. As we embraced, I felt something hard from his body press against me. I was repulsed and sickened with disgust, and quickly removed myself from him.

I had learned to ignore the circumstances of whatever happened to me, in order to keep my smile, so I pretended that all was OK as I walked outside to get into the car.

I did wonder, "Why did he hug me? Was he happy for my sake, thinking that coming back to the church was *my* real desire? Or was he happy in the fact he didn't have that mark against *him* for having an excommunicated child?"

We left for church after all of our family was in the car. Once again I said what the ministers wanted to hear. Standing up, I made a public confession that "I was sorry for what I had done" and "I believed that God had forgiven me for my sin." A vote was taken with a majority showing of hands, and I was re-accepted back into church fellowship.

Now I was a "Christian" again.

Not knowing any better, approximately at age fourteen, I accepted the guilt for the "sin" I had committed, and never could I get over it. With everyone else, life seemed to continue as normal.

Not only did I have a strained relationship with my father and I detested my Grandpa Schmidt; I now had an uncle whom I worked hard to avoid. At any family gathering I would enter a room slowly and gaze around, taking note of who was sitting there. If I spotted Uncle Dean, I would back out of the room, making sure I made no eye contact with him. The sense of shame followed me like a dark cloud.

Chapter 7

Love Doesn't Come

I was a sophomore in 1962. We still made frequent trips to Kansas to visit family, and I would be pulled out of school for a week or more at a time. Being absent from school brought much ridicule from the other students. I no longer felt any peace there; high school had become a place of conflict too. They jeered at me for being a teacher's pet, because of how the principal was trying to help me. I knew he must have sensed my pain and also my desire to do well in school. But after being absent one too many times, I had had enough, and just up and quit.

Right away I went looking for a job in Huron. Mom drove me to different interviews. I was sixteen years old and about to go out on my own.

I was hired to work for a couple, Richard and Allison Sanders. They were looking for someone to live with them and care for their six-year old son Johnny, keep house, cook and do the laundry. Johnny tells me he thought I was quite strange, with my hair all up in a cap, and he wondered who had invaded their house!

My Mom had never taught me to cook or iron, so the situation perfected the sense of insecurity and lack of confidence that had shadowed my entire life. I met myself with daily anxiety; *I am not capable of doing what they want.*

I tried. When it came to cooking, I struggled. I would get nervous as the dinner hour approached and they were due home. Was the food cooked right? Would they like it? The Sanders used china, real silver, and place mats, which were all new to me, as this was my first exposure to upper middle-class professional people.

There was a radio on the kitchen counter near the sink and I mostly tuned it to a station in Oklahoma City. I never got enough of the music. It was available to me with the turn of a knob, and in this non-Mennonite house, I was safe in listening!

In my spare time I always had silver to polish—bowls, candelabra, flatware—and then put away in the chest in the dining room. Ironing included using the "mangle," a machine about three feet wide that could steam press items such as sheets and pillowcases. If time allowed I would hang the laundry outside on the clothesline for the fresh clean smell that Allison loved.

Richard and Allison owned a flower shop, a block away from their house and they expected me to work there on a regular basis.

For the most part I liked it. I discovered I could make pretty corsages and bows without being criticized. It was great to work with the other women employees and we had a lot of fun laughing. We all wore cute smocks. I enjoyed waiting on the customers. How wonderful it was to be surrounded by so many beautiful and exotic flowers with their sweet fragrance! The perfume in the air enveloped me when I came in the back door to start my day, and I would linger among the scent.

The glass shelves were packed full of dainty figurines and vases. And they had to be cleaned frequently. I was always anxious about getting the windows clean enough or the dusting of the shelves done just right. The overriding fear in my mind believed that about anything I did, *was just not good enough.*

Richard and Allison had very opposite personalities. Working between these two became quite a merry-go-round. It didn't take long to notice that when it was time for Richard to make a floral arrangement for a funeral or a wedding, he would disappear! The more help Allison needed, the sooner he would be gone. She started urging me to ask him, as I could get Richard to do things that she couldn't.

Eventually Richard started flirting with me. He would take me out to the diner for ice cream and ask me to go on floral deliveries with him. In that respect, I was flattered by his attention, feeling all grown up. But when I was home during the day, maybe doing the ironing, he would show up, sit down at the kitchen table and make conversation. Sometimes he'd ask too personal questions about my body and it made me feel very awkward.

Once, he snatched a hold of me downstairs in the laundry room and kissed me, but it was slobbery and I did not like it. Richard was an older, married man! It was sad that I didn't have an honorable male figure to look up to, and that I seemed only to be noticed for my female sexuality by those around me.

Richard was very ornery. One day Johnny caught a bunch of tiny frogs, and Richard thought it would be amusing to put them in the bathtub. Soon the frogs jumped out and went all over the house. Of course father and son thought it was so funny. I sure didn't think it was, especially when Allison arrived home and I was given orders to bleach and scrub out the bathtub. Afterward, I found dead frogs in odd places.

Allison was the first person who influenced my life in a positive way, telling me I could be whatever I wanted. She had gotten a degree in business, but had dropped out of law school to get married. I think she regretted her choice. Perhaps that was why she encouraged me to go back to school and further my education. I appreciated her interest in me, but did not even consider her suggestions. As higher education was not an option in my religion, I didn't pay attention to her good advice.

One winter day, while the Sanders were out of town, my friend Marilyn stayed at their house with me. We wanted to have our own albums to listen to so we got really brave and decided to go downtown to Newberry's and purchase a record player!

We shopped very cautiously and made sure nobody saw us. Marilyn paid seventeen dollars for the player and I bought our first record album. It was by country singer Marvin Rainwater and our favorite song was *Gonna Find Me a Bluebird*. We hurried back home and played the album. Determined to have a "slumber party" we stayed up most of the night listening to the same songs over and over again.

We could get away with certain things at Marilyn's. My folks would not have allowed a record player in the house, and although we kept it in her bedroom, it was more acceptable at her house. In a short time we had purchased a collection of new albums, and we enjoyed listening to country artists such as Hank Williams, Kitty Wells or Johnny Cash.

The Miller family home was just south of Huron about three miles, close enough that Lyle would often come by to see me at the Sanders. In the evening he'd park his car in front of the house and we'd talk and smooch. Later, when I went inside, if Richard had seen us he'd shake his finger at me and say, "People can see you, you know!"

One night my former high school students were playing in a basketball tournament in Huron and I decided to go. Admittedly this was a bold move, because attending sports events was "worldly" and a big no-no. Most would never dare to enter a building where such events were held.

Happy, I was sitting with some old classmate friends, when suddenly Lyle appeared out of the crowd.

I was shocked to see him. "What are you doing here?"

"You don't belong in a place like this," he snapped.

Hurriedly he grabbed hold of me and escorted me out of the arena. My face flushed with embarrassment!

In 1963, I quit my job with the Sanders so I could go with my family when they moved to Montezuma, Kansas for the winter. My folks rented a small house on Main Street. Dad got work doing part time jobs to carry them through.

I went to work for the Schoens, a couple who owned a restaurant in Cimmaron, about fifteen miles away. I was hired to clean the house and waitress in the cafe. They had a little white frame house on a hill above the street. I lived in the basement, with my own room curtained off from their laundry area.

I would walk the few blocks to the downtown café, arriving for work by six o'clock in the morning when it was still dark. Occasionally the local cop gave me a ride. Usually people were waiting at the door to get in. At my young age of seventeen, I couldn't figure out why people got up so early in the morning and why were they in such a hurry for that coffee!

Our cook made the best chicken-fried steak, and delicious homemade pies. After my shift ended I would sit at the counter and have a piece of blueberry pie with vanilla ice-cream.

I loved to play the jukebox, and the traveling maintenance man always gave me quarters painted in red to keep the jukebox going.

I was working at that café when I heard the news John F. Kennedy had been shot. I was standing behind the lunch counter when a man, whose face I shall never forget, walked in, sat down on a stool and told us the news. We didn't believe him.

After working my shift at the restaurant, the first thing I did upon arriving home was to dip into my apron pockets and throw all my tip money onto the bed. Then I would spread the coins out with my hands, gleefully running my fingers over all the metal. As I counted, I put every dollar's worth into a pile. This was more money than I had ever had! And I got it for free! But I didn't get to keep much of it. The majority of my earnings went to my folks. Mom said it helped them pay their bills, as often Dad's income didn't cover their expenses.

When I wasn't working at the restaurant, I had to keep the house in order and do the laundry. Those were the days of white cotton shirts and I had to iron them by the basketful. It seemed a never-ending job, but I purposed to do it well.

The best thing about my job was that I didn't have to cook! We ate all our meals at the café. The Schoens were pleased with my work both in the restaurant and in their home. They were very nice to me and I always felt accepted by them.

During the course of this winter Lyle was living with relatives in Kansas also, four hours away. During his visits we talked about getting married in the spring, as soon as we got back to South Dakota. In March, he would turn twenty-one and I would be eighteen.

I knew we should not be getting married, because even though Lyle was in love with me, I was not in love with him. I felt we had nothing in common. I just liked being with him, he was around and our friendship was convenient. I did not know the meaning of true love, and so I accepted anything and went along with our relationship. After all, someone loved me!

In my illogical rationalization I *thought* marriage could be a way to escape the pressures of my family and church. I *thought* I could change what I didn't like about him. I *thought* I could be happy. To have my *own* home! Life would *become* perfect.

Lyle asked the ministers for my hand in marriage and they relayed information back and forth when I accepted his proposal. We chose April 19, 1964 for our wedding day.

Despite my feelings about the wedding, I was very excited the day that Mom and I went shopping for bridal things in Dodge City, twenty miles away. We bought material to make my dress, the bridesmaid dress and one for Mom.

In a specialty store, we found white Noritake china with a small pale pink rosebud and silver trim. I got every single piece that was available in that pattern. A set of eight silver-rimmed stemmed Fostoria glasses completed my tableware.

Our day couldn't be complete without purchasing the two items that were a necessity in every Mennonite bride's trousseau: a Singer sewing machine (I didn't even know how to sew) and a cedar chest.

It was traditional for girls to keep what was called a "hope chest." The purpose of the chest was to hold the special personal belongings that a bride would put in her new house.

Mine was nearly four and a half feet long by eighteen inches square, lined with cedar and it had a locking lid. The exterior wood was a dark walnut, and the front was decorated in a modern style, with a vertical ribbed pattern in the center and horizontal trim pieces on the left and right.

I filled my chest with linens such as embroidered pillowcases, tea towels, and handkerchiefs. This unique piece of furniture would follow me through all the turns in my life.

Soon it was time for my family and me to pack up and move back to South Dakota in time for our announcement in the church. Of course, it was springtime and Dad had to get back to attend to his farming.

Bridal couples are expected to have the minister involved when the courtship becomes serious enough to think about marriage plans. (Really, there isn't supposed to be courtship!) We were also counted on to keep it hush-hush after we had spoken with the minister.

As was customary in the church, the minister would "surprise" his Sunday congregation by making the wedding announcement about three or four weeks ahead of the big date. In our case, we didn't abide by the strict rules of courtship, and we had dated openly. So it wasn't much of a surprise.

Wedding gifts began to arrive from our friends and relatives. Other than that joy, in imagining using those gifts in my home, the days before the wedding were terrible. As the time drew near, I realized I did not want to marry Lyle!

Often, I paced the floor of my bedroom in turmoil, knowing I was about to marry a man I did not love. Still, there was no way I would cancel the wedding and endure the embarrassment that would follow. *I could not continue to live my life as it was.* So, undeterred, I forged ahead with the wedding arrangements. Maybe later, I reasoned, after we are married I will love him.

Two days before the wedding, the minister's wife, Anne, came over to visit. During the course of the evening, she asked to see my wedding dress. She probably had an instinct that I would try to get away with something barely appropriate.

I had chosen a cottony material with a lacy pattern in a pastel pink. (We were not allowed to wear white.) Mom had sewn it from a regular shirtwaist dress pattern but added the traditional designs; the long sleeves with a point over the ring finger and a row of covered buttons on the inside wrist. Twenty-five very small round covered buttons filed down the front from the small collar to the waist with its stiff belt. A pleated skirt came to just below the knees, called "street-length." Reluctantly, Anne approved it.

Wedding day was here! Naturally I woke up excited. But my heart was heavy, full of misgivings. This was supposed to be a day of love, only I knew it wasn't. Going through all the motions, I was putting on a show. I had kept my feelings a complete secret and no one was aware of my anxiety.

My wedding would take place at two o'clock in the afternoon.

Mom and I stayed home from church in the morning and just tried to relax. We were sitting in the living room discussing the day. At one point Mom said, "I have a book for you about 'the birds and the bees,' but you can't read it yet." She retrieved the book from her bedroom and handed it to me.

Peeking inside the burgundy cover, I could see that it was about marriage and sex and wondered what difference a few hours would make in looking at it. Being obedient, I rushed upstairs to my bedroom and tucked the *book* in my suitcase for the honeymoon.

Dad and the other children came right home after church. We all had a quick lunch in the kitchen.

I put on my wedding dress and when it was time, Dad drove all of us to church.

The members had recently constructed a new church building, and I was going to be the first to be married in it. Our wedding was a big attraction due to that fact.

After parking the car, we entered through double doors into a lobby. To the left were the women's coatroom, rest-room and nursery. To the right were the men's coatroom and restroom.

Our families went to their respective places in the pews that were directly behind where the bridal couple would sit.

From the lobby, double entry doors led into the sanctuary. This is where Marilyn and I met up with Lyle and his best man, Willard. As my maid of honor, Marilyn wore a mint green dress in the same fabric as mine. I lined up next to her and Lyle stood behind us with Willard. Nervously, we waited for the usher to open the door, as our cue to proceed.

When we walked in, the congregation began singing the hymn *Heavenly Sunlight*. The chorus goes like this: "Heavenly sunlight, heavenly sunlight, Flooding my soul with glory divine; Hallelujah! I am rejoicing, Singing His praises, Jesus is mine."

The front pew, left side, was reserved for the wedding party. Marilyn and I walked down the aisle together, with Lyle and Willard directly behind us. Then all four of us sat down at the same time with Lyle and me side by side.

Our wedding was a typical Mennonite wedding. Everything was quite plain, with no flowers, no candles, in fact no decorations at all in the sanctuary. As in a regular service, men sat on the right side and women on the left. The father of the bride does not give her away, and there is no flower girl or ring bearer. Because we did not use instruments, all music was sung *a cappella* from the hymnal.

The wedding service proceeded through songs, introductions, and a sermon. Then Lyle and I stood up to recite our vows, the minister led a prayer, and we closed with a final song. The ceremony lasted an hour and a half.

Our reception was held in the basement immediately afterwards. As Lyle and I walked towards the stairwell, he looked at me with a big smile and reached for my hand. I pulled away, not wanting to hold hands with my new husband.

Downstairs, Lyle and I stood with our two attendants in a reception line and shook everyone's hands. I reveled in the attention of our two hundred guests.

We and our parents would all sit at the "bride's table." It was decorated in pink and mint green, and bore a floral bouquet. For whatever reason, one small arrangement was permitted on the bridal table. Our table stood in the center of many long rows of tables laden with white paper tablecloths for the guests.

The church's Food Committee, plus volunteers, served the meal, which included ham sandwiches, cheddar cheese, pickles, lettuce, (each served on a separate platter) chips, applesauce, and desserts.

After we all had eaten, Lyle and I went to another long table filled with wedding gifts. According to tradition, we opened all of the presents right there, exclaiming about each one and then passing the gift down the line of guests. Family members squeezed in for the best spots, to be closest to the bridal couple. They wanted to hear every word spoken between us! Opening the gifts took a couple of hours.

Off to one side sat the groom's traditional present to the bride, a set of stainless steel silverware in a chest, open for display. The bride's gift to the groom is a Bible.

When we finally left the church for our honeymoon, the sun was down and we still had a long drive ahead of us.

Lyle and I arrived exhausted in Pierre, the capital of South Dakota. We found our reserved room at the Holiday Inn Motel and collapsed into bed. I lay there listening to the piped-in music, coming through a speaker in the wall. It all felt eerily strange, as if I had been dropped into another world. Too tired for romance, we did not consummate our marriage that night. We also lacked knowledge in intimacy.

For the next four days we toured the Black Hills area, visiting Mount Rushmore, Wind Cave, Crazy Horse and Wall Drug Store where I got my first prescription (I had taken it with me on the trip) of birth control pills filled!

While Lyle drove, to pass the time I read my new book. It seemed quite generic and I wasn't overly impressed, except for its appearance. The cover was well worn, and I thought it must be very old. I wondered: *Was this book given to my Mom on her wedding day?*

After the honeymoon, we moved into a tiny three-room house in Huron, near the Sanders'. I started working for them again in the flower shop and Lyle worked for a construction company building new houses.

In winter of 1965, Lyle's work had ended for the season, so we decided to move to Cimarron, Kansas. Lyle found a job as a co-op laborer and I went to work part-time cleaning houses.

Life went on. We decided to stay in Kansas instead of moving back to South Dakota. 1966 or 67 took us to Montezuma.

First we moved into a small four-room house next door to Lyle's parents' place on Main Street, as they had also moved to Kansas from South Dakota. Later we moved into a house two doors down that his dad, Harold, had purchased and remodeled.

Even though Montezuma was a small town, it boasted a Mennonite bakery with the best donuts, pastries, pies, and breads. It was common to get together with other women and I often picked up goodies before going to a friend's house for morning coffee.

For a while I was a housewife with lots of extra time. My pastime was reading and embroidery. Lyle spent many evenings tinkering on vehicles in the garage, or reading *Motor Trend* magazines.

Whenever possible, I kept a radio in the house. But I didn't want anyone to know! I panicked if I heard an unanticipated knock at the door. (This could happen quite often, as it was something of a custom to just stop by for a quick visit.) I would quickly turn off the radio, unplug it, and run to hide it in a closet. Then I'd answer the door with a pounding heart and flushed face, hoping the radio's volume hadn't been turned up high enough to reveal my secret.

Bored, and suffering from the strain of my religion and marriage, I got a job in Dodge City working as a sales clerk for Montgomery Ward, hoping it would fill the emptiness I had inside me. I did really well in my department (drapery), and frequently won "most sales" awards.

Though I had Mennonite friends, my closest friend was from the world. I met Sue Snodgrass as a fellow employee. Soon I was sharing with her my troubled life.

I felt totally helpless. My feelings for Lyle had not changed. I had not grown to love him. When I was young, I thought his antics were funny, now his immaturity and our differences became more than I could take. Thoughts began to fill my head about leaving him *and* the church. It was becoming too difficult to believe and accept all of the legalism, all of the "don'ts." Lyle was stronger in his beliefs, so we disagreed in our thinking where the church was concerned.

Living in such close proximity, Lyle's family became aware of my frustration. On one particular day, (I do not recall the exact cause) I was so distraught Lyle and one of his sisters had to physically hold me down on the bed in an attempt to calm me.

During this time of despair and indecision, I read a book written by a woman of the Amish religion who had gone through a similar situation in her faith. She left her religion and survived. Her story gave me courage.

I got the impression that Lyle's parents had problems in their marriage. His mother had tried to end her life when we all lived in South Dakota. As I was a teenager at the time and struggling myself, that came as a real jolt, wondering what would cause her to do something so drastic.

Lyle's dad was from the "world," and joined the church as a young adult, like my dad. His mom grew up in a good

Christian home as my mother had. I realized I had married into the same family circumstances as my own family: parents that had totally different upbringings. I asked myself, "What kind of a future do I have?"

It all put me into a great depression. I wanted to leave. But I felt trapped and thought there was no way out.

Members who "belonged" to the church just did not divorce. *It was unthinkable.* Inevitably, if I left my husband, it would result in excommunication from the church. I felt that *I* could tolerate the separation and avoidance that would bring, but I knew that my parents would be devastated. I was certain that they would worry most about what the church thought of them. They would feel disgraced for having a child divorce and leave their faith.

I debated long and hard. My parents were still young; I could not wait until they died before I made a change. So what could I do? I thought about suicide, but really, I did not want to take my life. I still believed there was something out there for me.

Chapter 8

Cycle of Contradictions

Five years after I had married Lyle, the dam of everything I had known, and was, in my life, broke and fell apart, never to be put back together the way I had been. I would be forever changed. I was twenty-three years old.

My now sister-in-law, Marilyn, had been expelled from the Mennonite church for quite some time, and she was planning to marry a divorced "worldly" man. The church felt that if you attended the wedding of an expelled person, you were condoning that marriage. Therefore it was forbidden.

Abiding by the church rules, all of Marilyn's immediate family, including Lyle, refused to go to her wedding. (The exception was one older, also expelled sister, Berdine.) Yet, I knew that after the wedding, her family would be together all the time. How could I treat my girl friend and family member in such a hypocritical way and not attend her wedding? Such contradiction! I was fed up with it!

After getting up and around on the morning of February 16, 1969, I nervously approached Lyle in our kitchen, "I'm *going* to the wedding today, with or without you. I want to do this. *Even* if I have to go alone."

He looked at me sadly. "You won't be coming home again." I wondered what he meant; what were his thoughts and reasons for saying that. Maybe he had an intuition. There wasn't anything more to debate, as we had covered it all in numerous discussions before.

So, on that cold Sunday with the ground covered in snow, I set out for the wedding, driving by myself. I took a country road to Ford, a small town near Dodge City.

I shivered with fear, shocked at the brazenness I felt each mile that I drove further away from Lyle, and towards the unknown. The long straight road ahead was desolate. I was very aware of the vacant seat beside me.

What would my punishment be for defying the wishes of my husband and the beliefs of my church? With my mind swirling, yet I held steadfast, gripped the steering wheel, and kept on driving.

I parked the car and entered the Methodist church. The only people I recognized were Marilyn's sister Berdine, her husband George, and her Uncle Carroll, all from Wichita. Everyone was scurrying around with last minute details.

Feeling awkward and uncertain of my surroundings, I entered the sanctuary and found a seat. I remember very little about the nuptials, other than having the sensation of being in a fog.

When it came time to go home after the reception, I said my good-byes and left the church as if all were normal, but on the road something happened to me. A sick feeling over-whelmed my heart, and a thought repeated itself: *I can't go on, I can't go home.*

I drove to the side of the road and stopped the car, not realizing Carroll was following in his car. He pulled up behind me, and walked over to see if everything was OK.

I don't recall exactly what happened next. It was like a blackout. I can only guess I was in some sort of shock at the bold decision I had made in going to the wedding. I told Carroll I could not go back to my house.

Carroll took me to Dodge City, and when I came to a sensible frame of mind, I discerned that I was in a room at the Silver Spur Lodge. I don't know what happened to the car.

Unbeknownst to me Carroll had called Lyle, who came right away, and was with his dad in an adjacent room. I think they came to my room to visit, but I can't recall the conversation. I believe I spent two days at the motel. Then they took me home.

I had to have some advice. But I didn't know whom to turn to....

Berdine was aware of my unhappiness and had always offered to assist in whatever she could if I ever needed it. Retrieving my mail from the mailbox at the street, I noticed a letter with her return address. Tearing it open, I quickly scanned what she wrote:

> *I was really surprised to see you come alone yesterday. But am glad for your sake, if that's what you believe in, that you had enough nerve to kick total conformity in the teeth!!!*

For a day or two I paced around the house, literally wringing my hands. *Somebody help me, please!* I felt I was going crazy. I didn't know where to go for guidance or answers. I couldn't go to the church leaders. I was confident they wouldn't have any solutions. I *had* no choice but to leave.

Berdine's words and offer to help tumbled around in my mind. After getting up the next morning, I told Lyle, "I'm going to Wichita to see Berdine."

"Absolutely not," he replied. "You cannot go."

"I'm going."

"I'll stop you."

"*There is nothing that can stop me.*"

I went into the bedroom and hurriedly packed a suitcase.

Seeing my resolve to go, Lyle walked over to his father Harold's house to tell him of my plans. Shortly after, I stepped outside, closed the door behind me and walked toward the car. They were standing beside it. Without a proper good-bye and with my heart pounding against my chest, I opened the car door and got in.

I turned the ignition. It wouldn't start. I tried again and again. Jumping out, I hollered, "What have you done to the car?"

"We fixed it so you can't leave."

"Well, I'm going no matter what."

We argued until they realized how determined I was. Lyle gave up, and said with exasperation, "Well, then I'll drive you."

We arrived in Wichita and Lyle took me to George and Berdine's. He returned to Montezuma.

The next couple of days were a blur. Berdine made an appointment for me to see her psychiatrist, Dr. Riordan.

Sitting in his office, Dr. Riordan asked me, "What is wrong? What is troubling you?" I had no response. I could only cry.

I was a mess. I absolutely did not know who I was or what I wanted. All of my life I had lived in a contradiction of everything that surrounded me. My parents were strict in some things, lenient in others. Some of my relatives on my mom's side were very strict, while other relatives on my dad's side cussed and smoked cigarettes. The church ruled me, but I didn't conform to it. My dad had controlled me, yet ignored me. I had never been taught that I could make a decision, *that I had any value.* And so I just cried some more....

He quickly determined that I needed hospitalization and wanted to admit me into the mental ward of the hospital, but there were no rooms available.

While we waited two days for a room, the doctor had me take a written test about my personality. It was very long, and I stayed up most of one night at the kitchen table, working on pages and pages of multiple choice questions. George sat across the table, speaking words of encouragement to finish it.

We got a telephone call from Dr. Riordan when a room became available. Berdine drove me to St. Francis Hospital in Wichita.

As long as I live I will remember that drive. I sat in the passenger seat, nervously pondering what was to come. What had happened in my life and world that now brought me to this place?

As we drove into the parking lot right next to the hospital, its red brick walls loomed over us. The entryway sat at the top of a huge wide flight of concrete stairs. Once those doors swallowed me, what was going to happen?

Berdine and I walked up the steps and through the doors and then up more stairs until we entered the open lobby area. She went to the counter to fill out my admittance papers. I waited for a long time, staring at a huge aquarium that divided the stairs from the rest of the room. Absentmindedly, I watched the fish swimming back and forth. Kind of like me, just moving about, no particular place to go.

Finally it was time. With my name typed on a blue wristband, I was taken to my room in the psychiatric ward, which was on the second floor of the hospital. It was a private room with a bathroom.

Chapter 9

Locked Up

I settled in at St. Francis Hospital and began a new daily routine, and a whole new life.

Right away, I made some friends among the other patients. Jim Stroud was one of them. He paid attention to me. "He likes me so I will like him!" After all, if I am worthy of being noticed, I owe that person.

Jim and I would hang out in the hospital's café in the basement or sometimes sit in the stairwell. There we could talk in private, and maybe steal a kiss, until a staff person found us and chased us out.

Every day I went to a large recreation room where I listened to the jukebox. The room was located in an adjacent building, connected by an enclosed sky bridge. Both sides of the hallway had windows that looked out over the streets below. Often, while passing through, I would linger a long while peering out those windows, observing all the people going about their usual life beyond the glass barrier.

Early on, Dr. Riordan said he wanted to give me shock treatments, called "electroconvulsive therapy." A pulse of electric current is passed through the brain, causing a convulsion. It was, and still is, used to treat cases of severe depression. At the time I had never heard of any such thing, but I agreed to the treatment.

On the day of the procedure, I had to drink some special medicine that was thick and gritty and flavored like orange juice. Quite horrible! (And it was years before I could tolerate orange juice again.) The doctors wheeled a machine into my room. They tied down my hands, feet, body, and head, because of how the body jerks during the treatment. I was given a general anesthetic and then they administered the shock. Each time, I woke up exhausted, and slept for the remainder of the day. I was given a total of six treatments while I was on that floor.

I cannot recall making a conscious decision to leave the church or divorce Lyle. But one day, it just happened. I walked into the beauty shop, next door to the café, and had the beautician trim my hair to shoulder length. Then she styled it into long curls around my face, finishing the look with hair spray. The sweet fragrance was powerful and over-whelming. It settled into my deepest consciousness, to be recalled many times.

Next, I hesitantly looked at the tubes of lipstick for sale, picked out a soft color and made my first make-up purchase.

I walked out of the shop down a long hallway and back up to my room a visibly changed person. As I passed by, other patients who were standing at the doorway to their rooms exclaimed how wonderful I looked. But even more, I felt *elated*. I had started down the path to freedom. In my heart, the restraints of my past life were now cut.

In addition to Dr. Riordan, I was seeing a psychologist, Dr. Velusek. Dr. Riordan would let me cry, always ready with a tissue, patting my shoulder or holding my hand. Dr. Velusek was stern, not letting me get by with any excuse.

Dr. Riordan was my primary doctor and as such, had to make decisions in regards to my getting better, even if he was usually softhearted towards me. During one of his daily visits he said, "Gladys, you are not dealing with your issues. We're going to have to put you in lock-up, where you won't have all these distractions."

Was he possibly thinking that one of them was Jim?

Whoa, I didn't want to go there! They kept you locked up! I had heard rumors about that place. I broke out in a sweat at the thought of losing my new friend. Dismayed, I tried to reason with the doctor, to no avail.

I packed my belongings and went with the attendants up to the third floor.

Anxiety overwhelmed me as I stepped off the elevator into a small entry room. I was losing my freedom again! I waited while they unlocked the massive barred door. As the attendants ushered me through, I suddenly felt that I was entering a real mental hospital. It wasn't really, but the cases here were more serious than downstairs. Some patients sat on the hall floor, staring vacantly. The second floor had been a safe place, almost pleasant, *like a vacation from my life*. I was removed from family and church pressures. But this place was only a different prison.

The attendants showed me to my room. They sorted through all my personal belongings and took away any items considered dangerous—I couldn't even have my comb. All the women on this floor had to share a large bathroom with open showers. My telephone calls were limited.

The third floor had no wonderful recreation room or music. Instead, we had mandatory arts and crafts therapy, in which we sat around a table and made things. I put together a small oblong dish with tiny squares of cobalt blue tiles. Tediously I set them in a pattern that matched the shape of the dish and finished it with white grout. I saw no sense in any of it and tried to convince the nurses. Why did I have to do that? What did crafts have to do with my problems?

I would walk around people sitting on the floor in the hallway. Sometimes, in the middle of the night, a patient would start hollering and the attendants would call the cops. I don't know if they were taken away or what they did. It was just so disturbing and noisy.

I sort of remember discussions with Dr. Riordan about my parents visiting. I don't recall if it was his idea or mine, but my family was not allowed to see me on a regular basis. I believe my parents came to visit twice.

We met in a small, cramped room, about eight feet square with a vinyl couch at each end. I cannot remember anything of what we discussed; I was only aware of the room's close perimeter.

Eventually Dr. Riordan told me, "I think you have improved enough that you may leave the hospital." I had been admitted in February and now it was early April. I said my good-byes and received my stored belongings from a nurse.

Berdine picked me up and I went to stay at her house, happy to be out of the hospital. I intended to stay with her until I could find my own place in Wichita, file for divorce, and get my life together.

Very soon I discovered how the shock treatments had affected my memory, as is so common among people who have received them. Some things happened in the hospital that I have never remembered. Berdine told me that Lyle came to visit me numerous times. I don't recall ever seeing him.

One day as Berdine and I were out walking in her yard, I commented on some pretty lilies planted next to the house. She said I had received them at the hospital. I wondered; did I look at them every day and now I have no clue of it?

I found out how concerned the family had been that I might attempt to take my own life while I was in the hospital. They told me how they were scared that I might jump out of a window, or take an overdose of my medications. I still have two empty containers with the prescription labels, on which Lyle had written the number of the pills so he could keep track.

George and Berdine were going to a family gathering planned for an upcoming Sunday in Montezuma. They offered to take me, but I was extremely anxious about going. *Should I even show up? What were people going to say? How would they treat me? Maybe it'd be better to stay away.* I decided to take a chance and go as my family was also going to be in town.

Miles of pavement rolled away beneath the car. When I could see the Montezuma grain elevator on the horizon, my heart beat faster, and my palms got sweatier as I knew we were getting close. I was so nervous I could hardly stand it. This is where I had a house. This is where I used to be a Mennonite. Now I was different, inside and out.

Driving down Main Street, we pulled in to Lyle's parents' house, and finding my parents already there, made greetings all around. Then we had dinner.

While the others visited, I walked back and forth between their house and mine. Everywhere I went someone followed me, as though they dared not let me out of their sight. I kept thinking, *"This* is my house; what do they think I will do if left alone?"

I thought it must be time to leave and I went back to the in-laws' house, but noticed right away that the car was gone. "Where are George and Berdine?"

Someone in the family told me they had left.

I screamed, "What do you mean, they're gone? I was going back with them! This can't be, they wouldn't leave me!"

"Gladys, it's for your own good."

"What gives *you* the right to think you can keep me from going back?"

We argued like that for some time, but there was nothing I could do.

I stayed the night at my house, sleeping on the couch in the living room. Lyle stayed in the basement in an unfinished bedroom, and Mom and Dad slept in the master bedroom.

During the night, Dad got up from his bed and came over to the couch. He knelt down beside me and spoke softly, "Gladys, I have a confession to make."

"Oh?"

"You know that I have always had difficulties with you throughout your life. Well, I have not loved you the way I should have, but now I do. Will you forgive me?"

"Certainly, I'll forgive you," I mumbled.

He left, and in the silence of the night my mind went over his words, *"I didn't love you but now I do."* Stunned, I lay there, my head spinning. Why did he have to tell me *that,* why did he tell me now, and how was that revelation going to solve anything? Wasn't it enough that I *already felt that* by his actions towards me?

Maybe he said he loved me now, out of guilt, over what I had just been through. Was he truly remorseful, or did he have some other motive? Right then I just wanted the heartache and the awful hurt in my head to go away. Fitfully, I slept through the night.

The next morning was just another day. I didn't mention the previous night's conversation. My families went back and forth between our houses, discussing what to do with me, because I told them I wasn't going to stay!

We were in Harold's house when I announced, "I'm going to Wichita."

"No," replied Lyle, "We've decided that we're going to admit you to Larned State Hospital."

I reeled, because I knew that was the state mental institution. "No way! I just got released from a place like that!"

I ran to my house, jumped into the car, and bolted. How could I know that they *couldn't* actually seize me and throw me into the institution?

Lyle, Harold, and Dad piled into another car and took off in pursuit.

Mom and Pearl stayed at the house, and later I learned how they'd gotten down on their knees and prayed desperately for the situation.

I headed for Cimarron, thinking I'd go to the county courthouse for protection. I watched as the speedometer got higher and higher. I didn't care. I pressed harder on the gas pedal, reaching one hundred miles an hour, in my attempt to outrun them. But they were close behind me when I got to the courthouse. I jumped out of the car and dashed up the steps, out of breath.

Once inside, I looked around frantically for the nearest clerk, explained my dilemma, and then had to sit in the lobby and wait for an attorney to arrive. *I felt very alone,* that my family was all against me.

When an attorney got there, we were all escorted into a small meeting room, where we deliberated back and forth. The men wanted to get me committed, but the attorney said, "In order for this to happen, Gladys will have to sign a consent form."

"Absolutely not," I adamantly refused.

Boldly, I got up out of my chair, walked across the street to the attorney's office and filed for divorce. Lyle would be served with the decree on May first, 1969. The men were gone when I came out of the building, got in the car and headed back to Montezuma.

I went back because I did not know what else to do. I had no money, no car of my own, and none of my belongings. I stayed at the house again that night.

Later I found out from George and Berdine that they had not wanted to leave without me, but the family insisted, "No, no, she's *home* now, so you might as well go."

I refused to go back to the normalcy of my previous home life. I told Lyle, "My life as it used to be is over." My mind was made up. For once, I knew what I wanted.

Seeing how headstrong and determined I was to go to Wichita, Lyle finally relented and said he would take me.

In the morning of the day I left, two ministers from the church showed up and walked straight into my house. Why did I let them in?

My cedar chest sat in the center of the dining/living room, and I paced around loading it with my china, silverware, and Fostoria glasses. Whatever personal things would fit, mostly my clothes, my sales trophies and a few books went into the trunk of the car.

The ministers sat watching me coldly the whole time, occasionally peppering the conversation with comments such as, "Gladys, you need to repent of this. You have a spirit of rebellion and pride. You need to be submissive. You need to change your ways, or you will be excommunicated from the church and you will lose your salvation and be condemned to hell."

I was tired of being threatened. I clenched with anger, my insides churning. In an effort to try and explain my indifference towards them, I told about my life growing up, how my married life began in disappointments and that I needed to recover myself from the hurt of my past.

To a certain degree, I shared my unhappiness with the church, but kept quiet about the strong feelings and animosity I felt towards the ministers. Repeatedly I voiced, "Well, I have left the church and I am going to divorce Lyle."

I just kept packing and eventually they realized they weren't going to change my mind. As they departed, I closed the door behind them.

After the ministers left, Lyle and I loaded the cedar chest into the back seat of our car. I took one last look around as I walked through the rooms of the house.

How strange, that I was leaving behind my furniture, pots and pans, bedding and personal items. I had no real desire to keep them. I wanted to move ahead. In my mind I thought it was my own fault for wanting to divorce, therefore it helped to ease my guilt if I left stuff so Lyle wouldn't have to buy new things!

I didn't cry but I was somber as I closed the door, it was such an incredible finality to my whole life.

Once again, Lyle drove me to Wichita. It was a quiet drive. Looking at the man sitting beside me, I could hardly imagine that he had been my husband. I was void of any personal feelings towards him.

We arrived in Wichita and while heading toward Berdine's on Oliver Street, we noticed an apartment for rent, so we stopped to check it out.

Sitting on the east side of Oliver, the unit was in a red brick fourplex. It was furnished and going for sixty-five dollars a month, so I took it on the spot.

We unloaded the car of my possessions. Lyle said good-bye and I watched him drive away.

After sitting down on the couch, I looked around and tried to comprehend everything that was happening. Freedom, and also apprehension about my future, was ever present in my thoughts.

I was twenty-three years old. I was in a big city. The only people I knew were Berdine and George and my doctors. Oh yes, I had Jim's phone number that I knew from the hospital. But I didn't have a telephone yet. I didn't have a car and I didn't have a job.

It didn't take me very long to unpack! My living, dining, and kitchen were in one room with doors to the outside on either end. Actually, my complete kitchen with one sink and a two-burner stove was behind two cupboard doors. The cedar chest became a divider between the brown couch and kitchen table with two chairs. A small bedroom and bath completed my tiny abode.

Berdine helped me settle in. I got telephone service. I walked to an appliance store and took out a loan so I could purchase a black and white television set.

I continued to see Dr. Riordan. At first I went for appointments three times a week. I would walk to his office five blocks away as the cars whizzed by on Oliver Street. To survive the mental anguish from my dad, I cried in Dr. Riordan's office a lot. He had two chairs in a corner divided by a small table with a lamp and a box of tissues. I would weep as he handed me the tissues and patted my hand.

The doctor's aim was to get me out of severe depression and into positive thinking, to listen and help me learn how to make my own decisions, although he never advised me on what to do.

Dad and Mom called frequently on the telephone. They could not believe I was in my right mind living in Wichita. Mom was mostly worried about my safety, and Dad spent a lot of time screaming about what I was doing to *him*, things like, "You are sending me to my grave." And, "Now the church looks down on us as parents, because *we* have a child out of the church. It's embarrassing. It reflects poorly on how we raised our children." His number one concern was how the church viewed him. Never mind how badly I was hurting.

Would my dad never let go? I couldn't help it that I couldn't make him happy. And Mom and Dad were convinced that my psychiatrist was brainwashing my mind to get me to abandon the church. Couldn't they believe that it had been *my* choice to leave? *I wanted to be free, to be released from bondage.*

Chapter 10

Worldly Balance

The first declaration I made was to drop my first name. "Gladys" had been Dad's idea, but I was sick of the name and all its baggage. I figured I would only be meeting new people, and I would introduce myself as Elaine, my middle name. Different look, different name, I thought they went together well. I would request the same from my family and friends. There was a lot of stuttering going on for quite some time as everyone adapted. It was the most difficult for Dad to call me Elaine.

Having no car, I walked everywhere. If I needed to do certain errands I would take a different, more sedate residential route than busy Oliver Street. I enjoyed ambling along the tree-shaded sidewalks, feasting my eyes on the colorful flowers and gigantic trees.

The old part of town had huge, stately homes with manicured lawns. One street boasted a Frank Lloyd Wright house built in 1915. Surrounded by a brick wall, only the upper levels of the home could be seen from the sidewalk. I could hardly stand the fact I couldn't see what was on the other side of the wall. I never got enough of gazing at it.

I had my first date in the "world." I don't remember his name. We went to the Lakeshore Club on the west edge of town. I feasted on shrimp, my first ever, baked potato with lots of butter and sour cream and fell in love with the taste of blue cheese dressing.

In May and June of 1969, I went a little wild. I sampled all of the forbidden things—smoky bowling alleys and drive-in movies. I was promiscuous. I dated Jim, my friend from the hospital, and a couple of other guys. One managed an all-night diner, where I would sit for hours listening to the jukebox as night gave way to a new morning.

Several times I went to a nightclub, put a quarter in the jukebox and slow danced to Buck Owen's song *Together Again*. Sitting at a table with an alcoholic drink and a cigarette in my hand, I was feeling "all grown up" and at the same time very uncomfortable.

One time I got drunk on a date and threw up at some man's house. Trying to be bold and adventurous, I was seeking my balance in the world. That only happened once, and once was one too many times. I felt horribly insecure and very embarrassed about the incident and couldn't believe what I had done.

Going about everything the wrong way, I was attempting to find self-esteem and confidence in myself, and who I was. While grappling with the up and down emotions of aloneness, the attention of men, my obliging them, and the never-ending conflicts with my father.

That summer, I felt like a butterfly coming out of its cocoon, observing life all around me. Everything was new and different. Now I was living in the "worldly" culture, and hardly knew what to do with it. In conversations with people, I didn't understand their jokes and I was unfamiliar with talk about television and radio shows. I wasn't comfortable with my makeup, having no one to show me what I should buy and how to apply it.

In general, I was trying to live a carefree and leisurely life. I made a routine of walking to the grocery store, drug store, beauty shop and a small strip shopping center that had a very nice clothing store, Lewin's.

I spent quite a bit of time shopping there, where I felt safe, figuring if I paid enough money the dress must be in fashion. The attendants were very helpful as I awkwardly determined *my* style, replacing all of my old dresses with modern fashion. Many of the new dresses were sleeveless, with a short flirty skirt, modest neckline, and white or bright colors. A favorite one was white with big red polka dots.

My next door neighbor thought I was a "Lady of the Night" as I often took a cab and was always dressed in a nice dress with nylons and high heels whenever I left my apartment. He didn't know that I didn't know how to wear jeans or shorts, or any kind of casual clothes. I didn't own a pair of tennis shoes.

I had a new hairstyle with no idea of how to fix it. One of my biggest expenses was going to the beauty shop. This was the day of the "beehive" hairdo. About every third day I walked to the shop to get my hair done.

I would have to sleep very carefully with my head propped up on my hand to avoid messing up those perfect curls. I bought a pink satin pillow that snapped around my neck to help keep every hair in place.

At first I did not work or even attempt to find a job. Wichita then had a population of two hundred and eighty thousand. It was by far the biggest city I had ever lived in, and I was a bit intimidated by its size. I had received a fifteen hundred-dollar advance from Lyle towards the divorce settlement and that was the money I lived on, but it didn't last long.

Bravely, I went out for introductory dancing lessons and took my first tentative waltz steps. Oh, glory be, how wonderful it felt to glide across the hardwood dance floor with the instructor leading the way.

He found that I possessed some natural rhythm and told me, "You could become professional in dance, but you'll have to dedicate yourself to training."

I loved dancing, the music and the glamorous atmosphere of the ballroom. Not wanting to make a commitment, I dismissed the fantasy and soon I was finished with my set of lessons.

I also had a new diversion....

Top: Me in front of cabin in Minnesota. Bottom: Me holding teddy bear.

Top: Our cabin and car in Iowa. Middle: Left to right, Elaine, Pearl and Mom. Bottom: Left to right, Pearl, Mary Jane and Elaine in park in Iowa.

Top: Osceola school. Middle: School slide in Ringwood, OK. Bottom: Grain Elevator in Oklahoma that Dad helped construct.

Top left: Elaine in hat. Childhood pictures of me. Bottom:
Left to right, Pearl, Mom holding Earl, and Mary Jane.

Top and middle: House in Osceola. Bottom: Train track that went through our property. (Homestead in background)

Top to bottom: Farm Place, Osceola Lake, Elaine in Huron Park, and Mennonite Church. (Brick addition added)

Top right: School picture of Lyle. Middle: Elaine in wedding dress in front of newlywed house. Bottom left: School picture of Marilyn.

Top: Mom and Dad at dinner in restaurant in SD. in 1968. Bottom: Earl, Dad, Mom and Mary Jane, weekend of Pearl's wedding, 1969.

First pictures I took after getting out of hospital. My eyes reveal how lost I am.

First portrait taken at studio.

I met Bob Anderson on the 4th of July holiday in 1969. I decided to take the bus to Dodge City to visit my dear Uncle Fred.

On my return trip, Bob happened to be the driver on the Continental Trailways bus. Wearing an impeccably pressed gray uniform shirt and navy pants, he stood at the door as I handed him my ticket and stepped inside. Always a little scared of going into the interior of a bus, I was lucky and found an empty seat right behind the driver. The front seat also provides the best spot to see what's up ahead.

Right away, he started flirting with me via the rearview mirror. Not to many miles down the road, he asked for my phone number. I was very flattered by his charm and his crooked smile, and we talked and teased the rest of the way to Wichita. By the time I got off the bus, he had my number. He called a day or two later and we started dating.

Bob was divorced and had been single about two years when we met. He had one young daughter named Tiffany, by his ex-wife Susan. He was of average height, a little over-weight and balding. But he could ooze charm if he wanted to. Bob had a way of looking at you sideways, with a little half-snickering smile like Elvis's, as if you were in on a secret together.

I became his puppet and fell completely under his spell. I latched on to him like a fly to honey. Nothing else mattered, but to be with him.

It wasn't long before we began sleeping together. He easily convinced me that he needed me. And I had one desire, *the desire to please him.* He would take me to some out-of-the-way, seedy motel on the far side of town. I noticed, but I did not value myself enough to question his reason or motives.

I received a few letters from the ministers of the Mennonite church. And then the letter of excommunication arrived. It read:

Dear sister Gladys: Christian Greetings to you.

This letter is sent to you to inform you that your spiritual condition was brought to the attention of the brotherhood in a council meeting on the 6th of July, 1969.

After repeated contacts with you endeavoring to help you in your problems and spiritual condition we found that your spiritual life had been very shallow for a number of years, that you were indifferent, carnally and worldly minded, self-complacment and self-centered which also affected your marital life between you and your husband, (Lyle) thereby causing strife and disunity to the extent that it finally culminated to the extent that you filed for a legal divorce. With this action pending we as a Church were compelled to give this attention. After presenting this before the Church prayerfully and in the fear of God, it was decided and agreed that such could not be born in the Church. This is now to inform you that you are now severed (excommunicated) from the fellowship of the Saints.

We your grieved brethren shall endeavor to keep the door open and the light burning, and we plead do repent and return home.

Lovingly your grieved and praying ministers, signed.

In early September, my divorce from Lyle was finalized and I received an additional fifteen hundred dollars in the settlement. He kept both vehicles and all of the furniture. Of course, I got to keep my "hope" chest!

My visits to the psychiatrist were reduced to twice a week and then tapered off. I felt I was ready to go to work.

My first job was in the Customer Service Department at Gibson's, a type of department store. I didn't stay there long. It was far enough from my apartment that I had to take a cab, and that quickly became too costly.

I was fearful about driving in Wichita. Bob let me practice in his car on a quiet street. As I got bolder, we picked busier streets. It was a long time before I felt comfortable driving on Kellogg, the main highway through town. But what a proud moment it was, when I accomplished that feat. Now, if his schedule permitted Bob would loan me his car while he was at work.

I found a job checking at an IGA grocery store five blocks from my apartment. Beginning wage was $1.10 an hour. I walked back and forth from work, on Oliver Street, sometimes as late as 10:00 p.m.

The first day I was on my own after training, I got called to the boss's office. They said it wasn't possible that I had balanced perfectly, with so many customers, and I must have done something wrong. "No," I replied to their inquiries, "I haven't cheated in any way!"

It was soon apparent that I was a fast and accurate checker. In those days, we had to manually punch every unit price into the cash register, and I found that I had an excellent memory for numbers. I could tell you the price of almost any product in the store, and soon the other checkers were asking me for prices on unmarked items.

But I discovered another horrible effect of the shock treatments: Sometimes, I couldn't remember what a produce item was called. For example, I could not tell a red potato from a white one, and how I needed to find the item on the produce chart. Same thing with turnips and parsnips. By the next day I had forgotten again.

Overall, I really enjoyed such a fast-paced job and the customers, and I stayed there for close to three years.

The neighborhood, where I had chosen to live, inspired rumors of petty crimes such as peepers and prowlers. I would get so very scared at night that I would go to bed early, figuring that with the lights out and everything dark, I would be safe. What I didn't know then was that every day my mother prayed for my safety.

Bob took me to a certain store where I excitedly purchased my first radio alarm clock. It sat on a shelf on the headboard of my bed. After going to bed at night, I would turn it on with the sound as low as possible, so it could barely be heard, as I didn't want a prowler to hear and think anyone was home.

I was now free to listen and the music was beautiful. But it reminded me of my honeymoon night with Lyle in that motel room where I felt like I had been dropped into another world.

So mostly I just listened to silence.

A few years earlier, after moving seasonally back and forth from South Dakota to Oklahoma, my parents had moved permanently to Fairview, Oklahoma.

Now in September of 1969, my sister Pearl was getting married, and I decided to go to the wedding. This would be my first return to visit the Mennonite church since being excommunicated.

I had told Bob all about my family, and he urged me to show my independence by renting a car and taking myself to the wedding. I agreed—I could do this by myself. I was capable and didn't need any help.

This would be the beginning of mentally torturous trips home. I would get extremely nervous. It was like stage fright, with pounding heart and sweaty palms. What would it be like this time? As each mile got closer, my heart beat faster. Upon arriving at my parent's home, I could tell it was going to be a tense weekend. Dad immediately went into his bedroom, leaving the door open just enough for me to see him sitting in his chair, hoping that I would notice that he was in a deep depression. When he came out he would hang his head like a person being punished, and shoot an occasional glare at me.

When it came time to go to church for the wedding rehearsal he said, "*You* can't go because your dress is too short."

We had a long argument, and finally I pleaded, "If you just close your eyes and hear my voice, you will realize I am the same person as ever! Why is this all about the length of *my dress?*"

In the end, I stayed home by myself, fuming inside but trying to maintain my composure so as not to completely spoil the wedding and cause a bigger scene.

The next day I attended the wedding, but had to sit alone (without my family) during the service and at the reception afterward.

As an expelled person, I was considered "lost" and church members and my relatives would tell me to my face that I was going to hell. Because I had known the "truth" and then left the church, I was treated worse than any stranger would be. A newcomer is welcomed because he or she has not yet been exposed to the "truth."

A favorite scare tactic told to me then and throughout the coming years was, "You will never be happy until you return to the church."

The church doctrine states that a member does not associate with an expelled member. When I had been a member in the church, and I would see a relative or friend, we would shake hands and hug.

Now most everyone, even my own relatives, had to keep their distance, even if they secretly desired to greet me. We just acknowledged one another with an awkward glance and a nod from across the room. I had just been through a very traumatic time with my hospitalization, but there I stood, all alone.

The majority of the people at the wedding did not show concern for me personally. They didn't talk to me. They dare not ask about my life. How could they? That might be construed as condoning my new lifestyle, and I was now a complete outsider. *They just stared,* as I once had.

After the wedding activities, night had fallen and I hurried back to my parents' house. I knew Pearl and Frank would be coming to the house to change into their travel clothes, so I waited in the car until they emerged to leave for their honeymoon, and I snapped a surprise photograph of them.

I returned to Wichita the next day, relieved that the wedding was over, and I was back to my world.

But, my world was filled with telephone calls and letters from my father. Indeed, it was constant. I couldn't heal myself; how could I persuade my parents to accept me, so they could heal?

One of the letters I received from my father reads:

November 14, 1970

Dear Gladys

I got up early this morning, have been wanting to write to you.

When I came home the other day, I sat down and read your letter, but before I got through I was crying. I felt that we were so separated and so far apart and yet you are so very close to me because you are my child and oldest daughter.

I know that God understands the heartache and sorrow, but still my grief often is more than I can bear, of course there is always a comfort when I can see my way through with the Lord. Often I have felt the great shame that has come upon our home because of the way that you have taken. I have also been offended and for this I am sorry and want you to forgive me. It is too hard for me to accept the way things are going.

Bob is a stranger to me and yet he has been brought into my home altogether against my will. Often I want to press you close to my heart, but when Bob comes around I get so depressed that I lose my senses or something.

It is hard for me to understand how for me to keep the avoidance and yet to show love and understanding. I know that you also have carried a heavy load and still are. All this has been so heavy on me that I feel on the verge of a mental breakdown. In my flesh I want to run away but I can't. All through the years to my boyhood days I have had tears, you know only so little of my life. I remember the day in Colorado when I made a vow that I would be true and faithful to God and love and be true to my wife and yet I have often fallen short of this. In all my life I need God to help me and you need him too.

I thank you for the nice cards you have sent me and when you write that you love me I want to believe you, and then I think why don't you want to obey me. I am sorry where I have hurt you and I don't want to hurt you anymore. But the future looks so dark. I wish you could pray for me. I will remember you. My

*tears are flowing everyday and my heart is filled with
sorrow. Good-bye my dear.*

*Love
From Daddy*

I could not get out of the sadness of my life. I felt terrible
about the grief I was causing my father and mother. But, the
more Dad fought me, the more I went to Bob for unhealthy
assurance.

I had a couple of girl friends, Sharon Jordan and Debbie
Laudermilk. I really liked to be with them, but they were
never a priority unless Bob was out of town.

I did not ask myself, why was I so clingy to Bob, and not
building other friendships? My number one thought was to
have attention and love from a man. I craved it. And in my
mind, when that thinking took over, other friendships, obligations and social entertainment became secondary.

My calendar *revolved* around Bob. I lived by the telephone, anticipating his calls. I'd tell myself, "I can't go
anywhere tonight because I've got to be here, in case he
calls." He'd tell me he would be back in town by a certain
time, and when he didn't call, I became petrified with fear
and anxiety.

When fear took over, I'd start thinking something bad
had happened to him, that maybe he had been in a car accident. I became desperate in the hours that the phone didn't
ring and I would walk the floor in pointless circles. Bob was
my lifeline and how could I survive without him?

The song *Help Me Make it Through the Night* was popular
at the time. I claimed it for my own as I sat on the couch next
to the silent phone, and sobbed, my stomach churning, while
I listened to the words and waited....

Then when he called, if I questioned him at all, he would become *furious* and go into a tirade. How *dare* I not trust him?

Once, I couldn't stand waiting any longer and took a taxi to his apartment unannounced. He poked his face out the door, livid with anger, and did not let me in. He put me in his car and drove me straight back to my place. Later it slipped out that Susan was or had been there.

Bob and I started having constant arguments. The majority of them related to where he said he was and where he actually was.

One night, his best friend Jerry was shot and killed as he walked into his own house. Jerry's family called me immediately, trying to reach Bob. I called his work, but they said he was not on duty. I kept calling his number all night long. He never answered.

As morning approached, I called another of his friends, and asked him to please try and find Bob. As the friend drove up to his apartment, Bob's car also pulled in. He had apparently been out all night. But what Bob told me was that he had put a pillow over the phone so he would not hear it ring, and he could sleep.

Bob had few friends; he said the only reason he had any was so he could use them for his benefit. Sometimes he told me about incidents at his work, and I heard things from other coworkers. One time he slapped a person, got sued and had to be put on leave until it was resolved. He was a very difficult person to get along with.

When I attended company functions with Bob, coworkers asked him, "How did you find such a nice girl?" They seemed amazed that I would date him and often teased me about it.

Bob would take me to visit his father, Joe, in Strong City, a cowboy rodeo town right across the river from Cottonwood Falls, a small quiet town. It was a ninety-minute drive from Wichita.

Right away I noticed an odd thing. When we entered the house, Bob would pull out a chair from the dining room table and turn it sideways while talking with his father, so he did not have to look at him. Slightly bent over with head down and eyes focused to the floor, he folded his hands between his legs, and nervously, gently clapped them together. I had never seen anything like it and was perplexed that he could treat his father that way. It took years of coaxing before Bob would look at his father face to face.

Bob told me he hated his father for how he treated him and his mother—controlling them to the point where they could hardly leave the house. According to Bob, as a child he once had a serious infection, but Joe would not let him go to the doctor. He could not forgive his father for those and other transgressions. Therefore, Bob grew up to be a bitter, hateful and angry man.

Of course, because of the relationship that Bob had with his father, he had no sympathy for my situation. Bob caused me to form a sort of deep bitterness towards my parents. I remember writing them a very strong letter—one which I later regretted sending, as Bob put the words into my head. I did agree with Bob on some points, my parents were suffocating me, but I could not hate them.

Another letter from my father reads:

Postmarked July 25, 1972

Dear Gladys Elaine

We got your letter today, thank you. We are still in Sidney, Nebr. It is raining every day.
For the last several weeks I have thought of you so much. The Lord placed a burden on my heart so I

have prayed much for you. I am so sorry that I as a father have failed to teach you the true way of life. I tried to teach you the word of God, but I have failed. You send me such nice cards and I appreciate them and your love so much. But why don't you obey me if you love me? You are giving your heart to your lover and turning your back to Mom and me. Where will you go when your lover is gone? When will you come back? We cannot give you our blessing. You deceived me in your first marriage so I will never believe in any more for you. You and Bob will not be able to eat with us because our fellowship is cut off.

This is simply God's word.

I am bowed down in sorrow. But I will live in hope. I am growing old fast. I am more weak. Someday I will give out and will be gone. How will you feel when I am gone? What can I hope for? I have been searching for a promise from you. Will you come to know the Lord? Or do you think I am an old man that doesn't know anything? I did not always treat my parents in love, but I am reaping tenfold.

I will close this letter by saying that you can do what you want to do, but may God help you to remember what you are doing to your father. My love shall always go with you. My desire is for that which is true. God has been merciful to me, so shall he ever be to all of us!

With all of my love,
From your Daddy

Thank you for that lovely card for Father's Day.

When Father's Day came around, I wanted to acknowledge him with a card. But it was difficult to find a suitable one. Plenty of them thanked "my Dad for loving me," or maybe "for being there in the tough times," maybe "for guiding me and giving me advice," maybe for "spending time with me." None of those would apply to our relationship. Often I would buy the most generic card that would say, "Have a Happy Father's Day." Then sometimes I would feel sentimental and would send Dad a loving card. He saved them all.

During this time, my relationship with Mom and Dad suffered greatly. We lost precious time in our lives because of our differences. Mom and I communicated via letters mostly, as there was not a lot to talk about. I could hear about her life, but I couldn't share with her what was happening in mine. My "worldliness" was foreign to them. We had lost what we had in common.

Bob and I spent a lot of time visiting his favorite sister, Norma Jean, who lived in Cottonwood Falls. Their old gray two-story home sat on a large corner lot filled with grand trees and a tire swing to one side.

I became very close to Norma Jean and her husband, whose name was also Bob. They became like surrogate parents to me, especially during the early years when I had little contact with my parents. I was able to fill that void with my visits to her house. Often, if Bob was working, I'd ride the bus to Cottonwood Falls and Norma Jean would pick me up. I felt very at home there, and I had a cozy guest room to sleep in. Her house became my place of peace.

Norma Jean was an excellent cook, fried chicken being her specialty. I would sit in the kitchen while she worked away. We always had lots to talk about. She loved to travel. Her favorite pastime was going to local auctions and collecting antique dishes that I "oohed" about. In the summertime we often made homemade ice cream, just like when I was a kid.

After almost three years of dating, I wanted to get married, but Bob didn't. He seemed to like having me around, and yet he wanted his independence. I was so naïve. I never imagined that he might have other girlfriends. Now, I am sure he thought he had it made: A hometown girlfriend who catered to his every whim, and probably, as they say, a girl waiting in every port.

I told him, "If you don't want to get married, then I'm breaking up with you. Three years is long enough to be together without a commitment. I'm going to start dating other men." That seemed to be OK with Bob.

In fact, a nice, good-looking customer at IGA had been asking me out, so as I was now available, I finally agreed to a date. He cooked me dinner at his house; we looked at his books and discussed our astrological signs (something that was very popular in the early seventies) and got along really well.

When I told Bob about my wonderful date and that I intended to have another, he quickly changed his mind about marriage. He let me know, in no uncertain terms, that he did not want me dating anyone else.

Shortly thereafter, on the 6th of July, he presented me with an engagement ring. The wedding date was set for November 6th, continuing the theme of our first meeting on the 6th of July 1969.

One month before we were to be married, I changed jobs after a persistent IGA customer convinced me to go to work for him. It was with a small company that manufactured aircraft parts. I got a good increase in pay and it was there that I began to attain my longed for office administrative experience.

Bob insisted that we apply for our marriage license in the town of Eureka, about thirty-five miles east of Wichita. He wanted to use a certain Methodist preacher there, a Reverend Johnson. I was a little suspicious, thinking how this would keep our names out of the "application for marriage license" column in the Wichita newspaper, but I had to go along with his plan. He didn't allow me a choice.

Chapter 11

Broken Tomorrows

W edding day arrived and started out like many other days spent in my life with Bob. I had a lot of things to do, including packing my belongings to move out of my apartment. But when I called Bob late in the morning, he was still in bed.

Bob was not accustomed to keeping a personal schedule and would sleep as late as he pleased. We were *always* late for our appointments.

Eventually he showed up to take my stuff to his apartment. The cedar chest was the first item to go in the back seat of his car. As the afternoon wore on, it became obvious *we were going to be late to our own wedding*. It was scheduled for five p.m. Bob called the courthouse in Eureka to ask for a clerk to stay after hours.

After dumping my things in his apartment, we then roared off to collect the flowers and a small wedding cake. Yellow frosting roses cascaded down the three white layers, with white bells on the very top. My bridal bouquet had white daises and miniature yellow and Tropicana roses, filled in with baby's breath and white stephanotis.

Finally Bob sped us onto the highway, while I clung to the cake in my lap. The car shook and rattled over rough spots and I watched with terror as little cracks appeared in the frosting.

We pulled into the courthouse around five-thirty. Bob hurried up the steps to pick up our marriage license.

A few minutes later we arrived at the church, where we found our wedding guests waiting. It was a very small party, Bob and Norma Jean who were our attendants, the preacher, his ten-year-old daughter who played the wedding music on the organ, and my best friend Sharon.

Hurrying into the kitchen, I quickly changed into my wedding gown. It was a beige street length dress of lace with an empire waist trimmed with small pearls and peach-colored satin ribbon. We pinned on boutonnieres and corsages and I grabbed my bouquet. At six o'clock, one hour late, the ceremony began!

Suddenly, I was standing alone at the entrance to the sanctuary clutching my flowers tightly and waiting for my cue. My photo of that moment shows an unhappy face, frowning in fear and apprehension. The others were already at the front of the church and facing me.

The organist started playing and I began my journey down the aisle. Nervously, with knees wobbling, I walked forward and stopped at Bob's side. He looked at me with a serious, almost scornful expression. His usual half-crooked smile now appeared to be a half-sneering smile.

Marriage was what I had wanted. I thought I loved Bob, but at this moment I felt trepidation. Not one of my family members was present. I had not even told them that I was taking this step. How would they react when they found out?

Bob and I solemnly spoke our wedding vows to one another.

I received a wedding ring, but Bob refused to wear one. He explained, "I want to wear my Masonic ring on my left ring finger. If I shake somebody's hand, I don't want a ring on my right hand." I believed him in a way, but still wondered if there might be another reason....

We spent the night back in Wichita at the Holiday Inn before leaving on a five-day trip to Houston and Galveston, Texas.

The wedding pictures show few smiles on our faces as we toured the area. I sent my parents a postcard from Texas telling them of my marriage and that I was on my honeymoon.

Bob had a fascination with prisons, and on our return trip we stopped at the Texas state prison and had a tour of the place.

Late on the last day of the trip, driving homeward, we were getting quite hungry. We looked quite a while for a restaurant. At last, we found one, went in and sat down. Bob picked up his spoon. "Look! It's dirty!" He asked for another one, it too was dirty. "I'm not eating here. Come on, let's go." He stood, and reluctantly I got up out of my chair and we walked out.

After getting back in the car an argument ensued, because I was hungry and there wasn't another restaurant in sight. We were still a long way from Wichita, but we drove home without eating—or speaking to each other.

Now I had to adjust to life on *his turf.* After we got home I went grocery shopping to begin my new life as a wife and a cook. I filled the cupboards with cooking essentials that had not been there before. In a small kitchen it was difficult to find space to fit everything, making it necessary to shift things around.

When he came home from work, I heard him yell from the kitchen, "Where are the salt and pepper shakers?"

"I had to move a few things around, as I needed a place to put the groceries."

"Don't mess with my stuff!"

"Bob, then where am I to put everything?"

This turned into another argument that made no sense. What were my alternatives, either not to buy groceries, or to put them on the floor? There was no reasoning with him.

I found out fast he didn't change at all with marriage. I felt helpless. I knew I hadn't done anything wrong—so why were we fighting?

I was always torn between two different ways of feeling in my marriage to Bob. Either, I felt like it was my fault, keeping me in a sense of total inferiority, or other times when I was sure I was innocent, it drove me almost to insanity. Because then I knew it was not in my power, and there wasn't anything I could do to change the situation. I had to suffer the screaming accusations towards me when I had done nothing wrong.

From the earliest days of marriage Bob used words to make me feel inferior, knowing their ability to cause hurt. He spewed lines such as, "You're worthless, you're no good, and *you are* a stupid jackass." One of his favorite taunts was, "You were a slut in the gutter, and I rescued you from it. You were *nothing* before you met me!"

It got to the point where I would beg him, *"Why don't you just hit me? You hurt me much worse with your words. I can get over a slap in the face, but I will never forget what you say."*

The topic of sex was a constant threat. Having an argument about something else completely, he would throw in the subject of sex. "I don't need you, I can get what I want anyplace!" Many times he'd say this and then leave the house.

Other times, he'd tell me he was going to see Tiffany, but often he wouldn't come home until morning. His explanation was, "I got sleepy so I drove to the side of the road and took a nap." This seemed peculiar to me, because he preferred night runs with the bus and he was very used to staying up.

Two months after our wedding, I received a typed anonymous letter in the mail. It told me about the person I had just married, how he was still having an affair with his ex-wife and other men's wives, how he used people and that he was very selfish, bossy, conceited, and cautious.

He's a b— —d. Don't think you can trust him out of your sight, honey. Don't mean all this to upset you but feel you need to know some facts, so you don't ever end up hurting too." Signed, *"Best of luck, you will need it. A friend.*

When I read the letter, and then re-read it, the strength drained out of my body. I trembled from head to toe. Unbelievable! Was it true? Who was it from? Was this why he got so angry whenever I questioned where he had been?

I turned the envelope over, looking for a clue as to who had written it, finding only a postmark from his hometown of Cottonwood Falls. I told myself, "I *have* to know who sent this. Who else knows my husband as that kind of person?"

My heart raced as I waited for Bob to come home so I could confront him with the letter. Evidence! Confirmation, that some person out there agreed with me that Bob was an evil person.

As soon as he sat down on the couch in the living room, I approached him and handed him the letter. His eyes and mouth drooped open in surprise, but he recovered himself quickly. "It means nothing. If you think it means more, well then you're just being an idiot."

I had listened to Bob's denials of his whereabouts for a long time before we married. The evidence that my husband might be cheating on me was more than I knew how to deal with. Still, I didn't put up much of an argument. Besides, at the time of any given situation, Bob could *convince me of anything.*

The note was not mentioned again, but I could not forget it. I kept the letter as a treasure, as though it confirmed to me that I was not a crazy person as he so often implied.

Bob collected Hummel figurines. One day while I was dusting around a figurine in the shape of a girl with a goose at her side, I found something attached. It was a love note to Bob signed, "From your little goose." My heart sank as I recognized the woman's name and I remembered other things she had given him.

With great anxiety I approached Bob about it when he arrived home from work. He assured me that she was "just a friend." Earlier I had believed him when he told me that. Now I wasn't so sure.

My suspicions got worse. One time, when I heard his car come home in the wee hours of the morning, I jumped out of bed and peeked out the living room window curtains. He was squatting down and combing over the passenger side as though looking for something. By instinct I knew; "*A woman has been there,*" but I rushed back to bed and pretended to be asleep when he came in. There was no use in mentioning that I had seen him go over the car. He would just come back with a ready answer.

There was other behavior that seemed strange. On the weekend or whenever I had a day off, I enjoyed going on the bus with Bob. Not particularly to be with him: but for the privilege to travel.

For a time Bob held a regular run to Joplin, Missouri, where he refused to take me. "The depot is dirty and you wouldn't like it there." Believe me, I had been in dirty bus depots many times before, that's just the way some of them were.

He kept an apartment in Lamar, Colorado, which I helped fix up, and then he never let me go there with him again. Was he in fact keeping a secret from me, I wondered? Was he being unfaithful?

I lived with the question of his fidelity. I couldn't *comprehend* that he was having an affair or affairs. *I refused to acknowledge the possibility, even though I dealt with the threats and worry constantly.* As a new bride, I couldn't even imagine leaving my husband. I needed him and I had nowhere else to go. So I endured his anger, his never-ending criticism, and at the same time, my family's unhappiness with my church excommunication and the fact that I had remarried.

Bob's ex-wife, Susan, and daughter lived in Cottonwood Falls, a block away from his sister Norma Jean.

Tiffany was about three years old when we first met. She was slender with long legs and brown eyes and hair.

On weekend custody visitations I would usually go along to pick her up, staying in the car while he went to Susan's front door. After he knocked, it would open ever so deliberately, as Tiffany would hide behind the door. Reluctantly stepping onto the porch, she stood close to her mother, who had to prod her to go on. With her eyes cast down, Tiffany slowly approached the car and then I gently coaxed her inside.

It had been told to me that Susan did not want Tiffany to see her father—or me, and she told Tiffany I was a bad woman who had stolen her dad away from her mother. No wonder Tiffany was afraid.

Of course, my eyes would be fixated on Susan, as much as I could ever get a look at her. She was short, a little on the plump side, with short dark brown hair and brown eyes. My mind tried to imagine how she had lived with Bob. The story goes, and it was a true one, that one time she hit him over the head with a frying pan during one of their fights.

Tiffany was a sweet and obedient child. I loved tucking her into bed and speaking kindly to her. It gave me great pleasure, a sense of motherhood. I enjoyed at least trying to make a positive difference in her life.

When she visited, Bob slept on the old couch, and Tiffany and I slept together in our bedroom. On her first visits, her body would shake violently all night. What frightful dreams must she be having?

Her father treated her well enough, although he could come across with a stern voice and cause her to quiver. He criticized her as he did me and was not affectionate towards her. Tiffany was mostly afraid because of her mother's malicious words about us. She probably expected us to be monsters.

Bob had told me how he'd never wanted to have children, and when Susan secretly quit taking the Pill and got pregnant with Tiffany, he was very upset with her.

Nevertheless, after their divorce he fought court battles over custody and visitation. I went along whenever he had his days in court. And he had a few!

Bob purchased a tape recorder that attached to the telephone so he could tape his and Susan's conversations, hoping that would be good ammunition for him to win his case. (She repeatedly objected in their phone conversations whenever Bob asked to see Tiffany.)

But often, he didn't want the things he would pursue; *it was most important to win, no matter the cost.*

Since Bob was an employee of Continental Trailways, we could get free bus passes to go anywhere in the United States. And that was good, because then we were able to take a few trips, albeit on a bus!

In October of 1973 we took a two-week vacation to Washington, DC and then on to New York City, my first trip to visit either city.

One morning in the hotel, I put on a new pantsuit I had purchased for the trip. As we left the hotel, I felt confident in how I was dressed and euphoric with the city around me, thinking, "Wow, I'm in New York City!"

Later, while we stood atop the Empire State Building surveying the view below, I asked Bob to take my picture. Curious, I questioned, "Why don't you ever compliment me if I look nice?"

He responded dryly, "You can *assume* that you do if I don't say anything. *I'll tell you, if you don't.*"

Something as simple as a kind gesture could not be given to me, but anything negative was spoken freely. Why was praise always withheld?

I desired to see the marquee lights and Rockefeller Center. We walked right past Radio City Music Hall! Excited, I asked Bob if we could see the Rockettes show. Immediately he retorted, "No, *I* have no desire to see them." Meekly, I kept walking along beside him on the busy sidewalk. Inside me, the sunshine of the day was quickly turning to gloom.

We did only what Bob wanted to do. He hired a taxi driver to drive us through the slums. We walked through dirty Chinatown. Why did he think it so important for me to see the filth of the city? Was he comfortable in that environment, or did he think I wasn't worthy of more?

We happened to walk by the Music Hall again and I stopped to look at the posters by the ticket window. I remembered how, as a child, I had cherished some pictures of the Rockettes that I'd clipped from a *Life* or *Look* magazine article. Now I was an adult and their show was within my grasp, and I could not reach it. Always on the outside, looking in.

I became *determined* to see the Rockettes. I was not going to let the opportunity pass by. This was probably my only chance at ever being in New York City. I more than begged. I was mad! Bob gave in and purchased tickets for the show.

What a spectacular theater! But as anyone knows, it is no fun to have your own way. I was thrilled to see their performance—and sick in my heart.

In every way I felt I was ugly and unimportant to him. I developed a horrendous, painful yeast infection from the stress and struggled through the remainder of the trip, counting the hours till I could get home to see my doctor.

To top it off, on our return we had a layover in Kansas City, one of the cities where he drove the bus on occasion. We stayed in a roach-infested hotel room. I shuddered when I saw the bugs in the bathtub. "Why do we have to stay in an old dirty hotel?" I don't recall his answer. I am now sure it was to stay away from better hotels where someone might recognize him with his "wife."

We came back to the daily routine of life. One night after an especially heated argument, Bob screamed, "Just get *out* of here!"

He took my clothes out of the dresser drawers and my ironed dresses that hung in the closet, hauled them into the living room and threw them down by the front door. He kept going back for more until they were heaped in a large pile. When I calmly said, "OK, if that's what you want, I will leave," he quickly slipped out the door and hid the car to prevent me from going. It was not possible for me either to go, or to stay. Confusion reigned and I was going crazy.

Barely a year into our marriage, Bob got physical in his abuse towards me. We were in the bedroom arguing when he threw me down across the bed. My leg hit the wood bedstead, causing a severe bruise that lasted for months. I favored my leg as it really hurt when I walked, but when people noticed, I pretended it was nothing. At the time, I told no one of the physical and emotional pain I was going through.

In between Bob's outbursts, I often sang the popular song by Donna Fargo; *I'm the Happiest Girl in the Whole USA*. Remembering the life I had led before, I thought I *was* happy, singing as my mother had, even in the midst of her trouble. Whatever hurtful abuse may happen one day, *I believed with my whole heart* that the next day would be better. It had to be; how could I go on otherwise? I kept dreaming, but I always encountered another broken tomorrow.

We went a few times to a marriage counselor, who told me, "You have two choices. You can either divorce Bob, or you can stay in the marriage and live with the fact that if he says, he will never change, then he probably never will." Bob told me, "I don't like this guy; I don't think his advice is any good." I didn't like him either because he wanted to hypnotize me, so we didn't go back.

Our social life consisted of bus company activities and the Shrine Temple. Bob was an active Shrine member and periodically drove their chartered buses whenever they participated in parades in other cities.

The Shrine organization had built a beautiful new two-story temple in Wichita, which we frequented. We went to their dinners and dances. Although I didn't get the chance to dance much, I liked being a part of the gaiety. I loved going up and down the grand stairway in the long stylish gowns of the day. Hotels, travel, conventions, meetings…I was in my element. I tolerated the bad in order to enjoy the good.

Whenever I had the chance I would go with Bob on his bus trips. On one chartered trip, I flew to Miami to join him and his group, whose plan was to take a three-day cruise to Nassau, return to Miami and spend the day sightseeing. Then I would fly home while he continued on his travels.

Our last evening on the ship, things went sour. At midnight, after dinner and a show, we headed to our stateroom. As we got on the elevator, the door began to close, hitting Bob's elbow and causing his drink to spill. He snarled at me, "You didn't step through the door fast enough!" Angry, he threw his glass on the floor.

We got off the elevator and walked through the narrow ship corridor. As we approached our room, he waved me off, saying, "You can't come in. Go away and leave me alone," and he locked the door. I was hoping no one could hear through the thin walls, as I was so embarrassed.

Not wanting to make a fuss in a public place, I accepted Bob's anger and didn't plead with him. I wandered around the ship for a while, finally sitting down at a table with another girl who was listening to the orchestra, in which her father was playing.

About two a.m. Bob came looking for me, grabbed my arm, and took me back to the room, only to order, "Pack your suitcase and get out!"

I stood in the hallway for a few minutes wondering what to do next. Suddenly he opened the door.

"You can come back in."

The remainder of the night I lay on the covers of my twin bed, awake and fully dressed, while I stared at the ceiling. We did not speak to each other.

Without saying good-bye the next morning, he left the room early and attended to his charter group. I debarked by myself, took a cab to the Miami airport and spent the whole day sitting there, waiting for my flight back to Wichita.

Later in another of our arguments he told me, "I was so angry that night on the ship, if we had been on an open deck when I found you, I would have thrown you overboard."

Chapter 12

Time and Again

In the spring of 1976, we bought a light brick house on Sheridan Avenue in the northwest part of Wichita for forty thousand dollars. The monthly payment was three hundred and seventy-six dollars, and we thought we were stretching it!

It had two bedrooms, a huge kitchen, dining and living room, fireplaces upstairs and down, a full unfinished basement and a one-car garage.

In back was an enormous yard full of trees and flowers that would bloom three seasons out of the year, yellow daffodils, tulips, iris, lilies, pink peonies, roses and in the fall, mums. To one side was a small patch of lily of the valley flowers. I thought they were especially beautiful and delicate and I watched over them with a gentle and protecting touch.

In my desire to please Bob, I often mowed the lawn. The task took hours. One day in particular, I couldn't wait until he got home to show him how nice the lawn looked and how he wouldn't have to spend time mowing. But he didn't notice the lawn; his only remark, "You dumped the clippings in the trash bins!" He then walked me way back behind the shed, all the while complaining that now he would have to dump them. "Why don't you know better? This is where the clippings are supposed to go." Not one word of how beautiful the yard looked and of the work I had just completed. I asked myself, why do I continue to spend my energy, to try and make him happy, only to be let down time and time again?

I had married a man just like my father!

I couldn't continue to live the way I had been, but I felt that I deserved the pain and abuse. It had to be my fault. If Bob wasn't happy, I must be the cause. And when he lashed out in anger, it was what I was used to from growing up. Furthermore, I accepted the hurt, because *I needed him* in order to make myself seem worthy. The perceived good deeds that I did were what kept me going, making me believe that I was *valuable* to him and he wouldn't be able to get along without me.

Bob and I were two emotionally sick people, in a codependent relationship. Why had I married such a person? I was drawn by his appearance of strength, thinking he would protect me. To the public, he projected a powerful image. Craving love in my life, I was attracted to a man whom I thought I could please, and therefore (unknowingly) get the approval I couldn't get from my father. But inside Bob was a wall that could not be penetrated, because it would mean having to deal with his emotions.

Once, Bob gave me a rare glimpse into his soul. I was walking through the house one late afternoon as the sun was shining through the west windows in the living room. I noticed him sitting in one of our matching olive green recliners. I walked behind his chair and gave him a peck on the back of his neck. "I love you."

He replied, "Well, what does that mean? I don't know what love is, do you?"

He seemed quite serious. What was he thinking? Did he have trouble believing that I could love him, as he imagined "love" to be?

I came to realize that he desired real love, but didn't really know what real love was. To be honest, neither did I.

After working for the manufacturing company for several years, I took a new job working for the First National Bank in the heart of downtown Wichita. This is where I met a wonderful friend named Judy.

I was employed in their customer service payroll department where outside companies hire the bank to do their payroll. While sitting at our desk's one day, we suddenly heard a loud pop. Thinking it was a car backfire we continued our work, only to be interrupted again by a sequence of shots. Rushing to the window, we witnessed pandemonium in the streets.

A sniper had gone to the twenty-sixth floor balcony of the nearby Holiday Inn and was shooting at the people down below. We saw cars strewn in the street, and people lying on the ground. Quickly, there were police sharpshooters hiding behind building corners in front of us. Our work stopped and we frantically waited for the carnage to end.

The sniper was captured in his hotel room. But not before eleven people were killed on that horrible day.

Later, as I stepped out of the bank building onto the empty and quiet street I felt a tremendous sense of vulnerability and couldn't leave the area fast enough.

I began to dread going home after work, with my stomach tensing up the closer I got to the house, wondering what I was going to face upon arrival.

Maybe I had left a bathroom drawer ajar as I hurriedly left for work in the morning. If I left a crumb or speck of jelly on the kitchen counter as I made my lunch, Bob would leave it there.

As soon as I walked in the door, he would beckon me into the bathroom to show me the open drawer or into the kitchen, and the lecture would begin: "Look at this counter, you left it dirty."

"I was in a hurry."

"That's no excuse."

"Bob, stop it! Quit treating me like a child!"

"You quit acting like a stupid idiot!"

The argument would escalate because I always defended myself. (I am not a sloppy person and didn't ever mean to leave a mess.)

I wasn't allowed to lie on our new sofa—"That's not what it's for!" And if I touched it with the vacuum cleaner while cleaning, that would cause a fight. I could do nothing right in our home, just as I could do nothing right for my father.

After a fight he usually would not speak to me for about three days. Then we'd have a brief respite, which I couldn't enjoy, because I feared peace and happiness. It felt very uncomfortable, and something I was not used to. Nervously, I waited for the next blow-up. Not wanting it, but at least then I knew where I stood.

I was determined to withstand whatever I had to, in order to stay married. I remembered what had happened with Lyle. I hadn't loved him when we married. When I took those vows, "Till death do us part," I was not being fully honest with myself, or with God, or anyone else. In retrospect, I justified divorcing Lyle.

But I loved Bob, and had told my parents so, many times in defending my reason for marrying him. Now, I felt that my own words obligated me to stay married. I made a vow to myself: *I was not going to divorce Bob, no matter what.*

Eventually the stress began to show. At night, my legs would turn numb. If I had to go to the bathroom, I would stumble getting out of bed, sometimes falling to the floor. Many times my legs refused to hold me up and I had to crawl like an infant.

Every once in a while after a fight, I would go to bed and he would kick me out with his feet. Then I would try sleeping on the couch, only to have him come in and push me off. So, I spent many hours lying on the living room floor. That made the numbing sensation worse and I crawled even slower. I wondered what was happening to my body.

Bob kept a small pistol in our bedroom in a dresser drawer. Sometimes he would say, "Just get the gun and shoot me."

After a terrible argument one night he went to bed while I was still in the living room. After a while he came back out, telling me, "If I can't sleep, then you don't need to either. I'm miserable, so you should be miserable too." He pulled me back into the bedroom with him, closing the door behind us.

On the floor in the corner behind the door, I cowered, all curled up like a child, fearing for my life. I often did this as a way to endure his outbursts and make it harder for him to hit me. Now, he was in such a rage, I wondered if this was the night he would actually go to the dresser drawer and pull out the gun.

Why had he closed the door? We were the only ones in the house. Very scared, I knew I had to keep quiet.

Although he reminded me of the gun, it stayed in the drawer.

He kept me up the remainder of the night, threatening and taunting me, telling me how "stupid" I was and how "good" I had it with him. What a contradiction!

Once in a while, after our fights, I would spend the night at the English Village Motor Lodge on East Kellogg in Wichita.

I felt very alone as I drove up to the motel, got my bag out of the car, and entered the room, with the darkened world all around me. Sometimes I wouldn't bring a bag, and then I was quite embarrassed to think that the motel manager might be curious as to why I was checking into a room.

In the quiet solitude, my spirit too broken to turn on the television or even read, I lay on the bed and sobbed.

Bob never tried to find me. I wondered if he ever worried about me, or wondered where I might be. Nary was a question asked when I returned home.

During my marriage to Bob, I did not think about God very much. A couple of times I went to a Baptist church a few blocks from our home, the first of any kind since I had left the Mennonite church.

The whole time I was sitting in the service, all I heard in my mind, over and over, was a voice; "You're going to hell, you're going to hell." After a few visits I did not return; it felt like a betrayal of my upbringing. Better just to stay away. And yet, it seemed like somehow I knew that was a place to get help.

There were times I would leave the house in the evening and drive around as though going crazy, sobbing and wiping the tears from my eyes so I could see to drive. Other cars sped by me, continuing on their journey.... Did the people inside those cars wonder why I was crying? Could they see my pain?

I would knock on church doors, hoping a person might be there, pleading to myself for somebody to rescue me, *please, please help me make the hurt go away! I can't continue to endure how Bob is tormenting me.* I didn't know that churches had parsonages, where I might have gone to find a pastor.

After staying away from the house as long as I could, I would return, exhausted and emotionally spent, having accomplished nothing. I wanted to go to sleep and not wake up.

In the early years, Bob and I saw little of my parents. Still, I was eager to show them the house I lived in, and pleaded with them numerous times to come for a visit. Finally they agreed to spend a Thanksgiving Day with us.

They arrived around noontime. Dad and Bob made themselves comfortable in the living room while Mom helped me in the kitchen. Shortly thereafter, Bob appeared in the doorway, beckoned me to the side and hissed, "Tell your dad to get his feet off the coffee table, now!"

I refused to say anything to Dad. My stomach was always churning when my dad was around, and I wasn't about to confront him on the issue.

Instead, I had to contend with an angry husband.

Mom, being very sensitive, perceived the coldness between Bob and me. But I assured her everything was fine, even though you could cut the tension at the dining table with a knife! Soon after we ate our meal together, my folks left.

Bob remained furious. Yelling at me for refusing to deal with my dad, he went to one of our recliners, got up on it in his shoes, and jumped up and down, bellowing, "What about this? *What about this?* If that's all you care about our furniture, I might as well do *this!*"

As time went on, we made more visits to Fairview, especially at Thanksgiving and Christmas. My folks did not ever take a liking to Bob, and Dad made himself pretty scarce if Bob came home with me.

The constraint I felt towards my father had not abated.

As soon as we would arrive, if Dad was not in the house, I knew he would be out in his shop waiting for me. Obligingly, I'd go out to see him.

His office was very important to him. He liked to show me how neat and organized it was with his papers carefully stacked in piles. Sometimes we'd walk together back to the house.

Then, I would sit and try to listen attentively as he showed me his history books, atlases, magazines such as *National Geographic* and *Farm and Ranch*, or Mennonite genealogies. I had no interest in history, geography or genealogy, but I listened in order to make him happy.

He would always pull out a map and tell us where some lake, mountain, highway, city or country was. That was his joy, when he could be showing us in detail where a river ran or about a particular magazine or book he was reading.

But afterwards, when he was no longer the center of attention, he would either leave the room or retreat to a chair in the background.

He never asked me how I was, or what was new in my life. I could not imagine what it would feel like to share inner thoughts with my father, or have any emotion other than unease.

I lived my life having a knot in my stomach when we were together, waiting for his judgment towards me. *I was never comfortable in my father's presence.*

Mostly he would be in his own world. He would sit aside with his head bent to his hand, vigorously rubbing his forehead, or else gaze around the room with a staring look in his eyes.

I never knew what he was thinking. Sometimes when I would stand or walk though the room, and as his eyes followed me, I wondered, "*Is he undressing me in his mind?*" Embarrassed at the thought of it, I would move quickly out of his sight.

Every once in a while, late in the evening, he would knock on my bedroom door and invite me out to breakfast the next morning. This was another act, a ritual of paying him attention. Submissively, I went along.

If one of his "coffee friends" happened by, he would proudly introduce me and invite the other person to sit down. He loved to show off his kids, and I am told, talked proudly of us. In the café with me, he was upbeat, with a wonderful wide smile on his face. There, he conversed amicably. He liked the sociable atmosphere. I paid for the meals.

Mealtime at home was different. One time I had asked the Baptist minister in Wichita on how I should handle the subject of avoidance with my parents. His advice to me, "Elaine, write your parents a letter and tell them you are not in agreement with the avoidance, but out of respect for them you will honor their wishes." So I did my best. Still, I approached each meal apprehensively, with my stomach churning, wondering how or whether the avoidance would be kept. This varied according to whom might be eating with us. When we had other Mennonites for company, my mother would set two tables side-by-side, with the expelled members sitting at our own table. If it were immediate family, sometimes I would just sit at the far end of our kitchen eating area.

Over the years, two of my siblings, Mary Jane and Earl both got expelled from the Mennonite church. By then, my family usually ate together buffet style, which meant we could sit where we wanted, having no formal table settings. Of course, who would want to take a spot too close to a church member, with the discomfort of knowing he or she was following you with their eyes, waiting to see where you would place yourself! So we still sat separately! One way to avoid all of this "musical chairs" was to dine at a restaurant, where none of this seemed to matter, and we sat side by side.

At the end of my visits, as I prepared to leave, Dad would start pacing around. Never failing, I could sense that another ritual would soon show itself.

Soon he'd shrink back into the hallway, peek around the corner and beckon me with his forefinger. He waited until everyone else was about out the door and saying good-bye. I feel sure he did this to avoid having any other person or persons involved in the conversation. He wanted privacy to attack.

"What are you doing to Mom and me? Do you know the great shame that has come upon our house because of what you have done with your life?"

What could I ever say that would appease him? I took his rebukes and would leave the house, my body trembling.

Driving back to Wichita, I would tell God over and over, how thankful I was that I didn't live like my family did. I sobbed, out of sadness and freedom at the same time. My hands tingled and my legs felt like they were shaking deep inside.

Arriving home depleted I would collapse in fatigue. I had to drag myself to work the next day. My coworkers could always tell if I had been home. The physical effects would often last for three days. Mary Jane told me she experienced the exact same symptoms.

Why did I keep going back? My friends would ask me, "Why do you continue to spend time with your dad?" A lot of it was guilt. It had been drilled into my head to honor my parents, and this included visiting frequently. Dad always told us, "It's your obligation as our children; you come home!"

So we did. We *were* a close family in certain ways. We couldn't stand to be together, yet we couldn't stand to be apart.

Although I really enjoyed working at the bank, after three years I was ready for a change. In March of 1978, I went to work for a fairly new company that owned a chain of restaurants, only a few blocks from where I lived.

What a great part of my life that turned out to be! To recall it brings back so many good memories. Some people go to their jobs to put in their eight hours, and that's it. But working for this company was a unique and enjoyable experience, one that I truly cherished.

When I came on board, the rest of the staff consisted of the owners, Tom and Sally, and their teenage kids. Sally was a short petite woman with curly brown hair usually worn shoulder length. With a passion for fashionable tailored clothes and shoes, she was always very put together. Tom, a handsome man, at probably six feet, four inches, towered over everyone.

I became their receptionist and first full-time employee. Tom and Sally shared the back room with desks that faced each other, and I sat in the front area. This was the total of our small office. We were located adjacent to one of our restaurants in a shopping center and often I could hear the sounds of the jukebox through the wall as Linda Ronstadt belted out *Blue Bayou,* one of my favorite songs.

In a short time, we became so successful that bankers were pounding on our doors, introducing themselves and wanting to loan us money! A little different from the early days when Tom had to go look for lenders. The potential for growth was phenomenal because of our novel product, and our sales quickly proved it.

Often when I went next door to the restaurant around five p.m. to take our soda glasses back to the kitchen from our office, rush hour was beginning. People were lined up so deep you had to literally work your way through the crowd to get to the counter. Feeling sorry for employees and customers alike, frequently I would stop and clean tables, work at the counter, or do whatever I could to help.

My job swiftly increased to include bookkeeping duties and payroll. With every store that opened, each daily task was duplicated one more time. As more bookkeepers were hired into the office, we were constantly rearranging to fit in another desk, and it got harder and harder to do in our cramped quarters. We became part of a close special family in more ways than one! Although we were thrown together in a limited space we worked towards one goal, in "growing the company," and we felt it was an exciting place to work!

As we grew, the owners prospered. All of a sudden he and Sally could go on trips and buy just about anything they wanted.

Soon enough the day came when Tom felt he needed to get around faster to all of his restaurants, as some were located out of state. He went shopping and purchased a small Cessna airplane.

Next he needed a pilot. He found Marty, who used to fly for Elvis Presley. We really enjoyed having Marty on staff, as he was a natural comedian. Of course, we always tried to get him to talk about Elvis. He told us snippets of when he sometimes got to take Lisa Marie back and forth to see her dad. But he was quite humble and respectful of Elvis (even though he was dead), and shied away from saying much about him.

During this time they bought a condo in Vail, Colorado. Generously, they allowed their employees to sign up to stay in the condo.

Occasionally Bob and I vacationed there during the summer months. Vail had a number of fine restaurants where we could dine outdoors. The weather was most agreeable, cool in the mornings and evenings and balmy during the day. The shops in town typically kept their front doors open. I was so amazed when I could just walk through an open door.

We couldn't do that where I came from because of the flies and bees and the need for air conditioning! I thought Vail was beautiful, with all of the flowers and aspen trees.

I loved to spend time at the condo, even during the tough times of my life. It was a good home base, while we toured the surrounding area. One time we convinced Bob and Norma Jean to go with us, but it turned out to be an especially difficult trip. My Bob was controlling of me and did not allow me the freedom that Norma Jean enjoyed. It caused a lot of friction and we headed home early as four unhappy people.

One evening while I was spending some quiet time alone and reading, my ex-husband Lyle called and asked, "I'm in town this evening, may I come over?" I said "Sure." Bob happened to be on a bus run, and I didn't give it a second thought.

With the sun still in the western sky, Lyle arrived shortly and I welcomed him into the house. I did feel a little awkward in that we had not seen each other since the divorce years ago. We sat in overstuffed chairs on opposite sides of the living room. He told me how he had done well financially in his business, and of his travels. Tentatively he inquired about me. He had heard that I was married to an abusive husband. I told him everything was fine in my marriage. We visited for thirty minutes at the most before he left.

The next night, when Bob returned, I had no misgivings about telling him of Lyle's visit. After all, for me, it had been an innocent thing. Why should I keep it from him? Lyle and I would have never given it a thought to do anything inappropriate. I guess you could say we were naïve in that respect.

Well, Bob flew into hysterics. Pushing me into the bedroom, he threw me onto the bed, held me down, and raped me. When he slammed my body, he sneered in my face, "Well, how do you like it? Was it like this with Lyle? Did you enjoy it? You're just a *whore*." I lay there as tears streamed down my face and past my ears, wetting the pillow beneath me. The emotional pain of such degradation left me feeling very sad.

Realizing our marriage was severely sliding downward, we agreed, "Perhaps what we need is to get out of town and talk things over." So we took a vacation to Colorado in December of 1978.

As it happened, the place we went was really a summer resort area (not the company condo) and there wasn't much to do in the winter season. Motels were closed and lodging was hard to find. Restaurants were closed or vacant, as there were few people around. It was a cold, barren and windy place. Just like our lives, hollow. It turned out to be an empty vacation—no warmth to be found.

On our return trip home through the scenic roads of Colorado, Bob drove and I gazed out the window. I had a sudden, intense intuition that something had happened to someone in my family. It was the 21st of December. Such anxiety filled me that I could hardly sit still. I thought I *had* to stop at a phone booth and call. But I didn't dare ask Bob. He would just say I was stupid. Instead I reminded myself that I had spoken with my folks the prior evening. I kept saying over and over that everything is OK.

But after we arrived home and walked in the door from the garage, the telephone was ringing and I ran to answer it. Mary Jane had moved to Hutchinson, north of Wichita a few months earlier, seeking her own happiness. On the other end of the line was the family with whom she was living. That afternoon, someone had tried to kidnap my sister!

She had just finished some Christmas shopping at K-Mart. As she approached her car in the parking lot, she noticed a man sitting in the automobile next to hers, parked in the opposite direction. She hesitated, but then continued. When she opened her car door, he jumped out of his car, grabbed her arm, and stuck a pistol in her side while trying to push her into her car. Screaming, she fought him off and ran back to the store for help, all the while afraid of a bullet coming at her from behind.

Police caught him the same day. He had been released from prison on a technicality a few months prior. They found rope already tied in a loose knot, duct tape, and a gun in his possession. The rumors strongly suggested that he was out to commit murder and may have been connected to one that had recently happened in a similar fashion near Hutchinson.

After dealing with the trauma of Mary Jane's horrific scare, I then listened to the trial. Ultimately the jury found the attacker guilty of attempted kidnapping charges. We were greatly relieved to know he was going back to prison.

Getting settled back into the daily routine, I soon realized that our "vacation" had not changed anything for the better.

Bob hit me more frequently. At least twice, he tried to strangle me. First time, he grabbed me by the throat and squeezed. The second time he threw me against the kitchen cupboards and forced my head backward onto the counter and then put his hands around my neck. I quickly gathered that his actions were life threatening and I had to stop any talk. I was scared out of my wits, and breathing hard, as he relinquished his hold on me. His words: "Next time it will be for good."

Work was my savior. It kept me going. It was incredible how different I felt there. My job allowed for a great deal of independence and I began to trust my intelligence and competence, although, sometimes my insecurities did make it tough for my boss to deal with. Whenever he called me into his office, I would usually start crying almost before he said anything! I was always ready to take the blame, even if there wasn't any blame to take. So he would start out the conversation by telling me kindly, "Now, Elaine, don't be so sensitive and take this personally." Over many years I did improve.

We moved into our new building with offices on one end and a warehouse on the other. With spacious offices, we increased our staff, as new departments were created for purchasing, training, construction and marketing.

We had a party to celebrate. The warehouse was turned into a country barn dance floor, with hay bales and everything. Gladly, food distributors provided us with food. They wanted our business! We hired the best local country music band, opened the warehouse freight doors and partied the night away.

By December of 1979, I became pretty reluctant to leave the office at the end of the day if I knew Bob was home. The minute I walked in the door Bob started in on me and I would want to curl up in a fetal position in a corner somewhere. I often wished I could bury my head in the sand like an ostrich, so I couldn't think.

One Friday night I stayed quite late. When I got home, we argued. I don't remember what it was about, but it probably didn't matter. Bob ordered me out of the house. "Pack your suitcase, take my pick-up, and get out of here!"

He took my house keys, checkbook, and all of my credit cards, leaving me with only the cash in my billfold, I believe, around twenty dollars. I made a call to my friend Judy and she said I could stay at her place.

Monday, Bob called me at work and said in sweet apologetic tones, "Would you please have lunch with me?" When needed, he was a master of smooth talk. Reluctantly, I met him at a nearby restaurant for lunch, and he pleaded, "I promise I will never be mean to you again."

I let him persuade me this time. I didn't *want* to go back, but I agreed to, because I could be talked into it for his sake, *always accommodating, for his sake.* His verbal plea would override my hatred of his abuse towards me and I didn't have the willpower, strength, confidence, or determination to follow my own heart.

But he did not do as he had promised. I left again. He never asked me where I was staying. He communicated with me by telephone at work. I stayed a few weeks at Judy's house, until he *begged* me to come back home; convincing me once again that he needed me.

We continued to make frequent trips to Cottonwood Falls. Bob always drove. I just stared out the side window as into another world, not thinking, not seeing anything, oblivious of the man beside me. I *was* conscious of my paralysis. I seemed to be floating in space, void and deserted. I felt like I was in a hypnotic state of being.

And when we headed home late in the night, I would lie down in the back seat of the car, and fall into a not-awake, not-asleep state, feeling every familiar bump and turn of the route. My life had become like this ride, the passenger swaying to every motion of the driver.

In May of 1980, I gave up on my resolve never to divorce. I served Bob with papers and a court order to leave the house. He ignored the order, saying, "There's no reason that we can't live here together, even if we are going to divorce."

There's always a once again, and once again he talked to me, kneeling down at my feet, crying and pleading with me not to leave him, promising to be good to me, even threatening suicide if I did not change my mind.

I dismissed the divorce action.

In June of 1980, we took another trip to Colorado. Kansas was having a record-breaking heat spell that summer and we decided to flee the heat. One particular evening, just as dusk was descending upon us, we drove down a hauntingly beautiful and narrow winding road from Canon City to Cripple Creek. My snack of apples and cheese made me sick. I did not know what was wrong with me and blamed it on the twisting road. In fact, for the rest of the trip I felt nauseous most of the time.

When the vacation was over, I went back to work. In the evening I would come home and lie down, still sick, day after day. Something had to be terribly wrong, but I couldn't imagine what. I thought I was a healthy person.

The sickness did not leave me, so I finally made an appointment to see the doctor. After an examination the doctor left the room. Shortly he came back and announced, "You're pregnant."

"That's impossible! I'm taking birth control pills!"

What the doctor said was true.

My mind quickly scrambled over the facts. I could not have a baby with what I was going through in my marriage. I knew it would be unending turmoil if I had a child and ended up divorcing, remembering how vehemently Bob had fought to have visitation rights with Tiffany. He had always made it absolutely clear that he wanted no more children. I couldn't discuss this news with him.

The doctor listened as I told him briefly about my troubled marriage. He wanted to know how I was going to deal with pregnancy. Sitting on the cold hard table in the doctor's office, I uttered, *"I cannot have a baby."* I repeated it over again, as if the doctor hadn't heard me. "Do whatever you need to do."

I felt there was no choice. I did not refer to myself as being "pregnant," and certainly refused to use the word "abortion."

I was such a mental wreck with our turbulent marriage I couldn't even fathom having a child. I couldn't consider it. It wasn't an option. Bob and I didn't discuss it; I just told him what I was going to do. He did not dissent, and immediately agreed that I should have an abortion.

In those days, it was a common practice for women to go into the hospital for a dilation and curettage, known as "D&C," to treat menstrual difficulties. This is what I told my family, friends and coworkers. That I needed to have a D&C. "Just a minor problem, everything is going to be OK."

Bob and I arrived at St. Francis Hospital in the pre-dawn hours of July 25th.

As I lay on the table before being wheeled into the operating room, an attendant came to my side. Leaning down close to my face she asked quietly and gently, "Are you certain that you want to continue with this abortion? You know, it's not too late to change your mind."

"Yes," I quickly responded.

I rejected any power of reasoning that came to mind as to what I was doing. *Impossible, there is no other way*, as I kept my thoughts focused on the words "D&C." I was whisked through the doors and the procedure was performed.

I was out of the hospital the same day. In the craziness of my life, *I lived in the moment—survival.* So that day was blocked out of my life. And I did not allow myself to analyze what I had just done.

Chapter 13

Breaking Free

Back in the days when I had worked at the bank, I processed the payroll for a local hotel. The employee in charge of their payroll was a woman named Jane. She and I never met each other; we only talked on the telephone. For whatever reason, we did not get along. Our dislike for each other had been spontaneous and intense. I think the cause of that stemmed from the fact it was my job to review her payroll, and she didn't like to be questioned. When I left the bank, I commented to myself, "If I never met Jane, it would be too soon."

In 1980, I found I couldn't keep up with all of my duties, and Sally told me she was thinking of hiring an office manager. That position would be responsible for the restaurant side of the business while I would be in charge of purchasing administrative equipment and supplies, keeping track of company cars, tags and expenses, organizing events, and all administrative billing.

I paid the bills for all company travel, entertainment, utilities, and rent. I approved and paid all the expense reports from our district managers, management personnel, airplane maintenance invoices and the pilot's expenses.

My office was right across from Sally's, and one day in August she called me in to look over an application from the person she had decided to hire. I commented to her that the woman sounded very familiar, and my curiosity was aroused.

Thinking about the new applicant and her resume, I finally realized with whom I would be working! It took me a while because she had married and had a new last name.

I panicked and told Sally of my concern, but it was too late. Sally had already offered the position to Jane—of all people! What could be worse?

Jane arrived for her first day of work and Sally introduced us. A look of shock passed over Jane's face when she learned my name. Our tension had not abated.

Tom boasted that I was the most trusted employee, and our controller, Keith, asked me to review Jane's work. Even though I did it discreetly, she could see I checked up on her stuff. This contributed to us getting off to a bad start. Adamantly opposed to anyone watching over her, she would voice her objection constantly, "I'm the office manager and I don't need anyone looking over my shoulder!"

Eventually, in order to maintain some sense of civility in the office, Keith told me not to examine her work anymore. Over time, we settled into our different job responsibilities and a sort of truce.

In the autumn, desperate to try anything to make our marriage work, I suggested attending an upcoming seminar on marriage at Century Two, our local convention center in Wichita. Bob didn't want to, and we argued.

Standing in the dining room, he grabbed me and pushed hard against my chest. I flew down the hallway, hitting my head as I landed on the floor. This was the most violent and hardest of his coming at me. The pain was excruciating, in my body and in my heart.

He then said, as if stating an inevitable fact, "If we don't do something about our marriage, I will end up killing you."

In December of 1980, I left again...filed for divorce again...and went to stay with Judy again.... This time Bob really negotiated: "Look, you can live in the house just like always. I will be at the house while you are at work and then I'll stay away while you're here. I promise I won't bother you."

I relented and came back to try it, as I didn't really want to leave the house. Things were quiet for a couple of days. Then late one night, after I was in bed, he came in unannounced and scared me spitless.

I told myself, "This is not going to work." I began to think about planning my next move. In the meantime, Bob took over the house again, as if we had never had the earlier conversation.

I called the pastor of the Baptist church where I had attended a couple of times and he came over one evening to counsel us. While we all sat together in the living room, Bob spoke freely to the pastor, revealing his inner thoughts. "I have always felt that Elaine is the better person. I've put her on a pedestal. I *expect* her to be perfect. But, I don't know how to handle her goodness, so I have to tear her down."

Before leaving, while we were standing in the living room, the pastor requested that we gather in a circle and hold hands while he said a prayer.

The next time I called for his help, the pastor said he could not continue to counsel us because we were not members of his church. I couldn't believe it. So much for that course of help, because I certainly wasn't going to entertain any thoughts about attending church on a regular basis, let alone become a church member.

I suggested marriage counseling and Bob consented. I looked in the phone book and found a counselor who had an office on 13th Street just around the corner from where we lived. How convenient! We went for a few sessions.

During one meeting, the counselor spoke directly to Bob, "Put *yourself* in Elaine's shoes and try to see her point." Bob looked at me and said earnestly, "I can understand what you go through, but *I* am not willing to change." The counselor concluded, "Elaine, if you want to stay in the marriage, you need to accept the fact that you will be treated like a floor mat and you will have to learn to walk on eggshells."

One day I was driving on Riverside Boulevard, a tree-lined avenue that follows the curves of the great Arkansas River. As I guided the car around the bends, I said to myself, "I'm almost thirty-five years old! I have too many years to live yet! I don't want to be that man's floor mat for the rest of my life." I squeezed the steering wheel harder. *"Somehow, I have to make a final break."*

I never divulged my marriage problems to my parents, although I am sure that Mom surmised quite a bit.

In February of 1981, I took Dad and Mom on a Continental Trailways bus trip to Phoenix, Arizona to visit our pheasant-hunting friends, the Carlsons. I was so happy when I could give my parents something that they could not have done financially on their own. This was our first visit to Phoenix and we were quite impressed with the balmy weather in the middle of winter!

One thing that amazed me was all the fresh oranges and grapefruit on the trees. It was a real treat to walk out the patio door and reach for a grapefruit for breakfast. Our time spent was quite relaxed and our hosts treated us royally.

On one perfect warm sunny day, we drove out into the countryside to see the crops in the fields. Dad was impressed with the layout, and I remember him getting out of the car, walking out into the field, pulling up a stalk of grain and looking it over. He brought the stalk back to the car and he discussed the grain with Roly Carlson. *It pleased me.* It was so rare to see him enjoying the day, just taking in the moment.

On our return trip home the last evening, my parents departed the bus in a small town in Oklahoma where they had left their car parked, to return to their home. I began chatting with the bus driver, as was my habit. We could always find a connection in coming up with the name of another bus driver we both knew!

Around midnight the bus pulled into the station in Oklahoma City. The driver reached out for my hand as I stepped off the bus and asked, "Would you have a cup of coffee with me?"

"Yes," I quickly replied, flattered by his attention.

Anxiously I sat in the terminal, waiting as he signed in, and then we entered the coffee shop together. As we sat across from each other at the table, I noticed how handsome he was. The radio played a slow, sweet cheatin' song, *Last Cheaters Waltz* by TG Sheppard.

We were enamored of each other, as much as two strangers can be.

A motel stood just across the street. I had a layover. He whispered sweet nothings and suggested we walk over. I couldn't believe I would entertain such thoughts! As a married woman, I had *never* allowed myself to look at another man. Now, I had given him an opportunity to flirt with me.

In the wee hours of the morning the temptation was powerful, as I felt so vulnerable, knowing my life with Bob was coming to an end. Like a countdown, I watched the clock speed away while he waited for my response. I came to my senses, telling myself an affair wouldn't be worth the price I would have to pay with my conscience.

Instead, we walked out of the coffee shop and parted ways with a quick hug. Then I sat down alone on a hard bench, absent-mindedly watching the passengers and the homeless walking to and fro until the bus arrived to take me home.

With each mile that brought me closer to Wichita, I became sicker and sicker with revulsion at the thought of facing Bob again. I knew this was it and I had to divorce.

The bus pulled into the terminal at eight in the morning. I looked around for Bob. He was off duty and knew I would be arriving, so where was he? "Why isn't he here to pick me up?" My mind spun numerous scenarios around in my head. Maybe he didn't want to get out of bed early. *Maybe I wasn't important enough.* I took a taxicab home.

When I walked in the front door, he met me with the command, "Take off your pants." No "Welcome home" greeting or hug. I obeyed. I realized what my value was to him.

Within the next few weeks I again decided to proceed with a divorce. I asked Bob to leave the house, saying that we needed to separate. He did for a couple of nights, then came back and announced; "You'll have to be the one to go. I'm going to stay in the house, period."

In a settlement the judge often grants items to the person already in possession of them, and I realized I could forfeit all of my belongings if I left the property.

I quietly mulled over the situation, planning my next move.

On March 18th, while Bob was out of town, I packed a small suitcase and walked out of the house.

This time, I decided I would not return to the madness.

I knew right where I was going next. I had been driving past an apartment complex called Stratford West, only a few blocks from where I lived, and right off two main arterial streets, Riverside Boulevard and 13th Street.

The red brick structures reminded me of a castle with Tudor-style trim, and two of the buildings had a turret on one end. I had been dreaming about living there *by myself* and even stopped once to see if the rent was reasonable.

Now, confidently I pulled up to the office and learned that yes, an apartment would be available the first of April. Yes, it had a turret. I *must* have one with a turret! I made a rent deposit on the spot, without looking at any other place. This was going to be *my* castle. A new life awaited me.

In the meantime, I was without a home. So I went to a familiar place, my old haunt, the English Motor Lodge. I still have the receipt.

I needed someplace to stay more cost-effective than a motel. The next day I went back to Stratford West and asked the apartment manager, Judy, if she had any suggestions.

"Well yes," she replied, "I do!"

Showing mercy towards me, she said, "I have an empty two-bedroom upstairs unit that is vacant and I will let you stay in it rent free until your apartment is available." I was so grateful.

Judy loaned me a cot so I would have a place to sleep. I bought one set of bath towels and a bar of soap to take a bath. It was cold and I had only my coat to use for a blanket.

I had such mixed emotions. It felt good to be alone and free, but the apartment was bare and hollow, and every step I took reverberated throughout the rooms. I would be glad to get my belongings and move into my new place.

On March 19th, when Bob returned from work, he came home to an empty house. Oh, the furniture was still there, but I was gone.

Bob recognized the fact that I wasn't coming back. He went to see a pastor, a counselor and a psychiatrist, all in the same day. I know this because each one called me later to say they had talked to Bob that day. And each one wanted to know if I would meet at his office, together with Bob. It appeared to be a last-ditch effort to reclaim his marriage.

But this time it was too late.

I received a letter in the mail:

My Dearest Elaine and Precious Wife

Please accept this letter as it is meant and that is with much love.

And in no way do I expect any commitment from you. You know in your heart that I love you very much. Again I ask your forgiveness for my stupid action and ways of the past.

Elaine, please consider moving in this house as you know you can leave anytime and it would sure be better for the car, you and everything due to the time I'm away from home.

Elaine I love you very very much and I want to be of help not hurt so I'll try my best to give you room. However you please feel free to ask for anything from me. I'd love to help. Please accept this offer.

Love you
your "Bob"

Top: In "worldly" dress early 1970's. Middle: In my apartment 1969. Bottom: At my cashier job.

Top: Standing in front of plane Bob piloted to take me sightseeing. Bottom: Elaine and Mary Jane in front of my apartment.

Wedding day.

Top: On vacation in Vail. Middle: Official Shrine portrait.
Bottom: Bob on our honeymoon in Galveston, TX.

Left: Tiffany and me. Right: Atop the Empire State Building. Bottom: Snapshot taken at our apartment.

Top: In New York City. Bottom: In Washington, DC.

Top: Bob and Elaine at Fountainbleu Hotel, Miami, FL. Middle: Bob on the job in St. Louis. Bottom: Our house on Sheridan St.

Top: Bob celebrating his birthday. Bottom: English Village Motel in Wichita.

Top: My 2nd studio portrait, 1976. (Lost and sad eyes, Bob refused to go with me.) Bottom: (Left to right) Mary Jane, Earl and Elaine in 1978.

Top: Serving lunch in the field in Oklahoma. Bottom: Picking fruit in Phoenix, AZ.

Top: (Left to right) Pearl, Earl, Elaine, Mary Jane, Mom and Dad around 1980. Bottom: My parent's house in Fairview.

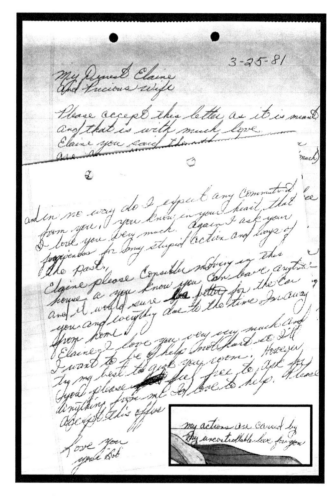

Letter from Bob and (insert) card with note from Bob.

I consented to meet with Bob's attorney, Russell Shultz. We met at his office, filed for divorce, and agreed upon what items I would take to get by on until we reached a settlement.

After getting the keys to my apartment and during Bob's next trip out of town, Russell and a team of movers met me at the house. I took only the most basic furniture, including my cedar chest and the couch that Bob never let me sleep on.

While the movers loaded the truck, I paced back and forth. Russell sat on the windowsill in the living room, observing the action. With urgency and bluntness in his voice, he said, "Elaine, knowing Bob like I do, if there is anything else in this house you want, *you'd better take it now.*"

I listened to his suggestion and then told him, "It won't be that bad, we'll be able to work things out. I want to be fair and not in any way take advantage. We can decide later how to divide the rest of the furniture and things like record albums and personal photos."

Why did I always think that tomorrow Bob would be kind? Why did I live in such a fantasy?

That evening I got to thinking about what the attorney had said and acknowledged he was right. I remembered how numerous times Bob had told me, "If you *ever* leave me, I'll make sure you'll get *nothing* but the shirt on your back. You had nothing when I met you, and you'll leave with nothing!"

With that thought in mind, I decided I had better get what I could from the house while Bob was still on his bus run, although it was now too late to get any more furniture.

Early the next morning I began like a tornado. There was no time to waste! I went to the house, backed into the garage, put the door down, and proceeded to throw things into the car. When the car filled up, I drove back to my apartment, and literally threw stuff just inside the door, then raced back to the house for another load.

I felt certain that if Bob came home early and caught me doing this, he would kill me. I kept a panicky eye on the clock as the hours sped away. My heart was beating so fast and I got tired, but I could not stop. I put linens, dishes, small appliances, and lamps in the car without packing anything, but not one item broke.

When I got back to my apartment with the final load, the first thing I did was to call my mom. I had already told her that I had left Bob.

"Please come help me," I cried.

Her suitcase was already packed; having anticipated this call, she came immediately. With her there, I felt better protected from Bob.

How was he going to react when he came home and saw what I'd taken? I expected the worst, but he was amazingly calm. As I recall, he didn't mention it. Maybe Russell had advised him not to, but I was sure Bob planned a payback time. That was how his mind worked. Revenge. Whether child custody or divorce, it was not the prize, but *who wins* that mattered.

Mom helped me put things away and said she was glad to be there. She stayed a few days and helped me get settled in before she returned to Oklahoma.

At last, I was by myself. No one to tell me I was no good, no one to get mad at me if I had a pimple on my face. I didn't have to fear another person's anger. My divorce was in process; I was actually going through with it!

Nevertheless, doubt began to creep in. Had I done the right thing by leaving? I badly missed Tiffany, and Bob's sister and her family; at that time they were closer to me than my own family was. We had spent most weekends, holidays, and birthday celebrations together. Was it better to be married and miserable and have family, than to be alone with no one…? This kind of thinking didn't last too long as I was soon forced back into reality.

I adored my little one-bedroom apartment. It was so cozy. I put green plants and white wicker furniture in the turret, which was part of my bedroom. I had a small walk-in closet. In the living room, built-in bookcases stood on each side of a huge stone fireplace.

It was springtime. The apartment manager, Judy, who had been so kind to me when I moved in, started inviting me over. She had a small, close-knit group of residents that got together twice a week at rotating apartments for dinner. I felt honored to be invited. To be accepted! For a while that helped me get over some of the emptiness and loneliness that I felt. They became my friends, and they were so nice to me.

Everything was perfect and peaceful.

But peace was not to be.

Bob started sending me cards and letters brimming with sweet-talk. He wrote such things as:

> *Elaine, I informed the pastor of how much I love you as best I could. I further told him how I had hurt you in the past and how I had begged for your forgiveness and told him that I want to change and make you the happiest woman in the world if I can only get the opportunity.*

> *I will further try to quit being so dominant and treat you as a full equal.*

> *I'm very sorry that you don't think marriage should be permanent. I took the marriage vows seriously and I thought it was "until death do us part."*

I just hope and pray that you have loved me as much as you say, and that you aren't a quitter.

I asked God to tell you how much I love you.

My actions are caused by my uncontrollable love for you.

He also assured me repeatedly that everything in the divorce would go smoothly. I tried to believe that, although I wondered if he was manipulating me to get what he wanted. He even told me, "I'll help you with anything I can. If it's the car, I should be the one to look at it."

I took Bob at his word. I went to the house for him to do an oil change on the car. Before I could leave, he pressured me into having sex. I quickly saw the real reason he had convinced me to come over. I didn't want to; his presence repulsed me more than ever, but fighting him would do no good. He said, "I can't help it, I love you so much."

It was time to see Russell again. The three of us met briefly at his office, and concluded that Bob and I needed to agree on our division of property.

Bob had a new idea. "Why don't you and I go to your apartment? We can make a list of what we each want out of the house. It'll save us some attorney fees."

So, dumbly trusting, I agreed, and we left the attorney's office.

The sun was shining. It was a beautiful warm spring afternoon.

As soon as we walked through the door to my apartment, he locked it and grabbed me. He was there for one thing only. Wrestling me to the floor, he seized my legs by the ankles and dragged me into the bedroom. He reached up under my skirt and tore off my panties, found a tampon in me, and yanked it out.

This time, it was as though I awoke to the degradation of his abuse. I had had enough of his brutality! I battled with all of the strength I possessed. Furious, I clawed him until blood ran down his back. Sometimes I slipped out of his grasp and ran for the door, but he kept catching me.

I screamed repeatedly, *"Please, somebody help me!"*

But no one came to my rescue. Maybe because I was a new tenant and they thought this was my normal behavior. Bob took a pillow and angrily said, "You'd better shut up or I'll put this pillow over your head and smother you!" I stopped yelling but kept on struggling.

Finally after an hour and a half I was able to calm him down. I quit fighting, feeling it was my only chance to survive. Bob was so hot and tired he just lay there on the floor, sweating and holding onto me.

He panted, "I need a drink of water."

I quickly replied, "I'll get you one! I'll just go to the kitchen; I *promise* I won't leave." He knew me to be a person of my word.

He released me. I stood up, raced to the door, unlocked it, and ran to the sidewalk of another apartment building. I was safe! Once I did that, there was nothing else he could do but leave.

Not another word was spoken. With head bowed, he walked swiftly to his vehicle. I stayed at a distance until he was gone.

Afterwards, when we were at the courthouse for one of our hearings, he told me his thoughts about that day: "When we were in your apartment, I wish someone had locked us in there so that we could have died together."

The next time we had to meet to sign some tax papers, I thought I would be a little smarter and suggested we meet in at Sambo's restaurant. He agreed, but when he arrived and walked over to where I was already sitting in a booth, he quickly told me, "I will not talk personal business in a public place like this. Come on, let's go sit in the car."

Not wanting to make a scene, I reluctantly got up and followed him out the door. He sat behind the steering wheel and I was on the passenger side.

After he finished signing the papers, I opened the car door. Before I could get out, he reached over to run his hand up my thigh, at the same time starting the car. When I realized what was happening, he was already driving out of the parking lot.

Scared about being alone with him again, I kept the passenger door open with my leg dangling out. I had to escape! When he slowed down at a light, I jumped out and started running. He stopped the car in the middle of the street, snatched me and forced me back into the car. However, seeing my continued determination to flee, he took me back to the restaurant parking lot and allowed me to leave. Trembling with fear as I got back into my vehicle, I wondered if he was aware of how he had just put my life in jeopardy.

Within six weeks our attorney, Russell, wrote us a letter that stated, "Elaine wants to hurry the divorce and Bob wants to drag it out. I cannot represent both of you in this situation and I have no choice but to resign from the case."

Getting a recommendation for a good attorney, I swiftly hired Don.

At our first meeting, after introductions were made, I sat down on the edge of the chair that was positioned directly in front of his desk. Pointedly, and with emotion, the words sprang out of my mouth, "You'll be dealing with a very difficult man." To my surprise, he seemed to take the warning in stride.

Our divorce proceedings continued—as did the fighting back and forth. I just wanted a settlement and an end to it all. Bob did everything he could to delay or manipulate the process.

I would ask the court to force him to give me my mail, and he would hand over just enough to say he cooperated. He always kept some back. In any transaction there had to be a trade. If I got something, he had to get something. I remembered when we were newly married, one day he told me: "If I get you glass of water, you owe me one in return." Was he serious? As it turned out, he was very serious.

Bob refused to do as the court ordered, and I charged him with contempt of court. For some reason, the judge found him "not guilty." After court adjourned Bob asked me, "Did you see the judge smile when he gave his decision?" It seemed to be a man's world back then. Bob appeared to relish in it and in the fact that he could get things his way.

On more than one occasion, he saw me at the grocery store. He would walk with his shopping cart in circles around me, and just snicker, a crooked snicker, without saying anything. He seemed to enjoy taunting me.

After a year's worth of delays, the judge issued his verdict and our divorce was final. He told my attorney, "Because Bob and Elaine are both unhappy, I must have divided everything right!" One thing the judge did do decently by me was to order that Bob pay the majority of my attorney fees.

The court gave me permission to go to the house to get the personal belongings that the judge had awarded me. When my attorney and I showed up at the time of our appointment, Bob was cool but cordial and let us into the house. He was probably hoping to see me alone! But as soon as it was apparent that I was there to really *take something,* he became agitated and refused to give me a single item, not even my wig. Wigs were popular in those days and I carried mine around in a big black round plastic case.

Don called the police. When an officer arrived, he looked over the court papers and said I was within my rights to take the items that were listed, including my green Schwinn bicycle. Bob didn't agree, and he put his hand on my chest and shoved me towards the door. The policeman pulled me aside and said in a low voice, "This man is not rational. It's best just to leave."

Many times after that encounter, I envisioned myself breaking into the house and grabbing my bicycle or my coin collection. I let it eat me up, that I could not take possession of my personal things.

Eventually I got a call from Don telling me that Bob had agreed to give me some of my personal items. I was to go to *Bob's house* to pick them up. *Were they crazy?* I was not about to step inside the door and be alone with Bob.

The attorney refused to go with me. He wanted nothing more to do with Bob. Finally it was determined that Bob would put them out on the front porch. I drove up in the driveway and got out of the car sheepishly, hoping no one would pass by and notice me picking my stuff up. I couldn't help feeling like a homeless person receiving a handout.

I walked away without receiving the dining room set for which I had taken a three thousand dollar loan and worked hard to pay. I thought it was so beautiful, and I hated to leave it. But Bob convinced the judge that it needed to stay in the house, as "it matched the decor!"

From the time of the divorce decree until everything was settled, another year had passed. Two years spent fighting over nothing! But it was finally coming to an end. As I was visiting with my attorney, I recalled our first meeting when I said Bob would be hard to deal with. Don told me, "Every woman who comes to my office says that same thing, so I didn't take your comment as anything different. Now, I can say you were right. I have never had a more difficult person to deal with in a divorce case."

I gave up on ever getting some things that I held dear. Those material things—were they worth fighting for? No, but at the time, they were all I had.

Most painful was losing my photographs. Bob liked to take pictures and it wasn't long before I had gotten into the act, finding that I had an eye for composition. I treasured those photos, especially the childhood ones of my little niece and nephew. They were the only pictures of them in existence.

In the ensuing years after our divorce, I often thought about asking my attorney to write Bob a letter and see if he would let go of my pictures. I would write out the sentences in my mind, just what I wanted Don to ask Bob. But in the end I was too afraid of the possible consequences, and could not afford the risk of any contact with him.

[See Postscript 1 for more on Bob.]

Chapter 14

Try Again

I continued to have fun at work. Being a private company, with the best bosses, we got to do things on the job that wasn't the norm. We might all go out to a Mexican restaurant for lunch and return to the office at three in the afternoon, or maybe attend an afternoon baseball game.

Tom's motto was "Work hard, and play hard," and that we did. The first couple of years they treated the employees to company trips with all expenses paid. Office staff, restaurant managers and all spouses were invited. We would caravan our cars or charter a bus to a resort in Missouri. Once there, we just signed a ticket for anything we wanted to do, whether it was golf, boating, horseback riding, bowling, or eating.

I remember one summer retreat in 1981, when we went to The Lodge of the Four Seasons Resort. For the first time, I didn't have Bob with me, and on this trip I felt a tremendous freedom in my life.

For a day's entertainment on the beach, we had a "Superstars" day. The idea came from a popular TV show at the time. We were divided up into eight or so teams, each with our own brightly colored tee shirt, with a huge white star on the front. We would then have contests on the beach, such as having to fill a glass with beer by running quite a distance with one teaspoonful at a time.

One evening we had a Hawaiian luau on a large wood deck that jutted out over the lake. In the soft breeze at a perfect temperature, I stood in awe of the view.

Towards dusk a helicopter flew over and dropped red carnations on us as we partied on the deck. The flowers falling from the sky was an incredible sight, but the helicopter flew so low the wind shear almost blew everything off the tables. So instead of enjoying the flowers, and the moment, we were scrambling to hold the table settings in place!

Later that night while Tom and I were dancing, (or rather standing and gently swaying) outdoors on the deck amid all the music, and with the moon glistening on the water, he asked to come up to *my* room. *Why on Earth would he want to do that?* I demurely declined, but felt flattered by his attention, knowing I was almost the only one he had danced with, other than his wife.

In the summer we always had an all-day picnic. One year we hired a caterer to grill steaks on site at a park. We didn't bother with kegs; a beer truck pulled up and cups were filled from a spigot on its side. A couple of times we went to Worlds of Fun, an amusement park in Kansas City.

One of my favorite job duties was planning our company events. The Christmas parties were the best. In the early days we usually went to a country club for fine dining and dancing, as Tom and Sally liked to dress up. Only problem was, the employees didn't.

One year, in an effort to make everyone happy, I convinced the owners to let us have two Christmas parties back to back!

The first night, a Friday, we dressed up for the country club formal dinner. The next night we had a casino party at the Broadview Hotel beside the flowing Arkansas River in downtown Wichita. With prizes ranging from new televisions to barbecue grills to luggage, I arranged it so every employee walked away a winner.

Employees thought the casino party was the best, as each employee received a gift, and they didn't have to dress up! After that the parties were mostly casual.

Some years for our Christmas party we would go to the dog track. We would have dinner at tables on multi-tiered levels where we could watch the races. As always, I was concerned with pleasing everyone. If it were a sit-down dinner, I would select two meat entrees to be served on each dinner plate.

Each employee and spouse was given a packet of crisp new $2 bills, which I had ordered from the bank and methodically counted out, enough to bet one on each race. If the spouse didn't bet, that meant more for the one that did!

I didn't participate very much in any of our activities. I was too busy pacing back and forth making sure everyone else was having a good time, and enjoying those pats on the back. That kind of surrounding was where I thrived, what kept me going.

Tom always acknowledged me when I did a job well in party planning. It made my heart about burst when he was happy with the way things went. I cherished his compliments.

The blessings and joy that I received working for this company were incredible. Over and over again, I'd receive free dinner certificates to the best restaurants in town, tickets to concerts and plays, college basketball games, and special events. One was a private party after an ice show to meet Olympic figure skaters. Another time, I watched the USA hockey team play shortly before they went on to win the Olympic gold medal in 1980.

Our pilot, Marty, was an important fixture around the place. Tom and Sally loved to fly, and sometimes they'd take off at the spur of the moment.

As the numbers and the distance of our stores grew, Tom thought he needed a *bigger and faster* plane, so they bought a Beech King Air and hired a copilot named Charles, a young guy, quiet and soft-spoken.

Marty loved to go sky diving when he wasn't flying. Tom really liked Marty, but not his dangerous hobby. He'd say, in a half-joking way, "How will you fly our plane if you break a leg? If something like that happens, I'll have to let you go." Guess what—in 1981, he broke his leg and he left the company.

Now missing a pilot, whenever Tom needed to fly he would go to the local flight training facility and hire a charter pilot from there. He became familiar with different pilots. One in particular, named Ted, really impressed Tom and he started to use him on a regular basis.

Tom got to thinking that he would like to travel faster yet. Fortunately, Wichita was the aircraft capital with factories that made Cessna, Beech, Boeing, and Lear Jet aircraft. Again, he went searching and brought home a Lear Jet. At the same time he put Ted on the payroll to be our full-time chief pilot. With a new jet and great pilots, Tom and Sally were flying happy.

Ted introduced Tom to fine restaurants, wine, and social manners. Ted had been around the world, so to speak, while Tom had grown up sheltered in the Michigan countryside. They often flew to Kansas City or maybe Chicago just for dinner or to Palm Springs for the weekend. There, Ted would take Sally shopping. Sometimes, she came back with particularly striking outfits, more elaborate than she would ordinarily buy. It seemed that Ted brought out an adventurous spirit in both Tom and Sally in ways neither had known before meeting him. He helped elevate Tom and

Sally to a higher social status, although they had no desire to be "society" people.

Tom and Ted developed a close and very personal friendship. Of course, Tom had to also put all his trust in this man who was flying him and his family all over the country.

We didn't see much of Charles. For some reason he stayed away from the office most of the time.

Unlike Charles, Ted would frequently stop by my office and we would have lengthy conversations. Sometimes he talked about his marriages. He had divorced his first wife and then married the baby-sitter, Holly. I did not get the impression that it was a marriage based on love. He told me he married her in order for his children to visit him from out of state, to give the appearance of a stable life.

Holly liked to drink, and it seemed she spent her days wasted on alcohol. At one Christmas party, before dinner started, she was already drunk, literally dropping her head on the table and into the salad. After stuffing her with bread, which didn't absorb the liquor fast enough, Ted quickly took her home and returned alone.

Ted treated me well enough, although I didn't quite know how to handle the attention he bestowed upon me. Occasionally he even brought me gifts. One time, returning from New York, he brought me a special New York cheesecake.

Tom and Sally almost always flew to each new store's grand opening. When the fiftieth franchise opened, they invited me to come along. What a special day that was. Upon arrival at the Houston airport, we were led off the plane directly to our waiting car. No going through the terminal with lots of people! I thought, "I could get used to this."

After spending some time at our new store, we went to dinner at a very nice restaurant. Driving up, I noticed the elegance of the place and the expensive cars parked in front.

Feeling intimidated in my everyday dress, a simple red in a floral pattern, I wondered if it would be appropriate. I was not looking my best.

After entering, we were ushered to our table where our restaurant manager, building contractor, construction and marketing people were already waiting for us. The walls were stunning, wallpapered in bold colors. The table was laden with fresh bouquets of flowers along with fruit trays. At a table next to us sat a movie star who was then in the popular *Knot's Landing* television series.

Our dinner and evening were lovely. I felt privileged to be there, sitting next to Tom with Sally on the other side of him and Ted next to her. Ted made it all feel right. We looked up to him and tried to follow his confidence in such surroundings. Enjoying every minute of the evening, I was on top of the world.

Our operations manager, Dave, handed a plaque to each person who had helped the company reach this milestone. I applauded, feeling I was one of them, complete, in my element, and where I wanted to be.

Our dinner came to an abrupt end when Ted got a telephone call. A storm was brewing and we had to leave immediately for Wichita in order to outrun it. On the way back we saw a lot of lightning, but we arrived safely.

Driving from the airport to my apartment, I got home around three in the morning and went right to bed. I lay there a long time, eyes wide awake, unable to sleep, thinking how just hours ago I was in Houston having a wonderful evening. The experience left me feeling elated. To think, that's how some people live all the time!

The summer of 1982 was a year like I had never had before. I was free to do anything anytime I wanted. My weekends were spent in leisure. Many hot lazy days were consumed reading in a lounge chair by the swimming pool.

I was about to enter into one of the strangest journeys of my life and meet a person that I would highly regret knowing.

It was like picking up a package that had the prettiest wrapping of all on the outside. But oh, how we can be so deceived when we do not look deeper, to see what is inside. When I entered my next relationship with a man, I did not think of the possible consequences. I saw only the wrapping and the captivating ribbon that tied it neatly all together.

I kept noticing this man at the pool. Though in his fifties, he was tall, tanned, and muscular, with sandy hair falling in waves down the back of his neck. His wide smile and piercing brown eyes were magnetic.

One day while I was indolently lounging at the pool with a magazine in my lap, this man was sunning nearby. I overheard him mention, to no one in particular, "Boy, I'd like a Pepsi." Immediately I said, "I'll get one for you," as I jumped up from my chair. Grabbing some change I had with me I walked over to the soda machine by the clubhouse and bought one for him. Then, pulling my chair closer to his, we introduced ourselves and started a conversation. His name was Bill Olson. He was distinguished looking and with his charming manner, I found myself attracted to him.

As the hot weather beckoned, each of us spent a lot of time at the pool, and we continued to run into one another. He started asking me out for dinner dates, and I accepted, although shocked that he appeared to be interested in me.

I couldn't help but notice that Bill seemed to always have lots of free time, so my initial impression was that he probably owned his own business and was partially retired.

With both of us living in the same complex and it being so convenient, we started hanging out at each other's apartment. We would sit by the hour, usually on the floor of his apartment as it had very little furniture, drink a Pepsi, and listen to a radio station that played big band music.

Many years earlier, while serving in the Army, he had played trumpet in the Army band, and he loved that type of music. In fact, he was quite knowledgeable about it. The station often had contests to see who could name the song playing on the air. Bill could usually name the tune in four notes or less. I was impressed.

During our long conversations sitting on the beige carpet, Bill shared with me his growing up years. I learned that when he was eleven, his father had died, and how his mother then had to become the breadwinner for the family.

Bill was proud of his two children. Living in Chicago, his son Dennis was a businessman and his daughter-in-law was a professional model. She graced a number of magazine covers, and Bill spread them out proudly for me to see. His daughter, Karen, lived close by in town.

As I got acquainted with his children, I considered them to be wonderful, kind and classy, a joy to know. Ex-wife Peggy lived a few blocks away.

Our relationship was idealistic. Bill treated me as I had never been treated before. He smothered me with attention and acted as though he were crazy about me. I ate it all up. I was flattered by his intentness.

After meeting Bill, my fellow employees asked me, "Where did you find such a good-looking man? How did you get so lucky? What a fine gentleman!" Although I thought, what does this man see in me? Still, I determined in my mind that I was not going to let my insecurity overcome the opportunity to date him.

He introduced me to some of the finer things in life. We had dinners at one of the most exclusive private clubs in Wichita. I was enjoying it all....

During this time my mother was sewing some of my dresses, which were plain and modest, but nice, and definitely cheap on my pocketbook, so I wore them. Bill wanted me in better things. He would say, "I want to see you in fashion's finest." So occasionally he would take me shopping, showering me with expensive clothes. A Cashmere sweater, dress suits, coats, handbags, and shoes. He loved it when I would try clothing on in the store and model for him. The only problem was that I loved frills and he wanted to see me dressed in a tailored style.

Bill would call me each day before I left for work.

"How are you this morning?"

"Great," would be my usual reply.

Then came the same question, as the day before and the day before that: "What are you wearing today?" I would then describe my outfit, including the color. His questioning bugged me but I chalked it up to flattery, that when he thought about me during the day he could imagine what I looked like.

After a short time of bliss, Bill's criticism of me began creeping into the relationship. When I heard his knock at the door and opened it, the first words out of his mouth would be: "Your hair is too curly. You need to fix it straighter, more stylish." My heart would sink. I didn't know how to avoid curling it too much, as no one had ever given me pointers.

I became more self-conscious, worried that my looks were not what they ought to be. I should've said good-bye! Instead, I ignored my own feelings and my life, and started living for him, in trying my best to please.

On Christmas Eve, our first together, Bill walked over to my apartment. It was cold, with quite a bit of snow on the ground. Hearing a knock, I opened the door and there he stood, his arms laden with beautifully wrapped presents. I looked past him through the open door and caught a glimpse of the snow. Then my eyes again took in the colorful gifts. It took my breath away. Truly it was Christmas! I couldn't believe it. Was I really worthy of all these gifts? Did he *really love me?*

Soon it was springtime. Life was comfortable. Then Bill moved in with me. I kept the fact that we were living together a secret from my family and coworkers. The thought of them finding out put me in a panic. Even so, I argued with myself that times were different now than in Biblical days. It was becoming common for people to live together outside the confines of marriage. Therefore it must be OK. That thinking was how I continually justified my actions.

In time I found out that Bill did not have a regular full time job. Off and on, he was a part-time sales clerk at a men's upscale clothing store. Occasionally he worked for a wealthy, prominent and influential man very well known in Wichita, driving out to check on this man's oil fields. To do what, I don't know. When I asked, he wouldn't give me a straight answer.

His favorite job was modeling clothes for a local retail sales catalog and their newspaper ads. He simply loved going to photo shoots at a luxurious home or out in the country, where he got to put on high dollar outfits. Business magazines used him in ads, all dressed up and professional looking.

Bill carried a huge wad of cash, which he would openly flaunt whenever he paid for something. He would make the transaction drawn out as he fanned the bills, while I stood to the side embarrassed by the lengthy production. It looked like he had a lot, but I guess that was all he had! One day in the pool during a casual conversation, he offhandedly told me he didn't keep any money in a bank account, because that way the government couldn't get it. I didn't know if he was serious or not.

Bill was always home just before or *just* after I got home from work. And if he were there before me, the minute I walked in the door, I would see him sitting there in his red leather chair waiting for me.

Fiddling with his watch on his wrist, the questioning would begin. "You're five minutes late. Where have you been? Why is your hair a mess? Why were you tucking your blouse in? Why are you chewing gum? Why are you putting on lipstick? What are you trying to hide?" He always found something wrong with me! In my mind there was an explanation. "Why, I stopped to fill the car up with gas." Or, "I wanted to look nice for you!"

These questions drove me nutty. He accused without directly accusing. I felt it incomprehensible that Bill might be suspicious of me stepping out on him. Never did I give him reason to, whether in his presence or away from him. What would it take to convince him of my total innocence and to trust me?

Yet at the same time, he was being attentive.

I'd wait on him hand and foot, and then he'd carry on about "How wonderful you are!" as if he adored me.

An odd thing happened. One day, arriving home from work, I walked into the bedroom and saw Bill sitting at his desk, just hanging up the receiver on his red telephone. He took a handkerchief off the mouthpiece. Curious, I quickly asked, "What are you doing?"

"Oh, I just called Peggy and I didn't want her to know it was me calling."

I quietly accepted his reason.

Sharing our lives together in the apartment brought about a lot of tension. Always having to defend myself, with Bill continuously picking me apart, I wasn't happy. This was not a relationship built on love, but on convenience. We had almost nothing in common, with vastly different backgrounds and lifestyles.

Six weeks after he moved in, the comprehension of what a terrible mistake I had made hit me. *He was just like Bob!* I needed to get out!

I blurted out, "I don't think it's going to work out between the two of us and it would be best if you would leave."

"What?"

"I am asking you to please move out of my apartment."

"No way! We made a commitment!"

"What commitment? The fact that I agreed to let you move in was an *agreement!* It doesn't mean that we can't separate."

"We are the same as married, just without the license."

"But Bill, we *aren't* married!"

"I will not leave. We made a commitment, in the fact that we live together."

In my heart, I didn't agree. We had not bound ourselves to a lifetime together. We had never discussed marriage, or even our future. On and on the argument went. And finally, for the time being, I gave up the fight.

I put on my happy face and didn't let anyone know this "gentleman" refused to leave my place when asked. To others, we had an idyllic life.

He continued to harass me on a daily basis, about how I looked, what I did, and where I was. Never-ending questions. *Every day* I had to defend myself. One day, preparing to run errands, I happened to put on a red outfit. He refused to let me leave the apartment dressed in that color. "Whores wear red! You will draw attention to yourself! You can't leave looking like that!" Believe me, that was the last thing I would ever look like. Defiantly, I walked out of the apartment.

To top it off, I was paying the rent and utilities and buying the groceries. Eventually it began to gnaw on my nerves. I started pressing him to help with the rent, but he always had a reason not to pay. After months of living together, I insisted and he started giving me two hundred dollars a month. What a bargain for him!

I began to distance myself from him, even to despise him. I don't like to use such words now, but there is no other way to say it; I was feeling pure hatred. One day as we stood in the bedroom fighting, after I'd asked him again to leave, I hollered in his face, "I hate you, *I hate you, I hate you,* get out of my apartment!" He didn't flinch, but calmly replied, "I'm staying." How could this be? I might as well have said nothing, as it didn't affect him whatsoever.

Time went on and the arguing got worse.

I didn't know how to change the situation. Having signed a lease, I couldn't walk away. I felt there was no way to escape this man. How in the world did I get myself into a position like this? I could not believe what I had done.

My home looked like a castle and felt like a prison. Sometimes at night I would stand in the darkened bedroom with my elbows resting on the windowsill and my face pressed against the glass, looking out at the streetlights and the traffic flowing by. With tears running silently down my face, I would whisper, *Oh, God where are you? What do I do?* Being trapped with a person whom I held in such contempt yielded the worst loneliness ever. Solitude would be far better.

Well, as I could not get him to leave, I came up with a plan that was really irrational!

I got to thinking, *"M*aybe I'm too possessive of my home." As I paid the majority of the expenses, the situation was more intolerable because I now felt he was invading my territory. I didn't want him there, yet I was paying for his upkeep.

As he would not move out I had two options; either I could have the police remove him or we could move and get a new start after my lease was up. Because I had the guilt problem when analyzing the situation, the easier of the two was to move, and thereby avoid hurting Bill.

One evening I approached Bill, "Maybe if we moved to a different apartment, we would get along better. If we had a new place with both of our names on the lease, we would be on more equal terms, financially and emotionally." Bill agreed.

For years I had driven by the Twin Lakes Apartments, fascinated by what it would be like to live there. Twin Lakes was considered one of the best places to live in town. I decided to drive over and check it out.

My eyes followed the beauty of the red brick Old English-style buildings, the property surrounded by a five-foot-tall black wrought-iron fence. After locating the office I parked and went inside, wondering if we would be able to afford the rent.

The complex was built around a twenty-five-acre lake with a small island in the middle. Peacocks, turkeys and Canada geese roamed the property, while black and white swans graced the lake. Paddle boats and pontoon boats were available for residents (mostly retirees) to use, as well as shuffleboard courts and five large swimming pools. Fountains flowed in the different courtyards. Trees and spring flowers lined the walking paths. This place was paradise! Maybe we could make it here!

On a cold, blustery day, Bill and I moved into our new ground level two-bedroom apartment. As I carried things to our unit, I fought a strong biting wind. The bare tree branches tossed against an ashen sky. Gray waves covered the lake and everything suddenly looked very dreary. I shuddered.

We got settled in, but guess what, our life only got more distressing. Bill's accusations towards me were nonstop. Soon he was calling me "bitch" and "whore." The apartments were supposed to be soundproof, but I felt sorry for the neighbor above us. I knew he could hear our arguments. Whenever we saw each other, he never said anything but gave me a sympathetic, if rather helpless, look. At the same time, I felt protected by him.

I didn't work on Friday afternoon. Normally I was home by one o'clock. I started getting harassing phone calls, with a whispering voice on the other end of the line. He called me by my name. Who on earth was this person? For the longest time, I thought it might be someone from my work place, because it only happened on Friday afternoon and my coworkers would know I was home. What was going on?

When Bill came home, his eyes immediately went to the telephone. He might say the phone was not in the same exact position as earlier—and the questioning would begin. "Who have you been talking to?"

"Nobody," I replied, "except for a hang-up call this afternoon."

"Well, you must have said something to *someone*, to *cause* him to call."

Scared, I wanted sympathy, not accusation!

I finally told Bill, "This arrangement is not working. We *must* separate!" Bill seemed to sense my total frustration and replied, "I'll speak to Beverly [the apartment manager] about breaking our lease." I trusted him to do as he said.

In the meantime I tried to make the best of things. When the days turned into weeks, I asked him what Beverly had said. He replied, "Be patient, I'm working on it. This is a touchy subject and it has to be handled just right or she will most certainly refuse to let us break the lease."

The weeks turned into a month and then another. I was going crazy. I could not live with this man, but I also knew I was under a contract to fulfill the lease on the apartment.

I suggested, "Maybe there are ways we can get around it. One of us could continue the lease in a smaller apartment."

He replied adamantly, "Things like this take time! But *don't you* go talk to Beverly about it; I'll take care of the lease."

In September, after living there six months, I said to myself, "No more! I'm taking this into my own hands." Without telling Bill, I marched up to the manager's office.

"Beverly, can I talk to you for a minute," I hurriedly asked as I sat down in a chair in her office. Extremely nervous, I inquired, "What's being done about our lease?"

She looked surprised. "What do you mean?"

"You don't know that I want out of our lease? Hasn't Bill spoken to you?"

"No."

I realized I'd been duped.

All these months Bill assured me he was working it out, all these months I had trusted him, had lived in misery, only to find out he had been lying to me.

Beverly must have seen the horror on my face. After I briefly told her my predicament, she suggested, "Elaine, here's what you can do. You can break the lease if one of you will continue living here. It'll be just like a transfer from one apartment to another one. It's no problem."

I signed a new lease on a small one-bedroom apartment in another building. *Then* I told Bill that I had spoken with Beverly and that I would be moving.

"Well, I'll just stay! I'm not going to move, which means your name will be on two leases."

But I retorted, "I'll take my chances. *I am leaving.*" And I started packing. I called my mom and asked her to please come help me.

Bill sat in his red chair, watching me while stroking the bridge of his nose with his forefinger, his gesture of disapproval. He was steadfast in his threats. I was concerned about his intimidation, but wasn't about to back down to his demands. I continued packing.

Mom arrived the next day. I remember how concerned she was. I love you, Mom. A mother's love is forgiving, kind and gentle and soft with compassion.

Despite his menacing, and letting me sweat, he finally started taking his things out. I had always admired his high-back wing chair and his grandfather clock. Knowing that, he insisted that I take those with me, for the time being. I hesitated, but really liking the furniture pieces, I acquiesced.

He moved into a private room a few blocks away.

Mom and I cleaned the apartment. She had met Bill earlier and formed an immediate opinion that she did not like him, so she was happy to see the relationship end. While we worked, she told me how she had prayed often for me, all the while not knowing what I was going through. Now I spilled my guts. Once I opened up, I told her everything.

Mom stayed with me for a couple of nights, until she felt confident that Bill was not going to come back and hurt me physically.

On the opposite end of the complex, my new upstairs apartment overlooked the lake. It was fall and the leaves were turning color. I opened my eyes—this was again such a beautiful place. For months I had only seen Twin Lakes as it looked the day I first moved into the complex, cold, gray and dismal. Even during the summer my focus was not on the beauty of the place.

In front of my picture window were large trees with golden leaves that rustled in the breeze. In the center of the courtyard was a water fountain, a girl statuette holding a vase with water gently flowing through. Beyond that was the aqua color of the swimming pool, and ahead, the allurement of the lake. I was mesmerized with the sights and sounds (peacocks, ducks, geese and birds) of my surroundings.

Now alone, I was forced to deal with the inner thoughts in my mind. I had been involved in a hateful wasted affair and the torture and guilt inside of me were almost as crippling as the abuse I had received from Bob. Then, at least I was under the covering of marriage vows, and I was trying to do the right thing. With Bill, there was no marriage contract.

On the outside I felt an exhilaration that I was by myself at last! I was content, and delighted that I could live in such a charming place.

At the same time, I was tormented. My hate for myself had become ugly. I despised myself. I couldn't even look at my naked body in the mirror. I hated the sight of me. I hated what I was on the inside.

And I hated Bill for the suffering he had put me through. Why hadn't I walked away a long time ago? Why did I continue to be manipulated by men? Why was I so gullible? I *was* a floor mat! Stomped on and wiped on, trampled clear through the mat. And I had allowed myself to be destroyed all the while he was bringing me flowers. Just like Bob, one day he would build me up and adore me, the next day he'd break me down, telling me what a slut I was. I could not comprehend how I continued to let men abuse me and mess up my mind.

I felt a new determination never to get into another situation like the one I had just gone through. In fact, I'd be satisfied not to get married again! I was finished with men picking me apart, and trying to get them to "love" me. I decided I had really learned about men and myself.

This time, I thought, *a new life will begin.*

During this unnerving period, and just after I had moved into my own apartment, I got a wonderful reprieve. As a perk at my job, two other employees and I were given an all expense paid trip to the tropical island of Tahiti. We could each bring a guest.

Bill heard about my trip and felt *he* should be my guest. No matter how many times I told him I would not take him, he was determined to convince me otherwise. And this trip would have been great for impressing his friends. Well, it didn't make any difference how desperate he was to go with me. I was *not* taking him to Tahiti.

Instead, I called my parents. Mom wouldn't fly, so I asked Dad to go with me. I got my love of travel from him, but due to his finances he wasn't able to travel as much as he desired. I felt the opportunity to include my father in this trip far outweighed the difficulties that might surround it. He was very excited and thrilled to go.

Certain people asked me, "Why would you do that for your father, considering how he has treated you your whole life?"

I did it because he *was* my father, and I have a soft spot in me that desired to see my family happy, therefore it made me happy. As much as I have given in order to be loved, I have given even more because I love to give, with no strings attached. I have given money to strangers with no thought of ever seeing them again.

In about two weeks, we obtained passports and were on our way. Our tour of one hundred people flew out of Oklahoma City to Los Angeles.

When we arrived in Los Angeles, Dad told me he loved the feel of the city. He turned to me and said in awe, "I can hardly believe I am sitting here in the same town as so many important people that I have heard about!" (He was an avid reader and knew about movie stars, even though he didn't go to movies, nor did he have a TV.)

The next day we toured the Howard Hughes airplane and the *Queen Mary* ship, where we had lunch.

At midnight our plane took off for approximately a ten-hour flight, to arrive the next morning in Papeete, Tahiti.

Our hotel was one of the best on the island, perched on a mountainside overlooking the city and the ocean. The rooms were built in terraces down the side, affording everyone a great view. Instead of going up to your room, you went down, as the lobby was on the top.

After checking in and getting the keys to our room, I unlocked the door and Dad and I entered. It was nice and roomy with two double beds overlooking a spectacular view of the ocean and the black sandy beach.

Dad made a fleeting comment that sounded like: "You know, this could make people think about incest."

I was mortified. My heart seemed to stop. I thought, *"Did he really say that?" And why?* I pretended to ignore his words and quickly went about my tasks, unpacking and getting settled. But his comment burned inside me as to why he was *thinking* in that way.

About three or four days into our stay, the majority of employees of the main hotels on the island went on strike. This meant no more cleaning service in our room. We had to make our own beds and if we wanted clean towels we had to go fetch them. We only had buffet service in the restaurant, because of the limited number of managers that were keeping the hotel running.

One evening before sunset, our group went to dinner at a restaurant that was located at the top of a mountain. The road was only wide enough for one vehicle. The driver used a walkie-talkie to keep in touch with other drivers, and at certain points one would find a pullout so the other could pass. Some of the people almost got sick because we were sitting at all angles on benches in the back of a truck and going quite fast! At the restaurant my father drank a glass of wine with dinner. His religion does not permit drinking alcohol of any kind, so this was an indulgence!

The next day we all took a ferry over to the island of Moorea. Dad got quite sick, either from the rough waters or possibly the wine from the night before. He spent the day sleeping in a hammock while the rest of us toured the island with its magnificent scenery. We drove through the area where the movie *Mutiny on the Bounty* with Marlon Brando had been filmed. I was sorry he had missed out on the steep mountain forest, white sandy beaches and their clear turquoise waters. He would have loved the scenery. Our return trip was by a short airplane shuttle.

For seven days we enjoyed the splendor of the island. One day we rented a car and drove the main road for miles. We took open-air bus rides to the downtown market. From our hotel, we walked a jungle trail down to the beach that was littered with flowers on the ground and in the shrubbery, whose scent surrounded us with a glorious fragrance.

Dad kept commenting how he hadn't swum for years, since he was a young man. On our last day there he finally got up enough nerve to say he wanted to go into the ocean. Hurrying into the hotel gift shop, I quickly bought him a pair of swim trunks and we walked down the trail to the beach. Due to his weight and lack of exercise, it was difficult for him to swim, but he paddled around for a little bit. In the whole trip, this was the happiest he looked—he grinned widely, with boyish abandon.

It was wonderful to watch my dad enjoy that vacation. Certainly, in the pit of my stomach I felt constantly the unspoken tension of our relationship, but my desire was to give him a lifetime adventure and that is what happened.

Even after a week, it was too soon to leave this glorious paradise.

Departing the hotel for the last time, we heard a commotion. A crowd of striking employees stood around the entrance, yelling. Someone on our bus commented, "It looks like we're getting out just in time, before any trouble starts."

I had been able to avoid any conflict with Dad until the last evening back in our hotel in Los Angeles. At dinner he began ranting about the food. I tried to get him to quit complaining and our dining companions and I stopped the discussion before it got out of hand. I sensed he could feel his life coming back to normalcy and the hostility and anger were returning inside of him.

Upon our arrival home, we read newspaper accounts of what had happened to our hotel in Tahiti. Within twenty-four hours of our leaving, the strikers nearly demolished the hotel and it had to shut down.

With Dad in Tahiti

Back to work and back to reality.

My nightmare was about to begin.

I had made a big mistake during my breakup with Bill when I agreed to keep the grandfather clock and chair that he had given me.

He started calling and pestering me. "I just want to see you and talk about things."

He was very persuasive in his pleas. By taking the guilt and the blame that he put on me, I let him manipulate my thinking. At first I would consent to his nagging and agree to meet him. After all, *I wanted to please.* And in doing so, I ignored my own inner feelings of what I really wanted.

I remember one particular evening. I allowed Bill to come up to my apartment after dinner. Once there, he made it clear that he wanted to sleep with me.

"So, I thought you wanted to visit, but that isn't enough?"

I threw my purse on the dresser. Fed up, I got very mad at him, and myself, with his unrelenting behavior. I felt I had no self-worth and he must have thought the same of me.

I screamed at him sarcastically, "Just put the money on my night stand. That's all I am to you, a prostitute!" With that proclamation, he saw my intense anger, and left.

Thoughts tumbled over and over through my mind. Had any man ever cared for me and respected me as a *person?* I felt I had never been truly loved for me, only by what I had to give, whether it was for sex, for finances, housekeeping or whatever.

On another day, after adamantly telling Bill I did not want to see him again, hearing him beg I consented once more to have dinner with him.

During the meal, he proceeded to threaten, "If you don't date me, I'm going to kill myself. I will do it in a way that won't mess up my face. No shooting, but maybe a car accident, or a pill overdose."

I told him, "Nothing you can say will change my mind. I'm sorry, but it's over."

One morning on my way to work, I thought I caught a glimpse of Bill's car behind me. I didn't think much of it. Then when I left at the day's end, was that Bill's car parked on a side street? I shrugged it off. Next day, the same thing happened. And the day after that. I started to get concerned.

When I shopped at the grocery store, I'd look up and see him walking toward me. In a drug store, I might glance around and there he'd be, watching from a distance. When I settled in at a table in a restaurant to eat, there he was, peering at me across the room. Why was he every place I was? I came to the scary realization that he was stalking me.

I remembered incidents from when we were dating, and later living together. Sometimes he would drive into the parking area while I was just getting out of the car after arriving home, or sometimes minutes later. I always told myself, *"What a remarkable coincidence!"* This happened over and over. Yet I never questioned it beyond thinking, how could it be such perfect timing?

Now I understood fully that he had been following me. And what about those harassing telephone calls I received only when he was gone? He had been the one placing them, to see how I reacted! To test my behavior, when out of his presence.

One time I had taken the bus to Dodge City to visit Uncle Fred and his family. When I went to the bus station to return home, I found Bill waiting for me. At the time I was shocked and really flattered, and thought he was so wonderful to make a four-hour trip to pick me up! Looking back, did he make that trip to check on my stated whereabouts?

Bill started harassing me at work and at home with telephone calls. They became so continual that sometimes the phone rang all night long. I counted thirty-six times one night.

I had my telephone number changed to an unlisted number. It made no difference. I asked him how this could be, and he told me he "had connections" which enabled him always to obtain my phone number.

The cycle of mental abuse continued to haunt me. In the evening just as I had dreaded going home to await Bob's harshness, now my body tensed up wondering if Bill was sitting out there somewhere just waiting for me.

He began leaving me notes and letters. Some arrived in the mail and some were put on the windshield of my car. They were similar to Bob's, in which he would do anything to win me back, after the fact. I am convinced that Bill believed his own lies. He seemed to justify his actions.

Elaine, Believe me when I say, this letter is not the beginning of a series of letters but only a humble effort to right the wrongs I have done to a sweet girl and for which I am truly sorry. Bill.

Bill continued to follow me, even more so than before. He would come to my workplace. Per my request, the receptionist would not let him come to my office to see me. He would then leave a bouquet of flowers for her to give me, or sometimes gifts or maybe a letter.

Elaine, I was trying to talk to you only to apologize. I don't want to part that way and have it on my mind the rest of my life. A short phone call is all I ask. I was wrong and want to tell you and that will end it. Signed, Bill.

Often late at night, usually at the stroke of midnight, (I think he maintained a time schedule) he would quietly walk up the flight of stairs to my apartment and check my front screen door. If it was locked, he knew I was inside, and he would leave. But if it were unlocked, he would tiptoe back downstairs and go sit in his car across the street and watch for me to come home. If I had the nerve, I would fool him and intentionally leave the screen door unlocked. At least this trick kept him away from the telephone so he couldn't call me. Thank goodness those were the days before cell phones were common!

Winter arrived and soon it was Christmas. Another note came:

Elaine, If you will let me see you through the holidays, I give you my word I will get out of your life forever. Bill.

Bill called to ask, "I bought you some presents. May I bring them over?"
"No," I said firmly.
After repeated attempts at another manipulative way to see me, Bill finally left them at my front door. Retrieving the gifts, I sat down on the living room couch to open the beautifully wrapped presents. I finally thought to myself, he was the fool for trying to bribe me, and so I would just keep them. One gift was an expensive gold bangle bracelet. Bill had the bracelet engraved with the words "Elaine Christmas 1983 Bill"
Another note from Bill:

I loved you much more than you knew and that is why I have handled things so badly. These are not excuses, these are feelings I can only express to you and you alone. When this is over I want your friendship and respect even if we never meet again.

Chapter 15

Stalked

At work, I was planning our company Christmas party. It would be our best and most elaborate ever.

Party day arrived. Our banquet room was in a restaurant adjacent to a wing of the hotel. As I busied myself setting up the party, I would glance out the large picture window every so often. Suddenly, there was Bill, watching me from the other side of the window. I became weak and my knees wobbled. *Would he never go away?*

When my fellow employees went outside, Bill would question them about me. Then they would come tell me. This became quite a stressful situation, as I was in charge of the festivities, keeping track of food and drink service, gifts and entertainment.

Finally, going outside, I confronted him—"Go away, get off of this property!"

"I have a right to be here! I'm helping the band, and I rented this room close by so they have a place to do their drugs in between sets."

I contacted the hotel/restaurant manager, but they said there wasn't anything they could do.

After the party ended, as the band was packing up their equipment and a few people remained to help clean up,

Bill came inside and started to harass me. At that point the manager called the police.

The hotel had reserved a room gratis for me, for booking a number of hotel rooms for our out-of-town restaurant managers. My accommodations were in a part of the hotel located across the street in another building.

When the police arrived, they asked Bill to leave the restaurant. The officers escorted me to the front desk of the hotel and then up to my room. I was sick with embarrassment.

That night, the coldest wind blew that I have ever felt in Wichita. If I recall, it broke some sort of weather record. It howled from the north and seemed to come right through the windows into the room. Earlier, I had been so eager to retreat to my suite after the party. I had thought, maybe I would sit and relax by the large window that overlooked the city.

Now, I was so miserable, shaking from the cold and from nerves that I went straight to bed. Even there I shivered. But I would not call room service to ask for additional blankets. I was petrified that somehow Bill might find out which room I was in. Instead, I threw my coat over the covers and tried to sleep.

In the morning, I was in no mood to read the Sunday paper and enjoy a leisurely breakfast, which I had looked forward to. I checked out immediately upon awakening.

Sure enough, there was Bill standing outside his room, watching as I drove off.

I was desperate to sever any connections to Bill. In order to do so, I knew that I had to relinquish the two pieces of his furniture that were in my possession. By now, I realized he had wanted me to have those pieces in order to keep a connection with me.

The next few times he called, I asked him to pick them up. He refused, until days later when I firmly stated, "I am putting them outside my apartment door as soon as I hang up this phone."

With a panicked voice he replied, "No, you can't do that! The weather will harm the clock. I don't have any way to get them on such short notice."

"Bill, you've had time to work on how you're going to transport them."

"Elaine, please let's get together and talk about it."

"There's nothing to talk about. I *am* putting them out, and that's it, I don't care if you don't get them. They can rot! Good-bye!"

He was very angry, but I kept my word and out they went. A few hours later, I watched out my peephole in the door, as he and his son-in-law came by to pick them up.

I had thought in time Bill would quit stalking me, but time didn't matter to Bill. I made a vow to myself that as of January 1st, 1984, I would never speak to him again no matter how persuasive he was or how many times he called me. I would totally ignore him. I kept that vow, although it did not change anything. I reported his harassment to the police numerous times, to no avail. What could the police do?

Next I asked Beverly what our options were to keep him off the premises. Like anybody else, she had a hard time believing me at first. Not Bill! He wasn't the type, or capable of such behavior! All I had to do was point out her office window. He was almost always sitting there in his car, in plain view across the street.

After a couple of visits like this, she believed me and agreed to help. She called her attorney and had him place a restraining order against Bill.

It made no difference.

Beverly told me how she ran into Bill walking across the lawn one night around midnight. He must have climbed the fence to get in. When she told him he wasn't supposed to be there, he told her he was just returning some pictures to me.

Beverly then asked him for the pictures saying she would get them to me. After some discussion, he finally admitted he didn't have them. She ordered him off of the property.

On a cold morning in February, I approached my car and saw Bill standing by it. I ignored him and his words, got in the car and tried to remain calm. The windows were thickly coated with ice, but above all I wanted to avoid any conversation with him. I didn't know what else to do, so I stayed locked in the car and let the engine run till the windshield finally cleared of ice enough for me to leave. It made me late getting to work.

When I arrived, I learned that Bill had already called my boss, and told him that I was late because I had been out all night. He implied that I had been drinking and whoring around. Keith was used to calls like this. He had heard it all, and knew they weren't true. Grinning, he said, "Well, I hear you're quite the wild one!"

Bill pestered my coworkers for information such as, was I seeing another man? It became a daily ritual going through all this between Bill, my boss, and my fellow employees.

When I worked late at night I could see Bill across the street hiding his car behind the semi-trucks, watching and waiting for me. If he noticed that I saw him as I was leaving, a note of justification would come.

Elaine, My only reason for following you was to explain why I came to see you. Bill.

My mom became very worried that he would do bodily harm to me. Likewise, I was concerned, but deep down I felt he wouldn't hurt me physically.

The phone calls were incessant. When I didn't answer, he would let the phone ring, over and over. I changed my number again, but to no avail.

At some point I started calling his daughter, Karen, who lived a few blocks away from my apartment. She always listened to everything I said, yet maintained her silence with no comments.

One night I had my *final* last straw with Bill.

A coworker from my office, Gary, came to my apartment to set up a stereo system I had purchased. He was dark, handsome, and nice, and I would have dated him if given the chance. I had an enjoyable evening with Gary, but I was aware of Bill's car outside the whole time. I watched out the window as Bill left when Gary did. Gary lived way across town, and I wondered if Bill would trail him. Sure enough, Gary called to say, "That car followed me all the way home."

I wondered what would happen if I ever did date someone, and I became furious. I paced the floor of my apartment for a while and thought about it, then arrived at a bold decision. *I can take it no more.*

At almost two in the morning I got in my car, drove to Karen's house, and knocked on her door. Sleepy-eyed, she answered the door....

"Karen, I'm sorry for the lateness of the hour, but I go through this all the time and I wanted to let you know the seriousness of it."

We had been visiting for a few minutes when suddenly Bill burst in the door unannounced! Focusing his anger intently on me, he asked, "What are you doing here? What right do you have to come to my daughter's house in the middle of the night?"

"How did you know I was here, unless you have been following me?"

Karen looked stunned. There were no words that could have convinced her better of his harassment, than seeing Bill standing there.

It turned into quite a family discussion, with Karen's husband getting up and joining in. What a scene! They questioned Bill in detail and soon they were letting out some of their own frustrations with him. Apparently he had a habit of walking into their house anytime he pleased, day or night, without even knocking first. They demanded that he give them back their house key.

Bill, realizing he had been beaten, walked to the door with his head down, and left. Then Karen opened up and told me what life was like with her dad, and how he had tormented their mother with the same kind of harassment. He'd demand she be called out of business meetings in order to talk to her, just to prove she was there. Well, now I knew why he had quietly been on the phone so much when we lived together.

Of course, I had to receive another letter of explanation:

Elaine, I'm so sorry for the hard times and nervous moments I have given you since Christmas. That night at Karen's was a bad scene and my all-time low but it was what I needed to bring me to my senses. My reference to your private life was based purely on gossip I had heard and I regret very deeply saying what I did. I am offering a sincere apology for my behavior.

In later conversations, Bill's children Dennis and Karen told me more about their dad. For example, their grandfather (Bill's dad) was alive and well, not dead as Bill had told me! But in Bill's mind, he considered him dead. His dad had walked out on his mother when he was eleven years old. Bill hated his dad for leaving them, and as an only child, it then put an obligation on him to become the man of the house. That's when Bill began living a lie. Even his last name, Olson, was made-up, and not his real name.

Bill often got into scrapes financially and his children had to bail him out. They said he bought high dollar things he couldn't afford, such as a boat one time. Not surprisingly, he had some trouble with the IRS. (I remembered the time he confided, "If I don't have money in the bank, the government can't get any of it!")

Whenever Bill had driven the two of us anywhere, he had the habit of checking the rear view mirrors continuously. When I questioned his manner he said, "It's always wise to see who's behind you." I wonder if he was concerned that someone might be checking on *him*.

I continued to be wrapped up in my job. My work place was my sanctuary and once there, I tried to forget my personal problems. But I found myself in a quandary at the office too, although the circumstances were quite different.

Sitting at my desk and looking over our pilot Ted's expense reports, I started to get concerned about all the money he was spending on travel. One day I decided to add his hotel bills up for the previous year. The amount was astronomical. Then I divided that amount by three hundred and sixty five days. The result was a huge daily amount, but he was not out of town every day of the year, making the amount even more exorbitant. I knew what the average expense should be for the type of hotel where he usually stayed. How could he possibly spend that much money?

I knew I had to talk to Tom. Sitting at my desk, with butterflies in my stomach, I picked up the phone and called him in his office. It took a lot of bravery to go to Tom about anything. He could put out vibes that intimidated some people who might approach him, but I resolved to be strong.

"May I come up and visit with you about a concern I have?"

"Sure."

With much trepidation, and my numbers in hand, I walked upstairs towards his office. While sitting at his desk, he pushed a button, which opened the window-paned oak door. I whisked through and sat down in a soft, brown, pigskin leather chair directly in front of him.

He looked at my paper and set it aside, not showing any concern about the numbers and saying little more than "Thank you." I got up and walked out dejectedly, after feeling so high and like I was on to something. What a twist of emotion! Ted had Tom's complete trust, not only as his personal pilot, but also as a friend and confidante.

As the one paying the bills, I was the only person looking at them in detail. Ted knew my bosses didn't look over my shoulder at my work, as I was a trusted employee. He probably thought I was too dumb or too busy or whatever to catch any kind of discrepancy. He didn't know me!

Typically, Ted would enter my office and sit down in the chair in front of my desk. Always with my door closed, Ted might stay in my office for hours chatting about various things. In some conversations he would drop information in a most casual way. I am sure he planned every word. At the time I accepted what he said. He'd announce, "Well, I just came back from Texas."

"Did you have a good trip?" I would ask dutifully.

"Just great, but I did have to stop in Austin and have some repairs done on the plane. Can you believe they charged me a hundred dollars for a replacement bulb?"

"Are you serious?"

"Yup, maintenance on a Lear jet is really expensive. I'll send you a copy of the bill. I already paid it, so I need to keep the original. You can just write a check to reimburse me."

And so the talk went. He would let me digest the fact about the very expensive bulb, and get it ingrained in my head that it was OK. Then when I got the bill for a replacement bulb for one hundred dollars, I paid it. I had already been told how expensive it was. Most important, Ted had approved it with his signature, and that was good enough for Tom.

But I absolutely *knew* something was wrong and determinedly set out to find proof. Undaunted, I watched very closely all plane and hotel expenses.

Bill's harassment continued, in spite of our discussion at Karen's that early morning, and his letter of apology.

It was now spring and summer of 1984, and Bill was everywhere. He was still following me back and forth to work.

More snippets:

I did not intend to write again however after running into you recently at the Union Nat. Bank I want to explain a couple of things.

Hi Bambi,

After that unpleasant phone call only fate could have put us in David's (a department store) at the same time.

Now, I want to tell you my real reason for turning around and coming back today, even tho it's embarrassing to admit, I have no secrets from you and you know better than anyone else what I've been going through.

I am not proud of my performance in your parking lot Monday morning. It was inexcusable and I regret it very much. I am so sorry for the things I said to you.

I am really stunned at what happened in the grocery store. It's very hard for me to believe that you would even think of calling the police.

It seemed as though he made a career of tracking my activities. When I went outside to empty my trash, I'd see him parked across the street. If I went to the swimming pool and looked towards the west, there he stood across the lake, with his binoculars trained in my direction. I would retreat to my apartment. I could not spend time outdoors without being spied upon.

It was a horrifying awareness to *constantly* sense the nearness of an unwanted person around me, not knowing what he might do. A feeling of helplessness. A total invasion of privacy.

The residents told me that during the day (while I was at work) he would come onto the property and troll around the pools, prying information and trying to convince them of my naughty behavior.

Eventually Bill began calling my personal friends on some pretense. In the course of conversation he would subject them to inquiries about me, putting them in an uncomfortable situation.

Now just about everyone I knew had been pulled into the middle of my private life, my boss, coworkers, neighbors and friends. None had been left untouched by his harassment.

Below are a few fragments from other letters, in which he repeatedly tried to win me back:

Something else that means a lot to me is the kind of person you have always been.

Keep those principles and high ideals you have lived by since you were a young girl because you have a lot of class.

You know I have always adored you Elaine. You are something lovely that passed through my life and you will always be a part of me that I can never forget.

You have been a beautiful part of my life. I will always remember.

All of Bill's notes and letters came after our breakup. And each time that he said he would not do something, he would do it. His explanations were always the same, just a different time or place, or a different reason as to why he needed to see me.

I was subjected to a man's words telling me what a wonderful person I was, *after we had broken up*. It once again confirmed my feeling of unworthiness. "You think I'm of value now that you no longer have me, but when together I am only good enough and beloved when I am doing something for you. And then you tear me down."

Bill built me up in his letters to get back what he had lost. They were self-serving words. Desperate words.

The letters also made me angry. I wanted him out of my life. Would it ever end?

Bill and Elaine in Vail, Colorado.
Notes from Bill.

Chapter 16

Duped

As always, I poured myself into my job. Confident that something was amiss with our airplane and travel costs, I was going over Ted's expenses with a microscope.

On one Thursday afternoon in 1984, I noticed an odd charge on a credit card receipt. It appeared to be for nine headsets. What in the world did we need that many headsets for? The pilot and copilot only used one each. And besides, hadn't I just paid for some headsets? I checked a recent receipt, and sure enough, it showed nine more of them!

Suddenly, after trying for a long time to piece something together, just like that, there it was. I knew I had discovered what I was looking for. My palms got sweaty and my heart started beating rapidly. I was excited and ecstatic and scared spitless!

With my heart thudding, I went to Keith, who was now Vice President of the company, and showed him what I had found. What was Ted doing with eighteen new headsets? Could it be that he was stealing from us?

Immediately, Keith called Tom, who was on a nearby golf course. Someone from the clubhouse had to go fetch him. When Tom called back, Keith anxiously told him, "Please come to the office right away. We have a problem."

Tom arrived shortly and went directly to Keith's office. With the receipts on the desk, Keith showed him what I had found. At that time the dollar amount was just under a couple of thousand dollars. *Not thinking it through,* they made a rash decision and called Ted to come to the office immediately to meet with them.

When Ted got there, he scurried into Keith's office and they closed the door behind him. I could not hear, but with my office directly across from Keith's door, I could see some of the activity. Later I learned that when Ted was confronted, he became very nervous and apologized for buying the extra headsets for his personal use.

At one point, Ted stepped out of the office into an adjoining one to use the phone. We later found out that he had called his attorney and filed for divorce. When he calmly returned to Keith's office, they all agreed that the next morning, Ted would bring money in to reimburse the company for the headsets.

Then we let him just walk away.

After Ted left, Tom and Keith finally got to thinking. As a safety measure, they decided it would be best to disable our jet, in case Ted wanted to take off in it. They placed a call to the hangar office and asked to have the plane disabled.

Somehow during that night, Ted did show up at the hangar. It's a mystery how he got there, because his car was later found parked at a local shopping center quite a ways away from the airport.

When he couldn't take our plane, he simply crossed the street to the airport of the International Flight Safety School. Another company's jet was being filled with eight hundred gallons of fuel, which will go about two thousand miles. After refueling was completed, Ted walked over to the plane's door and joked with the technician, "Maybe I'll fly to Mexico." Then he climbed in, took off, and disappeared. It was almost eight-thirty on Friday morning.

Just like that, he stole an airplane! The cost of the plane was 1.87 million dollars.

About the same time Ted was taking off in that stolen jet, I arrived at work, eager to see what would happen when he arrived with his payment of money. But he did not show.

Almost immediately, I heard news reports about a stolen airplane. When we called the hangar and found out Ted had been there and had tried to take our plane we easily put two and two together.

No one knew of the previous day's happenings except the owners, Keith and me. We called the Federal Aviation Administration.

A Federal Bureau of Investigation agent showed up at our doorstep around 10:30 a.m. The receptionist called my office and said I had a visitor, and I told her to send him in. Nervous as all get out, I ushered him in, shut the door and closed the mini-blinds. He asked lots of questions, including whether we had any pictures of Ted. Fumbling through a box of some company pictures I had taken, I was able to provide a snapshot of him taken at one of our store openings.

It was a tremendous high, knowing how involved I was with such a big news event. I didn't get any of my regular work done that day. Suspense was rampant in the office, as the employees wondered what was going on.

I was told to keep quiet. That was difficult, as the newspaper headlines and television and radio blared the news about the stolen airplane. All weekend, out grocery shopping and running errands, I kept hearing the gossip. I wanted to scream out, *Yes, and I know the person who stole it!* But I couldn't say a word.

By Monday morning, the news media announced the culprit's name. It was indeed our Ted who had taken off in the airplane. Along with the theft came the news of the embezzlement from a company as the probable reason for why the person had fled. In our office the employees were shocked, but they now understood the secretive and mysterious behavior that had taken place.

For the next month, I was relieved of my regular duties while I tried to determine how much money Ted had embezzled from us. Keith brought Charles in whenever I needed help to answer questions about fuel and airport locations, training facilities, and so forth.

I started calling aircraft related businesses, asking them to verify the dollar amount of a particular invoice. It frequently turned out that my copy of the bill showed a different amount. For instance, a ninety dollar hotel charge somehow became nine hundred dollars. Ted had computer equipment at home that enabled him to change the invoices so they still looked original.

Ted purchased aircraft parts, charged them to us, then turned around and sold them and kept the money. He set up his own fake company names and submitted aircraft repair bills to us for payment. We thought we were paying a company Ted had contracted, when in fact we were unknowingly writing checks to Ted. It would be hard for us to spot the difference between a real and fake company, because many aircraft businesses have similar names.

In research, we found out that he'd purchased his own small airplane and a helicopter. In all probability, some of those parts that we paid for went to his aircraft.

He also used our credit card to obtain cash. Ted would pay in advance for flying instructions with his company credit card. Later he would tell them, "I don't have time to take the lessons, so will you just refund the money to me?" He then pocketed the cash.

I asked the flight school manager, "How could that happen?" He replied, "Corporate companies will take offense if you quiz them. Pilots are trusted."

I contacted the place that maintained Ted's own airplane. One woman who worked there told me, "Ted is such a nice guy. Who would question *him*? I'd trust him with my own kids."

When I went to our bank and discussed some of the methods Ted used in the theft, the manager of the credit card department made the comment, "He did stuff I never even knew could be done." A month later, *that* manager was caught embezzling from the bank where he worked.

In the end, we learned that Ted had stolen more than three hundred thousand dollars (a lot of money in those days) over a span of about three years. The first theft occurred just weeks after we hired him. We realized his crime succeeded because he was the first pilot connected with our new jet aircraft, which enabled him to get by with anything, *and he knew it.*

Ted had formed a very close bond and trust with Tom, to whom this was personally devastating. Tom swore, "I will never fly again with my own plane." And he didn't.

Well, after Ted disappeared we found out lots of other things. I never could understand why our copilot, Charles, rarely came into the office. Now, he admitted that Ted told him to stay away. If he hadn't, Charles might have slipped and mentioned something about their extra travel adventures. On some of Tom and Sally's trips to California and other places, the pilots would drop them off and then fly to Mexico. When the FBI found cocaine in Ted's safety deposit box, we wondered whether he had been trafficking drugs.

We discovered that he'd been putting money into a bank in the Cayman Islands. In that type of banking institution, a person's account is kept confidential and there is no way to get information. Even the FBI could not get everything they wanted to know. We couldn't get to that money, no matter how hard we tried.

We were eventually able to obtain some of his assets, but that was short-lived. As an abandoned wife, Holly took us to court and was able to get from us the cash that we had obtained by selling some of Ted's assets! It seemed so unbelievable the day we wrote that check out to her. Also, we were liable for taxes to the IRS on the embezzled money. I cannot remember exactly why, but I believe it was because we had accounted for it as going towards business expenses, but the expenses were false.

I remembered Ted's trips to my office and now the reasons why suddenly became obvious. When he spent all that time with me, was it because he liked to visit, or more realistic, was it just to sweet-talk me and gain my confidence? When people are loyal friends, it becomes hard to tell on one another.

And for all the negative comments about his wife, he did not divorce her until the day he fled. Even her alcoholic addiction covered him. If she stayed drunk, she couldn't know all he was doing.

We learned that it would have been better for us not to have our jet disabled. If Ted had stolen our plane, we could have collected insurance. Now it just sat in the hangar while we kept making expensive monthly payments. Eventually we were able to sell it.

The FBI posted a reward for Ted's arrest. We spent a lot of time speculating where he might be. All we knew was that Air Traffic Control had watched him traveling south for a while. Then he dropped the plane down and literally flew under the radar, thereby escaping being tracked.

What happened next? Did he fly to some small island and sell the plane? Did he change the plane's identity and then use it for his own business? Did he crash—fly to South America—maybe ditch the plane at some abandoned airport—change his looks and live on some tropical beach?

I heard rumors that some employees knew where he was and they wouldn't tell. I personally believe he had everything in order to start a new life on the day he was found out. The FBI kept a close watch on his possible whereabouts for a number of years. When one of his parents died, federal agents cased out the funeral, but he never showed up. He did not see his children. The federal agents never found him.

A very successful and popular television show contacted us and wanted to do a story on Ted. We considered it, getting to the point where we received a script. I would be on TV! It was a good story and they were quite confident that Ted could be caught via the show. But just when it was time to sign the dotted line, Keith backed out, not wanting the publicity. In my last telephone conversation with the television producer, I reluctantly had to tell him "No." His parting words reverberated in my ear: "You have made Ted a very happy man."

Chapter 17

Soul Mates

One of my pastimes was walking around the lake (or attempting to). There seemed to be a short window of time in the evening, when Bill would disappear and that is when I would walk.

A cool breeze would blow across the lake, and sunset painted the water a different set of colors every night. I drank in the beauty of it all, as that time of day was so peaceful and calming. Living here was like being on vacation.

I was now thirty-eight and confident that I was becoming a better judge of people, more discerning. I truly wanted to start a new life, and I was working hard to get past Bill's continued stalking. I was content just to enjoy life on my own; I would be happy never to get married again. But this determination didn't last.

Near my apartment the sidewalk passed a small dock, about ten feet by twelve feet with a wood railing, where I often saw a certain man fishing—in dress slacks! He was tall and slim, with wide shoulders and a dignified bearing. I noticed he wore thick glasses and a beautiful smile. We would nod to each other as I meandered by, and I began thinking, "*Who is this person?*"

The next night and then soon another night, we repeated the game. I walked by, and he nodded.

After quite some time observing one another, one particular evening I said "Hi." He smiled and remarked, "You're such a pretty woman." As I continued on my journey, my heart beat a little faster whenever I recalled his compliment.

I was quite interested in getting to know him, and I wondered why he didn't make a move to get better acquainted. On one gorgeous July evening after doing our usual acknowledgment, I got brave and walked up on the dock and introduced myself.

"Hi, I'm Elaine."

"I'm Jim."

After the usual introductory comments about the weather etc., I asked, "Would you like to come over for a Coke sometime?"

"Yes!"

"When?" I anxiously asked out of fear and delight at the prospect.

"How about tomorrow night?"

"Well, maybe I should go ahead and make dinner?"

That indeed brought an easy smile to his face.

I was surprised at his eagerness and thought, "What on earth am I going to cook on such short notice?"

After stewing all the next day at work, and talking to the "girls" on what I should serve, I put something together.

We had barely sat down at the table to eat when Jim calmly announced, "The green beans aren't done." He said it in a matter of fact way, not meaning to hurt me. Even so, I was shocked and embarrassed, but also impressed that he could be so honest.

After dinner I sat on the living room couch and Jim sat opposite me in an overstuffed easy chair. We talked, and he began to reveal more about himself.

I learned that he was an elementary school principal, he was twenty-one years older than I, and we loved many of the same things, such as reading and country music. Jim was always smiling, and I found him very easy to talk to.

Late in the evening, apparently waiting until I told him quite a bit about myself, Jim dropped a bombshell.

He told me about a professional acquaintance of his named Bill, whose ex-wife Peggy was a school librarian. (This put them in the same school administration circle of people). This "Bill" had repeatedly been calling Jim and telling him scandalous gossip about a certain woman, thinking that Jim was dating her.

Jim told me, "After a while it dawned on me, *he was describing you.* I got curious and asked him, 'If she's such a bad person as you say, then why do you keep calling *me* to talk about *her*?' He just stuttered, not knowing how to answer that! I didn't want to say anything to you tonight until I felt confident in what Bill was saying about you wasn't the truth!"

Jim and I discussed how the rumor of us dating could have started. Then it dawned on me. Bill, in his stalking, probably saw me sometimes as I walked over to the apartment building that Jim lived in. (Of course I didn't know Jim at the time!) I went to that building because it held the exercise room!

Shocked that I could not seem to escape the wrath of Bill, I was nevertheless intrigued by the fact that Jim knew Bill.

Jim told me his interest was definitely piqued to meet me, but considering our apparent age difference, he thought I would have no desire to become acquainted. His ego did not allow him the possibility of being turned down by a woman. He held himself back until I made the first move, and then he was ready and anxious, if I would only agree to date an older man!

Even late into the evening, too soon he had to leave. Standing at the door, he lingered, grinned and tousled my hair. "So can I see you again?"

"Sure, when?"

His immediate, definite reply: "Tomorrow night!"

But earlier I had set up a double date with a girl friend and was not able to cancel the plans. I went to dinner and the movies that next evening, and had the most miserable time—all I could think about was Jim....

The very next night Jim and I went on our first real date. It was at a nice restaurant on the east side of Wichita.

We were already feeling enamored of each other, when a girl vending fresh roses walked by our table, and Jim bought me a red rose. We had such a great conversation during dinner. I was totally smitten.

After dinner we went to a club in an adjoining room and sat in a cushioned private booth with tied-back drapery. We held hands while listening to a live band. Pretty soon he leaned over and we kissed. When our lips touched, my heart fluttered! We talked about feeling the electricity. And then we touched again. For the first time in my life, I felt real romance and the sparkle of stars. We fell in love then and there.

Everything about Jim attracted me! Though you might not call him handsome, he had a presence. Whether sitting or standing, his bearing was both relaxed and dignified. In conversation, his long arms and fingers made continuous graceful, open gestures. He gave you his whole attention and smiled constantly.

When we were together, we were always touching or embraced in some way. Jim was very affectionate with all of his loved ones—grown children were snuggled close for a hug.

I noticed Jim's sensitivity right away. He could shed a tear easily watching a sad movie. I loved that softness. But because of that, he also couldn't share certain memories if it meant he had to dig down deep within himself, so he simply avoided saying anything that would bring out his personal pain or heartache.

Along those same lines, he did not like to dwell on any sort of negative talk, saying, "I prefer to be positive and upbeat." I had always lived in what I would call "negaholic" surroundings. Understandably this was quite a change for me, and because of his attitude, I loved him even more.

His honesty continued to impress me. And he never criticized me personally.

I was in love with Jim and he felt the same about me. Still, I had doubts that I could just be loved for the person that I was. Something rooted deep within compelled me to do things for the one I was in love with. (Not an unhealthy desire, given a healthy relationship.) I was nobody unless he *needed* me; then I felt worthy, in my own mixed-up way.

I would drag my vacuum cleaner over to Jim's apartment and clean it. There was no obligation on my part to do that. But I thought the only way he would love me was if I did something for him. In deference, by nature I am also a servant and I loved serving him, as I did other people I knew.

Once a week he would go out to play cards with the guys, his most desired hobby after golf. Usually afterward, at his request they would drop him off, drunk, at my apartment. As I had never been exposed to people getting drunk, I had no idea this state of drunkenness could be a pattern in a person's life. I would think nothing else but that I needed to hold and comfort him because he was sick. I was his rescuer! In my mind, that made me important to him, so then he would love me.

Jim loved to dance. His favorite was the waltz. I also loved to dance, but had never really had the opportunity to learn. He quickly pronounced, "I'll teach you." The kitchen in my apartment was open on each end, allowing us to dance a full circle through the kitchen, living and dining rooms. Evening after evening we would make that circle.

The first time we went out dancing in public, after sitting a little while he whispered, "Elaine, may I have this dance?" and he led me out onto the hardwood floor. My knees were knocking and I was shaking so badly, Jim could feel it. He held me tightly, as I slowly relaxed and soon we were twirling around the dance floor to the beat of country music, all swept up in each other.

We dated every day except for a three-day school trip when Jim went to St. Louis. Usually we went to the Twin Lakes Club (located adjacent to our apartment complex and in the Twin Lakes shopping center) where they had a live band. After dinner, we danced or sat and listened to the music, while Jim would enjoy his alcoholic beverages. Charlie, the bartender, liked Jim and made sure he poured in a strong shot of liquor when mixing his drink.

Ironically, now Charlie got to meet me, the girl he had always seen Bill spying on with his binoculars, peering out across the lake from the parking lot of the club.

We made the rounds of three nightclubs that always had live music. If the band noticed us walk in when we went to the Crown Room or the Fireside, the next tune the band usually played was *Milk Cow Blues,* one of Jim's most favorite songs.

No matter where we were, at home, in a car, or at a club, whenever we sat listening to music, Jim would hold up his thumb and index finger and sway back and forth, keeping time. Sometimes he took my index finger, causing me to sway with him. He called it "arm dancing." This was the first time I saw someone enjoy music so much, indulging every style, sucking in every little beat.

I had grown up without music, except for the times I listened secretly. No one I had ever been close to embraced music as Jim did. It was a huge part of what made Jim the person he was. Now I was enjoying music in all its glory. And it drew me closer to him.

On our dates, Jim told me stories about his youth. He grew up in Ada, a small town in Oklahoma. He would often tell me, "I can't wait until I can take you to Ada. I want to show you the swimming pool and the lake where I spent a lot of time fishing!" It was his favorite place. And of course, it seemed huge when he was a boy!

Jim's parents had owned a restaurant downtown. Sam and Vera raised their two sons in the hotel quarters above the restaurant. Jim and his younger brother Bill could often hear the fiddling music of the jukebox playing below. That's where Jim fell in love with country music, listening to Bob Wills and others with their strong country rhythm.

Jim and Bill grew up with little supervision as their parents were usually managing the restaurant. Around the ages of seven and five, the two of them were playing in a tree, climbing around as children do. Jim accidentally pushed Bill and he fell to the ground, causing permanent damage to his leg.

They never acknowledged the consequences of the incident, but Jim was reminded of it every time he saw Bill, as he walked with a limp, and he never forgave himself for what had happened. It made a sad indelible mark on Jim at an early age.

Sam was an excellent cook in the restaurant and he had a caring, sympathetic heart. He would serve food to beggars who knocked at the restaurant's back door. Sometimes he had to add a lot of liquid to stretch the soup, but he always had enough.

Jim said he made the best chili ever! (Jim also loved to make chili, and with every batch would take pure delight when giving me a bite, savoring the taste with me, exclaiming how delicious it was. "Why, it's almost as good as Sam's!" he would tell me.)

Jim was proud of Sam, of his soft heart and his delicious cooking. He played up his father's good qualities. However, Sam had a downfall and that was alcohol. Sam frequently got drunk. As a youngster, Jim would have to go pick up his father off the street, literally dragging and carrying his dad home. It was terribly embarrassing for him.

Jim told me often how much he had loved his mother and how he admired her strength. She had to lead pretty much her own life because of Sam's drinking. Anger started building in Jim as he watched her endure a painful marriage.

Once, Vera took him and his brother and ran off to California with another man. But Sam came right after her and talked her into coming back home. This contributed to Jim's anger and insecurity, as he was hoping for a normal life in California and wanted to stay there.

Fresh out of high school at age seventeen, Jim was ready for adventure. He was anxious to join the Navy. Underage, but not wanting to waste any time, he convinced his parents to sign the military papers so he could join up early.

Grown up and on his own, and a natural at being the life of the party, in his free time on the ship he started drinking, boxing and playing cards. He also drank so he didn't have to deal with the pain of life in remembering the sad things of his growing up. *He wanted to be happy.*

Jim's position on the ship was a gunner. He lost some hearing while in that job as he stood next to the guns when they were fired. His tour of duty was over when World War II ended. I often heard him tell the story of him being on a neighboring ship in the ocean and watching (as the world did) when General MacArthur waded ashore in Leyte, Philippines in October of 1944. That was his proudest moment.

Jim then went off to college to get two teaching degrees. He married his high school sweetheart, Cindy, while still in college. After graduating, he moved to Kansas and became an elementary school teacher and soon afterward a principal. Jim and Cindy had three wonderful children, two girls and a boy in the middle.

Jim and Cindy later divorced, and he married his school secretary. I believe their marriage lasted around ten years. Jim had been divorced a year or so when we met.

In mid November, Jim asked me to marry him. I readily accepted, and on November 30th, 1984, a short five months after meeting, we got married.

Each of us lived in a one-bedroom apartment at Twin Lakes and we decided it would be best to move to another apartment. Jim said we would coordinate our wedding date around finding an apartment, and quickly there was one available that we both liked. It was in a building situated in the middle of the complex on the 3rd and top floor with lots of windows looking to the west and over the lake. The views were incredible and the apartment large.

During the time we were courting, Bill not only continued to harass me but also did the same to Jim. He would call our apartments to find out where we were, sometimes coming to Jim's door on some pretense. He followed both of us, keeping track of our every move.

On our wedding day, Bill called Jim a number of times. When Jim came to pick me up for the wedding, he only half-jokingly said, "We should have just given Bill our itinerary!"

At our appointed time we went to the courthouse. The wedding was very simple. Jim's best friends drove up from

Oklahoma City to witness. I wore a simple long-sleeved, cream-colored street length dress.

As we stood in the judge's office at five p.m., the setting sun beamed through the window, and by coincidence, the church bells began ringing. A cross and a painting of Jesus looked over us while the judge read the wedding vows and then a poem, which was lovely and meaningful. The judge put such sincerity into his words. I took it all in, absorbing everything he said, and concentrated on the significance of the vows. I held onto my man and grinned helplessly. I was totally in love and happy!

Our honeymoon was delayed and combined with a school convention Jim had signed up for in March of 1985 in Denver, Colorado.

We called ourselves "soul mates." We were in love and our positive sides were very compatible. We both liked to get up early in the morning and take our time reading the paper, luxuriating with a cup of coffee. Jim happily ate anything I'd cook for him. We were content.

In the summer of 1985, Jim retired from the school system and would not be returning in the fall. I was a little disappointed, as I had enjoyed being a school principal's wife, being able to go into his office and sneak a kiss and be by his side at his school functions. But I completely supported his decision to take early retirement. I knew he would enjoy it.

Top: Jim fishing at Twin Lakes.
Middle: The fishing dock where Jim and I met.
Bottom: Our apartment at Twin Lakes. (Between the
      trees)

Top: Waiting in the judge's office
Bottom: After the wedding vows

Chapter 18

Not Again!

As Jim and I settled down into married life, things were happening again at the office. We were in for our biggest and most shocking surprise yet.

In the spring of 1985 we franchised about a hundred restaurants. Our office manager, Jane, had been with us about four years. As the one entrusted with paying the rent and bills for our restaurants, she had control of the books and computer system.

One day while visiting with her, I noticed the diamond-studded bracelet on her wrist. How it sparkled! Later that day in Sally's office, I commented, "Jane must have robbed a bank in order to be wearing that gorgeous bracelet!"

She was in fact robbing us.

I had been discretely watching her side of the business for a long time, as in certain things we overlapped each other's work. One day a bank (it happened to be the one where I used to work) called with a question on a company check that I couldn't answer, so I transferred the call to Jane. "I'll handle it," she said, too quickly. I became suspicious and stayed on the line a minute to listen to the conversation. (I believe that is the only time I did such a bad thing!) Her frantic reaction to the bank's questions caused me to realize something was not right.

Immediately I left the office without telling anyone where I was going and drove directly to the bank. I was so nervous my knees were shaking, my palms wet and my heart pounding as though it would burst through my chest. I felt as if Jane knew what I was doing. In fact, she had no way of knowing. Nevertheless, when a person plays sleuth, it can be unnerving.

I obtained the check in question and determined that it had been deposited to her personal account, although it was made payable to a company name. I brought the check back and hid it in my desk drawer, under my other papers, petrified that Jane would catch me with it. She had just committed a crime, and I was the one feeling guilty! How would I behave toward her? What would I say to her?

As I sat pondering what to do next, in walked Jane. She sat down right in front of me and went into a long story to justify the check in question. My heart beat faster and faster as I listened to her explanation, all the while knowing it was a lie. I wanted to stand up and scream; "I know what you're doing! You are stealing money! I have the check right here! Look, look!" I kept quiet, wondering once again, *"How can a person sit six feet from me, look directly into my eyes, and lie?"*

As soon as she left, I hurried into Keith's office and closed the door. Oh, my, I thought to myself. "How do private investigators keep their blood pressure under control?" The excitement was too much. I had a hard time staying calm while telling him what had just transpired.

Once again, Keith placed a call to Tom.

Trying to remain composed we waited until 6:00 p.m. and everyone was gone from the office, including Jane. After locking the doors, Keith, Larry (the new controller), and I lugged all the ledger books and bank statements upstairs to the conference room. We spread them out over a huge oblong table and got to work.

This time it was easy. It was so obvious and plain to see once we started looking. Jane had been writing checks to various company names and then depositing them into her personal bank account. We had to determine and separate them from the real companies with which we did business. Sometimes the fake names showed little imagination, some using initials, with a twist of her real name.

I signed checks for the company, and she even forged my signature a couple of times. After a while, we noticed another pattern: Every check she had issued to herself was endorsed with the same color ink pen! Forget trying to determine who the legitimate companies were. All we had to do was open a bank statement with the checks enclosed, turn all the checks over and we could pick them out, like a deck of cards.

The first check that had alerted me was in the amount of ten thousand dollars. We found many more like it. Jane's little operation had gone unnoticed as the amount might be typical for a rent payment. And she wrote the checks to herself at the same time she issued the rent checks, so they intermingled easily.

While we sat, stood, and paced around the conference table, the drama continued to unfold with each passing hour. Keith kept in constant contact with Tom, calling every little bit with a new and larger total dollar amount. Fifty thousand, one hundred thousand, two hundred thousand, then three hundred thousand. We shook our heads in constant disbelief, and kept counting.

The charges we found that night added up to over four hundred and sixty thousand dollars. We discovered that she had destroyed certain records for one year. If she continued in the same trend for that year, then it means she likely had stolen more than a half million dollars. Our company had even been audited in depth by a national accounting firm and they missed it.

It became obvious why she had been so determined to work alone. The first check she wrote to herself was within six weeks of employment with the company. And the most incredible of all for us to comprehend, was that she was stealing from us at the same time I was diligently picking apart invoices on Ted's embezzlement.

At midnight we gathered up our stuff and decided to call it a night. I drove home in a daze. Emotionally exhausted, I told Jim of the day's events. It was a short night.

The next morning Jane arrived at work at her usual time, only to find Keith and Tom standing at her desk. She later said she knew immediately that she had been caught, before a word had been spoken.

They all went into Keith's office where she signed a confession in a fairly short time. Tom called the police. Then he called her husband, who came immediately to the office. He acted shocked, as though he knew nothing of her scheme. Jane told them she mostly took the money to cover her husband's business, as it was in financial trouble. Supposedly, she had told her husband the money was from an inheritance account of hers, and he apparently took her word for it.

Three months later the couple filed for bankruptcy to the tune of almost seven hundred thousand dollars.

Jane's employment with the company was terminated when we had her arrested. But soon she was released while Tom and Keith discussed whether to prosecute. The owners were reluctant to collect any more publicity. Finally we agreed to press charges and in December she was sentenced to seventeen years in prison, eligible for parole after twelve years.

I remembered most of the jewelry she wore, and at Keith's request made a list of it, including her wedding rings, other rings, earrings, necklaces and the diamond-studded bracelet. She turned it all in. My hands went over the pieces as I recalled the little pangs of jealousy I sometimes experienced when she wore her beautiful jewelry. Now it was all for naught. I wondered, "How she could do such a thing, and if she thought it was worth it, only to lose it all."

Keith gave me the job of hawking the jewelry. Buying jewelry is expensive; selling it is cheap. There was one particular pair of earrings I would have loved to have. I was hoping that the owners might give it to me as a reward, and I hoped until the last minute when I handed them over to the jeweler. But it was not to be. As partial repayment, Jane and her husband also turned in an automobile and some cash.

Our attorney recommended we file a civil suit against Jane, so we could attempt to collect money after her prison release. Keith was embarrassed with the weight of the additional publicity so soon after Ted's embezzlement, and fed up with paperwork, he ignored the advice. Contrary to the attorney's strong recommendation, we declined taking any further legal action.

Next came one of the hardest things for the company to accept. The Internal Revenue Service got wind of what happened and came calling, again. We had to pay income tax on the money Jane had stolen from us!

Her sentence was later modified and in one year she was up for parole. I went to the parole hearing and pled with the board for her not to be released. That kept her in prison for another six months, after which she went free.

Her original sentence awarded us about forty thousand dollars. A civil suit would have allowed us to keep going after her income. I guess we thought she wouldn't be released so soon and go back to work, thereby earning dollars we might have collected.

After being released from prison, she went to work in another company's accounting office in another city. One newspaper article commented, "There are people who still trust her with money."

Those years were trying times for the company. The economy was down. Competition was growing up all around us and getting tougher.

Tom had health problems and he and Sally started having trouble in their marriage. Their animosity towards each other leaked into the office. Keith and I were frequently caught in the middle. Keith leaned toward Sally, leaving Tom out of some decisions. I went through a lot during this time as I became a pawn between them. My natural tendency was to please Tom rather than Sally. He was the majority owner, but she told me that she had priority over Tom because she had hired me. So who was I to mind when they each would give me different instructions in the same thing?

One day Tom decided to remove Sally's name from all the business bank accounts. He told me to meet him at the bank and we redid all the accounts. Afterwards, the bank called Sally to ask, "What's going on?" I was very uneasy about this, I felt guilty for what I had done, and very saddened by the result—Sally and Keith were deeply insulted by the way I had betrayed her.

For a long time the tension was high. Keith wouldn't even look me in the face, and always closed his office door, which at the time was directly across from mine. Eventually even he admitted, "What could you have done? It was a Catch-22." Still, I made a mistake I wish I could have retracted. My relationship was never the same with them after that day.

Tom and Sally's marriage kept getting worse, and eventually they divorced. Sally bought Tom out of his share of the company and made Keith the President.

Chapter 19

Ups and Downs

In December of 1985, after we had been married a little over a year, Jim got up in the middle of the night, not feeling well. After being up for a while, he awoke me. "My blood pressure is extremely high and I'm concerned. I think we need to go to the hospital right away." I hurriedly dressed and we drove to the emergency room at the nearest hospital, St. Francis. (This was the same one into which I had been admitted after my breakdown sixteen years earlier.)

The doctors ran some tests and determined that he had unknowingly suffered a mild heart attack earlier in the day. In fact, while Jim was carrying a box inside the house, he said he had felt a strange sensation. Attributing it to making a wrong move with his body, he let it go. The tests also showed he needed to undergo carotid artery surgery, even before heart bypass surgery. He was immediately checked into a room, and the next day they did carotid surgery on his neck. The doctors found ninety-nine percent blockage of one artery.

It was Christmas time and I was in the midst of my usual party planning at the office. Three days after Jim was discharged from the hospital, I was putting on our Christmas party at the Broadview Hotel in downtown Wichita. Without missing a beat, we got a hotel room for Jim so he could be close by while I oversaw the party.

The next day, we once again walked up those steps to that same red brick hospital building. Both of our hearts pounded in anxiety over the upcoming bypass surgery, although I was more visibly nervous than Jim.

After Jim got situated, I purposely walked to the lower basement level where I had been a patient so many years before. The hospital had been remodeled and the restaurant and beauty shop were now located in other parts of the building.

Eerily, now the hall seemed sterile, so full of gray concrete and emptiness. There were no people coming and going, only silence.

Yet, I could almost taste and smell the emotions of so many years ago. The beauty shop. The hairspray! I imagined the booths in the coffee shop where I had frittered away time.

This was the place where I had finally rejected the religion of my upbringing. A part of who I am, and will be forever. I made decisions, both big and small, that dramatically changed the course of my life.

I wanted someone to wrap their arms around me, to take the chill away. I wanted to remember it all. I wanted to feel, to sit down on the floor and revisit my life there. All the same, I knew no one could totally comprehend my thoughts. They were mine alone...I was the only person in the world that experienced exactly what I had gone through. So, instead of lingering too long, I moved forward, slowly...down the hallway, still grasping at every remembrance.

Holding tightly to my memories, I proceeded to the door, noticing the clang of the door as it closed, and went back upstairs to attend to my husband.

The next morning Jim underwent quadruple bypass surgery. After the average length of time for the surgical procedure had lapsed, I waited for a word from the doctor, anxious to hear how the surgery had gone.

Finally, the doctor appeared and said they were having difficulty in getting Jim to come around. The doctor said there was a possibly he might not survive.

"It will be touch and go for a couple of hours. But with every minute, will be one more minute of the probability of him pulling through. Time is on our side."

I loved Jim so much. He couldn't leave me! We were still newlyweds!

In all my life I had never experienced the slowness of time as I endured those hours. Each minute felt like an eternity, as I paced back and forth in the waiting room. Jim's brother Bill was there beside me, although he just watched me pace. I would come back to him and we would discuss how much time had elapsed. Then I walked again.

After what seemed an endless amount of watching the clock, the doctor said we could go see him. Enough time had passed and he believed that Jim would make it. All hooked up to monitors, he was still a beautiful breathing person to see.

For seven days Jim stayed in the hospital and I cared for him around the clock. I slept in a recliner right beside his bed, going home only in the morning to shower and then return within the hour.

Jim came home from the hospital just before Christmas. We went out New Year's Eve with friends as we had planned much earlier and even danced to one song. He never complained.

By February, he had gone back into the hospital twice to have an angioplasty done. Jim's son was serving in the Peace Corps in Africa and he was able to come home to see his Dad. It was a scary time for us. The doctor said if scar tissue appeared for a third time, they would have to open his chest back up and perform another bypass.

We were anxious and hoping that Jim would heal speedily, and as each day passed, we were confident that he would not have to undergo another surgery. We were keeping our fingers crossed that we would be able to take a two-week vacation to Disney World and a cruise that we had scheduled months before his heart attack.

An hour before we were to leave for the airport in Wichita, our tickets were lying on the bed and I happened to glance at them. *I* about had a heart attack, as I discovered the travel agency had scheduled us to leave on the next day! We were getting on a cruise ship so that wouldn't work. I quickly placed a call to the agency and tickets were dropped by at the complex office as there was no time to give her our address. The trip down turned into a mini nightmare, as we got to the airport, planes and luggage were shuffled, and the agency had forgotten to also change our hotel reservation in Orlando. Jim and I both worried about the stress of that day on his heart!

It happened to be unusually cold in Florida that winter, but our hearts were warm as we enjoyed our first big trip together, and Jim's recovery. The weather in Wichita was warmer on our return than it had been all the while we were in Florida and the Bahamas.

As Jim was recuperating from surgery he watched a lot of television. He enjoyed a particular fishing show that came on in the afternoon. Its theme music went something like this:

I'm a happy man
Don't have time to be sad

Jim excitedly told me about the song. He said the words kept him going while he was sitting there alone in the apartment and I was at work. I made it my mission to find that song for him. I could not find a recording anywhere. After contacting numerous television stations across the country, I was finally able to obtain a cassette copy. The enclosed letter told me,

The ballad is no longer in print as a pressed record or available in any form to the public. It is a beautiful song and a favorite. Hope Mr. Davis is recuperating rapidly and sincerely hope he enjoys the tape.

Jim was thrilled to get the tape and he made several copies so that he could play it everywhere—at home and in our vehicles. It became his theme song. Every word seemed to fit the circumstances he was going through.

I'm a Happy Man

Woke up this morning, a smile on my face
Looked out at the world, what a beautiful place
The sun's shining and a blue sky above
A home and family surrounded with love

(chorus) And I'm a happy man, a happy man
I won't take time to be sad
And I'm a happy man, a happy man
Who's thankful and so glad
That I've been taught not to pity myself,
But live every moment of life that's left
There's just not enough time to be anything else,
*   anything else*
But a happy man.

I won't be bitter 'cause I won't take time
For that kind of thinking to clutter my mind
A man just has such a little while
To spread a little joy and give a smile

(chorus) So I'm a happy man, a happy man
I won't take time to be sad
And I'm a happy man, a happy man
Who's thankful and so glad
That I've been taught not to pity myself,
But live every moment of life that's left
There's just not enough time to be anything else,
    anything else
But a happy man.

I've had misfortune to visit on me
To break my weary spirit and bring me to my knees
But a man can never learn to appreciate this life
Till his joy's been mixed with trouble and strife.
So I'm a happy man, a happy man,
I'll take the good with the bad

(chorus) I'm a happy man, a happy man
I won't take time to be sad
And I'm a happy man, a happy man
Who's thankful and so glad
That I've been taught not to pity myself,
But live every moment of life that's left
There's just not enough time to be anything else,
    anything else
But a happy man.

The song personified Jim. I knew he had lived every word. I heard it over and over, but I didn't mind. To see the joy and the smile it brought meant so much to me.

262

Each morning, as I left for work, he called out with a smile, "Be happy!" But amidst his portrayal of happiness was the other persona of Jim. And that was his continual drinking.

Jim's natural personality was to be happy. And I loved that. On the flip side I had to live with the anger that emerged out of him. At first, when things didn't go right, I would not allow the hurt to stay with me. Because when the hurt is new, as in a new relationship, a person ignores it, as love overtakes the heartache. As time goes on, the pain becomes deeper.

In the early part of our marriage, Jim and I were active socially with Jim's school administration friends. We would go to their homes for dinner and parties. Jim liked to have a good time. Everybody loved him and wanted him happy, so they made sure to keep his glass full. But I became very uncomfortable in a room where there was a lot of drinking going on. Jim usually drank so much that I had to then drive us home, and that made me really upset. I was glad for our safety that I could drive, but I became increasingly irritated at what I felt was his irresponsible behavior.

After getting home from a party and going to bed, I would be afraid to go to sleep. After excessive drinking, during the night Jim might get up to use the bathroom and urinate in odd places, such as in the bathroom sink or on a lamp in the living room.

After a while it became harder and harder for me to agree to be with his drinking friends. Eventually, I begged for us not to go, and our social life dwindled.

Certain things seemed to make him angry. If I wanted to take chairs out to the gazebo for a picnic, he wouldn't let me. "No, don't move the chair, that's not necessary." Everything had to be done in order and in his way or he would erupt with great anger. In essence, don't change any plan, don't do anything if it caused a disruption. He could be a very happy person, and he could be a very angry person. Between the two was a fine line.

I would come home from work and find Jim on the sofa with a drink cupped in his hand with the television on. For a long time, it didn't occur to me that he was an alcoholic. I had never been around anyone who drank. I had never read about alcoholism. I didn't know the symptoms.

But one day I described his behaviors to a widowed friend, Hazel, whose husband had been an alcoholic, and she replied, "That's how alcoholics are. An alcoholic cannot handle change; their world has a pattern and they do not like to break it."

Later, one of his children remarked to me that when they were young, they almost preferred that when their dad came home from work he went for a drink right away. This child told me how at the same time she didn't like her dad's behavior when he drank, she would sometimes fix him one and greet him at the door with the drink in her hand. That way they knew the plan for the evening. He would be asleep and they wouldn't have to deal with his fits of anger with words that hurt so much.

Alcoholism can be a disease of denial, and Jim refused to admit he had a problem. He hid his liquor bottles far back in the cupboards. His day would begin with vodka in orange juice, or Bailey's Irish Cream in coffee. For the rest of the day he would find any excuse to drink. Maybe it was for a low golf score, a great game of bowling, for a holiday or someone's birthday. It was just to celebrate, right?

The anguish of watching someone I loved doing this to himself became a heart-wrenching burden that I put on myself.

At night while he slept, I would be aware of how his heart medications, along with the alcohol in his body, seemed to slow his heart rate and I couldn't tell if he was still breathing.

I'd lean over his face, holding my own breath, listening, terrified that I might lose him at any moment.

After asking Dad and Mom numerous times, I convinced them to come visit us. It was both Easter and my birthday. To celebrate, Jim and I wanted to take them to a special restaurant that was out of town. While driving, my husband shared with my dad his thoughts about the *Happy Man* song. He had the cassette tape along, so he played it. As I have already mentioned, it was about being a happy man no matter what the circumstances, because there is still so much to be thankful for.

Dad growled, "Well, I do not see anything good in that song. *I have no reason to be happy.*"

A huge argument developed as Jim, Mom and I tried to convince him otherwise. By the time we arrived at the restaurant, we were all very upset. As soon as we got out of the car, Dad took off walking around screaming at all of us, while waving his hands back and forth in the air. Guests going into the restaurant were observing this strange behavior, looking at us, and wondering what was going on.

Mom, Jim and I discussed taking him to the psychiatric hospital that was nearby. Without health insurance, and being out of state it would be inconvenient, so we determined that it wasn't the right time.

Dad eventually calmed down. After a while we went in and had a quiet and somber meal. By then, none of us were joyful and in a mood to celebrate. Such were the times with my father.

Around this time my parents were in the biggest financial crisis of their life. The church deacons and his friends would offer remedies, but it did no good. Dad wasn't interested in solutions concerning financial management. He had to do things his own way, and the strain this caused our family was immense.

Mom was working full time to buy groceries for the table, their clothes and her car. In fact, she carried the burden of paying most of the household upkeep. She also needed to get away from the house in order to maintain her sanity. Even so, Dad continually called her at work to vent his problems. She says, "He lived on complaining. *It was his sustenance.*"

Mom had for years, and continued, to take care of people with Alzheimer's disease. It worked out—as her patients didn't fully comprehend her own weariness and sickness.

My sister Pearl lived close by, so she had to deal with it on a daily basis. It put her in the hospital a number of times.

Pearl writes in her notes:

I was always the one closest to Dad, but eventually that closeness left. He wanted help…but he wouldn't listen. We finally just about gave up trying to have a conversation with him. Any little thing could throw him into a rage. Something innocently spoken…but he would take it wrong. But, he wanted visits, again and again…It didn't do any good, it would always end up bad. So we avoided it as much as possible.

I wanted to help…but I couldn't. Dad was pulling me one way and Mom another. I was so torn. I finally broke away from Dad and said, "You're the problem—not Mom!" Then he'd get angry with me. I felt so awful…all of my life, from little on, I had wanted to please him and escape his wrath. And now I had actually turned away from him – the pain was almost too much to bear. I still wanted his love and affection, but I had to take a stand for the right and speak the truth. Dad was the problem, had always been…he was the one to blame. But oh, the pain of separation...the hurt of it all. How I prayed and hoped for a change—that there could be peace and a togetherness.

Mom writes in her notes:

Pearl had endured so much for many years. I would go to her with complaints. Ben would call her, telling her she needed to help fix me. So she was literally being torn always—she in turn would go to the preachers, and they would call me in, and that's how the cycle continued.

The beast in our place was mental illness, and we were assigned to live with it.

Part of a note from Mary Jane to Dad reads:

Dad,

I'm glad we had a good visit—but if it's really real what you have with the Lord as you've been telling me—then you would have been the mature Christian and let me talk without you interrupting me. I let out my forty years of anger to you...and I can't say that for that I'm sorry. You need deep, deep therapy; you don't really know your real problem.

Love,
Mary Jane

Dad would call me on the telephone filling my ear with his troubles; then Mom would call and cry. I couldn't do anything but listen to them. When I did call home, if Dad answered the phone, I would hang up on him. The guilt I went through doing that to my parent.... Still, I couldn't bear to talk to him if I could avoid it.

My parents were bruised, battered and bleeding, but what could I do? I was torn between sympathy for Mom and bitterness towards Dad. I don't remember the details of most of our conversations. I do remember the anguish I felt every day having to live with my parent's problems, but not able to fix them.

Pearl summed it up in a letter she wrote to Dad:

What can I, as a child, give in the way of instruction to my parents? It doesn't feel right for one to advise very much.

At one point, one of the cafés in town forbade Dad from coming in again, because of his behavior and temper. (A contrast from the times I had spent in cafes with him.) If Dad was visiting with someone and they disagreed with him, he'd go into a rage. One time he made the comment, "Don't ever challenge a Schmidt...if you do, there'll be war!" So, if the rest of the family wanted to eat out in peace, we'd go to that café.

In many respects, living with my dad and his finances was like dealing with a substance abuser. All an addict wants is their fix, until that wears off, and then all they can think about is the next fix.

If I gave my father ten dollars to pay the bill that was most pressing, immediately there would be another. His bills were so many and he would only be able to make a payment of five, ten or twenty dollars towards what was owed. Dad could think of nothing else but how he was going to get money to pay his bills.

The mortgage lender kept threatening to foreclose on their home. Mom was afraid. She would call me, saying over and over, "What should I do? If they repossess the house, will they also take all the furniture?"

Dad would get crazy sometimes, hollering and demanding answers, but never listening. As he could no longer borrow, and Mom had good credit, he kept asking her to sign loans for him.

During this time, Mom had a couple of nervous break-downs a few months apart and ended up in a hospital in Newton, Kansas, close to Wichita and well known among the Mennonites as a place to receive good mental therapy.

Mom and Dad went in together for one session. The doctors counseled Dad. They recommended some changes that he could make to better his life and marriage, but he again wasn't interested in resolutions, in what they had to say. He refused any more counseling. There wasn't anything wrong with him; they needed to fix Mom!

Searching for answers, Mom got some books on mental illness and determined that possibly Dad suffered from bipolar manic depression. In the early years of their marriage she blamed his behavior on his background, growing up with poverty, filth and anger. Now she saw some similarity in manic depression and Dad's illness.

My Mom's notes describe so well my own thoughts:

> *The fact that most people don't see what goes on inside the house and have no idea what the family is dealing with makes it all the more terrible. All the awful emotions consume a family, and no one under-stands or empathizes.*
>
> *A simple "no" can trigger a nuclear explosion. A bipolar person has a great sense of grandiosity and perfectionism and must be in control.*
>
> *I lived with the perpetual anger, put downs and 'self-righteousness' which often goes along with this*

and the pride so high you can't reach it. Leaving scars so deep, one can't comprehend.

My gut hurt so badly, like a hole in my stomach, a feeling I could never describe. I didn't realize how mentally sick he was, and that he didn't love himself, so how could he possibly love me or anyone else?

I can't tell you how many times he got up after 'retiring' and would start yelling at me, walking the floor, waving his arms in his demon possessed misery. At times pulling the covers off me and stalked me from room to room as I tried to escape his wrath. He would stand over me and want me to talk, saying he needed some d— answers.

According to a counselor Dad's emotional quotient was about the age of five. But his IQ was perhaps quite high.

He was humorous and charismatic. He was a tender, soft person inside and did not want to be the way he was. He fought his demons.

I spent my entire life trying to understand my husband. I loved him so very much—why is he so mean to me—why? And why is he so angry? We used to say that love will bring anyone around—not exactly true of mental illness. "The voice of anger is louder than the voice of love."

When he was so sad, it broke my heart, and it melted my heart towards him over and over again. When one lives with this kind of person, you forgive thousands and thousands of times over and always go back to him in love. Until the next time he hurts you bad again. Then you go into a corner to heal the wounds, sometimes it takes longer than other times, depending on how severe the damnation on you and how sharp the words.

I lived with constant hope that he would change.

I knew I needed help—I drove myself to Halstead, Kansas, to see a doctor my friend had made an appointment with. My sadness was great, I felt like Abe Lincoln when he said, "I am now the most miserable man living. If what I feel were equally distributed to the whole human family, there would not be one cheerful face on the earth. Whether I shall get better, I cannot tell; I'm afraid not, but to remain as I am is impossible. I must die or be better." As I was driving, I lost my way a few times, partly because the flowing tears blinded me. I wondered as I passed the houses, are they as sad as I am?

Mom's words reflect to a great degree my relationship with Bob. And as I am reading her words as I write this, I am awed at how similar our lives were at one point. My mother's words were my words in my marriage to Bob, my words, her words, her pain, my pain and my pain, her pain. All twisted up in life with my father, and in the choices we both had made.

In the summer of 1986 or so the situation was noticeably affecting Mom's health. It seemed as if she was losing her mind. On a trip to Arkansas, she acted like a zombie, just out of it. She was going through the motion of accommodating us girls on the trip, but she didn't have the desire to do anything. Yet, we were most important to her and she wanted to be with us.

I really noticed something wrong one time I took her and Mary Jane on another short trip to Eureka Springs, Arkansas. Mom was not thinking clearly and she became fearful.

When we went into a store, she clung to us like a child and would not leave our side. "I'm afraid I'll get lost," she said in a pathetic voice. "Where's the car? We won't be able to find it." But we had parked right outside the door! No amount of reasoning would satisfy her.

When we arrived back in Tulsa, she said, "I cannot go home."

"Do you want to stay in Tulsa with Mary Jane?"

"No, no...."

"Do you want to come home with me?"

"No, no...."

Well, this didn't leave us any choice, so I took her back to Fairview. Oh how I hurt, what could I do for my mother?

Her face contorted in distress when she saw her house. "I can't explain it," she said. "It's like Hell. I can't stand to be in there; it's such a strong emotional torment." Where does a person retreat to when they are sick? Home. But home was where her pain was.

I cried after I left her at the house.

Mom could endure no more from Dad. Depression was coming upon her full throttle. Whereas the curtains had always been fully opened in the house, now the shades were pulled shut.

She moved into her own bedroom and put a new lock on the door. Her comfortable recliner went in with her. The sewing machine was close by and she made pretty dresses for her doll collection. That was *her* place of escape. Whenever we girls went home, that's where we spent most of our time. Visiting in the bedroom with the door closed, always keeping a wary ear out for the sound of Dad coming into the house.

Dad got the church leaders deeply involved in their marriage. The ministers came calling, telling Mom that she should sleep with Dad. The church insisted strongly that in order to be right with God, she had to forgive all and share a bedroom again.

My dad wrote many letters. I have a box full. They are so very sad and full of heartache. In literally dozens of notes and letters he begged for help and compassion. He spoke often of having a demon or devil spirit in him. Or, the rejection he felt especially from Mom, when she would close her bedroom door in the evening and then he knew he had to face another night alone. He said he had a broken and empty life and yearned for her love. He would say he hurt physically so badly also, but he didn't have money to go to a doctor. He said the grief in his soul was enough to kill any man.

Dad recalled how in the early years, he would stand outside the kitchen window and listen to Mom sing like a mockingbird. Then he took away her song by bringing such sorrow into her life.

Here are a few of Dad's notes that he wrote late at night, and then Mom would find them in the kitchen upon her awakening the next morning.

Oh, God, please do not leave me, for I cannot stand to be alone.

Please help me.

I not only am a child, I am also half crazy.

I need you to talk about my soul and life but I don't know how. Pray for me! I am nothing, nothing, nothing!!!

I want to show my love and affection to you but I am so intimidated and feel so cheap. I pray every night and day that God will make me a loveable person, to take away from me everything that is ugly. I see my self as a very ugly person. My self-esteem is too low. So low that I cannot be thankful as I should. I do not know where to go to be accepted. The only rock I have is Christ. As all my life's dreams are shattered.

*I come to you with all my heart and ask that you
please pray for me. I cannot bear this anymore that I
was so cruel to Elaine as a child and baby. I have to
talk to somebody how to be delivered.*

I also have a box of Mom's letters in her responses to
Dad. Their back and forth writing is very difficult for me
to read. I believe that without God, my dad would not have
made it through life. Mom did not have the history of rejection as much, so she was stronger.

The strife was getting quite intense and we kids became
even more involved. By 1987, we could not deal with the
situation any longer.

The folks had been seeing a counselor, Barbara, indi-
vidually and in a group setting with other people for about
a year. The other participants told Dad what he was like
and what he needed to do, and he got more depressed each
time after he and Mom left the session. He often threatened
suicide. Barbara warned Mom that he could likely commit
suicide and to be prepared for this. Sometimes Dad would go
to Barbara's office and she would tell him there was no more
she could do for him. But he still went. Frequently, he'd take
his songbook and sing to her!

Mom attempted to get Dad to go to a medical doctor and
get prescription medicine to alleviate his severe depression.
He refused any and all suggestions.

After several conversations with her and Barbara, my
siblings and I decided we must have an intervention with
Dad. Maybe if we all got together, we could convince him
to change his thinking. At this time we felt it best if Dad
would declare bankruptcy. We coordinated our plans to come
home.

The day arrived and we—Mom, Pearl, Mary Jane, Earl,
and myself—all met with Barbara at the courthouse in

Fairview. We went over the rules that the counselor suggested and agreed that we would be honest with Dad and convey to him our love and our desire that he make a change.

Then we headed for the house.

I will never forget the moment when we all drove into the yard. So many emotions flooded me, nervousness, but hopeful anticipation.

Dad had a smile on his face a mile long. All of the kids were home! What was the occasion? He thought it was for something special, and he strutted out to greet us, as if honored.

Then we all went into the living room. I sat on the floor and the others in various places around the room in a circle. Dad sat on a hard chair at the edge of the room.

The counselor explained to Dad our reason for being there. The details of the conversation now become blurry to me. The thing I can remember is Dad telling us, "All my life I have wanted to be a leader, a great man, maybe a preacher or teacher." He also disclosed to us, "I have always had the desire to be right."

"Even at the expense of your family?" asked Barbara.

"Yes. Even so."

"Dad, we love you! Please, let everything go that is a burden, and we will be so proud of you. Declare bankruptcy. We are not a family as long as you have this severe financial problem. It keeps us apart. Then, we can all start over as a family together again."

We begged and pleaded with him. "Please, please listen to us. Change your life and your thinking. We love you and want nothing more than to be a family."

But he just sat there frowning and shaking his head.

He rejected all of our reasoning. It was most important what he thought. And he thought he was right. He would not consider any of our suggestions.

Forget that all of us were saying the same thing to him. We became discouraged and the meeting ended. There was nothing that was going to change our Dad.

He became very upset and left the house angry, saying he might as well go and kill himself. Pearl followed him out the door and onto the yard, grabbing hold of his hand and begging him not to. "No Dad—don't, please don't."

He got into his car and drove away.

We were concerned. "He won't commit suicide, will he?" we anxiously asked Barbara. The hours lingered as we paced back and forth while we waited for him. Finally, he came back *and everything stayed the same.*

Upon my arrival back in Wichita, I recounted everything to Jim. I told him what had happened in the meeting. All my feelings about my Dad surfaced. Anger, resentment, hurt, shock, I felt it all.

For two hours I walked back and forth across the room, holding nothing back, verbally letting out every thought that entered my mind.

"All my life," I hollered, "I've tried my very best to be a good daughter to my father and now *he told us, we didn't matter to him!* I'm carrying Mom and Dad on my back, and they're determining my daily decisions. Every day their phone calls interrupt my life. It's enough. I have had it. I accept who I am, and what I tried to be to my Dad, and the fact that if I never see my father again, *that is OK.*"

That day, the weight was lifted off of my shoulders. No matter how much time I spent with my father, how I couldn't measure up to his standard for me, no matter how much money I gave him, no matter how he tried to make our family feel guilty for not doing enough for him, I let it all go.

In a way our intervention had been a success, only not in the way I had envisioned. I was healed of self-condemnation for being a failure as a daughter.

Chapter 20

Mixed up Muddle

In the spring of 1988, Jim and I had been married almost four years. When Jim retired he had let his life insurance lapse. Then after his heart attack the premium was too expensive to renew. Concerned for my future in case something happened to him, he thought we should own our own home, so he found us a cute condominium in Derby, a bedroom community just south of Wichita and often teased for its one stoplight.

Our complex, named The Woodlands, sat on a sprawling ten-acre property with twenty-one units. A concrete walking path made a loop through green lawns in the shade of trees, and a creek wandered in and out. A gazebo sat in the midst of it.

On the 15th of April, we moved into our small one thousand square foot two-bedroom condo. The tulips were blooming all along the path and the trees were covered in a green haze. I had been happy at Twin Lakes, but was thrilled to own our own place. I was anxious to decorate, to put up wallpaper and do all the things a person can't do when renting. The condo was only five years old, but we had some remodeling done before we moved in. I thought I would live there forever.

However, a place does not make a person happy. As much as we loved each other, the difficulties were becoming more obvious in our marriage.

The next couple of years took their toll on our lives. Jim really seemed to be two different people. As a school principal he had been confident, efficient, knowledgeable and very intelligent. At home—well, it was very different. In the "real world," life isn't always a party, and he could not deal with the responsibility of maintaining a home. Consequently I did the cooking (outside of chili!), laundry, house cleaning, home maintenance, shopping and other errands. As a full-time working person, I did wonder why I was picking up his clothes from the cleaners and getting his prescriptions filled.

I'd been brought up to believe that the man should provide the main support. Yet, I felt I had to contribute so much financially that I sometimes didn't have enough money for my own essential needs. We had separate checking accounts. He made the house payment and I paid for the utilities and groceries, and everything else that went into running a household.

Jim either played golf or stayed home and practiced golf while watching TV. And as always, there was that glass in his hand when I got home. Our evenings became quite stressful. We no longer went out as much because of his drinking. So instead, I had a husband who slept on the couch after dinner with the television on, while I tried to escape to another room to drown out the sounds.

As I loved to go places and my job gave me lots of vacation time, I coaxed Jim into traveling more. At first he was reluctant, but with time he really got into it. We took cruises and numerous driving trips to Texas, Arkansas, and Branson, Missouri.

Every year we went to Las Vegas at least once, and yes, Jim gambled a little. The both of us loved Vegas and never tired of it. We relaxed in the morning and strolled around during the day. Jim played poker in the early evening. I did not gamble, but would sit close by on the sideline. With a book in my hand, I would end up just watching the people wander by. We would close our day by going to dinner and a show.

When on vacation, if Jim paid the airline, I paid the hotel and vice versa. Sometimes, even when he offered to pay, I felt I had to do it anyway. I felt I was never worthy of anybody's generosity to me in words or actions. I lived a contradiction in my mind and my heart, as I also *never* wanted to put a hardship of any kind on people that were close to me. Jim frequently reminded me that he was living on retirement money and therefore had to be on a budget.

One time I asked him, "How would it be if I wasn't working?" He replied, "I wouldn't have married you." Well, that blew me away! It only confirmed that I didn't have value unless I contributed money!

I got tired of living this way and started thinking, "Why am I taking care of this man? Why am I enduring his bursts of anger? Why am I watching the one I love get drunk? *Why am I married?*"

At first, I was so in love, I put the problems in the back of my mind and would do whatever it took to keep our marriage intact. After a few years, the "love is blind" theory wears off, and the truth of reality set in.

Finally, I came to the conclusion that I did not want to spend the rest of my life with a person camped forever in denial, drinking so he would not have to deal with the complexities of life. And I had had enough of his raging anger.

Jim had brought so very much into my life that I'd never had before. We were soul mates, remember? The only person I felt I had truly loved. But I actually prayed to God, asking Him to take my love away from Jim so I could divorce. I felt it was the only way I would be able to separate from him.

Up to this point there had never been anything spiritual in our marriage. We did not go to church. Jim had a large beautiful dictionary on its own stand, kept in a prominent place, but we didn't keep a Bible on the shelf. Oh, I owned a couple of Bibles, but I kept them in a drawer, hidden away. I didn't deny God; I believed in Him, but He wasn't a part of my life.

God answered my request. My love for Jim diminished in a fairly short time. And when love recedes, people get hurt. Our storybook life of intense passion and love was ebbing. Striking back and power became the strong force in our lives. A contradiction I know, but buried way underneath it all was an undying love for each other, never to wane.

It was Christmas Day morning, 1991, when I told Jim that I wanted our marriage to be over. Without much of a discussion, he went ahead with our previous plans and spent the day with his children at his ex-wife Cindy's house. I moved into the guest bedroom.

To initiate divorce proceedings was one of the hardest and saddest things I ever did. Facing separation, Jim did not react with anger or resistance; he seemed neither for it nor against it. In fact, Jim told me that he hadn't expected our marriage to last more than a year because of our age difference. "But," he had thought, "If it is *only* for a year it would still be worth it."

When I informed my coworkers of our forthcoming divorce they were shocked, to say the least. They had never witnessed anything but love and joy between the two of us. One woman was standing in front of my desk as I told her.

Her mouth dropped open. She said, "I thought you guys had the perfect marriage. If you and Jim can't make it, then who can?" Because of how people held Jim in such high regard, I had never spoken of his alcoholism and our difficulties to anyone outside of our families and my closest friends.

In February 1992, after finding an apartment, Jim moved out of our condo. I felt this was the ultimate hurt that I had ever done to another person, as I watched him move out of our home when I cared for him so much.

On the evening he left, he lingered beside his car, resting his arm atop the open door. I stood just inside the open garage. There we were, hearts aching toward each other, neither of us able to say good-bye. He jingled the car keys in his hand and finally asked, "Could I see you two or three times a week for a date?"

I demurred, "Maybe, *once* a week or so."

The silence stretched out into uneasiness. There were no words to say.

Then he was gone.

Returning inside the quiet house, I dropped down into the recliner, and sobbed uncontrollably. What had I done? The best thing that had ever happened to me was no more. I was alone once again.

It had always been difficult to have deep emotional conversations with Jim. He was so very passionate about things and didn't want to discuss anything that might cause him pain. Yet arguments sometimes bring lots of pain. After one heated discussion he told me, "The louder I talk means the more right you are." Jim had deep fears within himself that he didn't admit to anyone. Instead of addressing his fears he vented through anger.

I was separating our books after Jim had moved, to give him the ones that were his. While leafing through a book, out fell a folded up yellow legal page with Jim's handwriting on it. What could it be…what was so important that it was hidden away, in the pages of a book? Nervous, and with my hands shaking, I sat down in a chair and quickly opened up the papers to read the contents:

Goal: To please and support in a loving way.
Love can only pass from person to person
Love is communicated in what we do. But often fear gets in the way of love—fear of the unknown, fear of danger, and fear of loss. There are many reasons why we fail in love and they are familiar reasons: pride, <u>anger</u>, <u>jealousy</u>, envy, lust, sloth, gluttony. Every one of them can be traced to fear in one form or another.

<u>*Anger*</u> *is a strong emotion of displeasure. It is usually prompted by some injury or hurt. The fear of suffering that hurt again, leads to hardness of heart and suppressed rage. Fear gets in the way of love.*

<u>*Jealousy*</u> *is the unpleasant suspicion or resentment arising from fear or mistrust of another. Jealous people are always afraid of losing something or someone.*

Fear suggests the presence of danger from without. But the real danger is within. What is more dangerous than my own anger and jealousy—the things that keep me from being a really loving person.

Two things I can do to overcome fear—first, use the reflex principle of inducing calmness by the repetition of a familiar saying: "the greatest thing I have to fear is fear itself." Repeated over and over again this is a direct challenge to the inner disturbance that fear creates.

Second, do something positive. Fear can be immobilizing when it strikes. Resist the temptation

*to negative reactions. Fear is often only a nervous
symptom. Self-respect is my most precious possession. To keep it, I must struggle with the challenge of
loving and the elimination of fear!
 Harness the energies of love.*

He had revealed his innermost thoughts on paper! I knew
he dealt with jealously and fear, though he would only *imply*
that fear to me, never able to admit what a strong hold it had
on him.

I was shocked to read his writing, and I read the note over
again. Then I gently folded up the yellow sheets, feeling like
I had spied on someone, and hid them away.

I never mentioned the note.

Jim had rented a small apartment in Wichita at the private
Tallgrass Country Club where he had a golf membership. He
kept the brown sectional he had brought into our marriage.
Now he purchased a bed, and I helped him buy a few things
such as kitchen place mats and towels. The apartment was
sparsely furnished.

I kept asking him, "Why don't you buy more furniture for
your apartment?" He'd say, "No, this'll do." Only much later
did I hear his explanation; He told me he had been convinced
that we would get back together again, so he would just get
by with what he had. In retrospect, maybe that was why he
took the divorce in stride.

We both said that we did not want to spend money on
individual attorneys, so the two of us agreed on a divorce
settlement and hired one attorney. With my usual guilt in
hand, it was easy. I kept the house, as I had personally paid
for the improvements on the equity that we had gained, and
he kept all of his money, which included a good amount of
savings. In actuality, neither of us gained monetarily, nor did
either of us lose.

After Jim had moved out, I was rearranging furniture at the condo, and I sustained a back injury while lifting a chair. That put me in bed for a couple of days.

When the day arrived to see our attorney, I was still really hurting and not able to drive. So Jim picked me up to go to our appointment. The attorney gave us a private room to fill out our paperwork. Being as I was in such pain, I was unable to sit totally upright in a chair, and had to lie flat on the floor while Jim asked me questions and wrote out my answers. A humorous scene, that was!

Being the gentleman that Jim was, he volunteered to be the one to make an appearance in court at the hearing. Our divorce was granted in July of 1992.

I agreed to see him with the stipulation that he must know one hundred percent that it was not with any intention from me that we would get back together. We would date for the sake of companionship only.

Jim had a habit of saying, "Look, we could live *here*. If we put our rents together, we could get a really nice apartment." It both made me mad and broke my heart. He never gave up that kind of thinking.

Yet he never complained about living single. A mystery to me, he almost suddenly enjoyed cooking and would tell about this or that dish that he just whipped up.

He enjoyed the personal freedom of partaking in his hobbies of golf, fishing and playing cards.

But he always asked, "Why did you *really* divorce me? I know you still love me, don't you?"

He knew we still cared for each other. I did not tell him the truth. That no matter how much we had loved each other, unless he acknowledged his alcoholism and anger, our marriage could not succeed. And Jim could not do that. He would never confess that he was like his dad. Too much pain involved. So, why rehash bad memories and talk about it again?

He kept my picture displayed on his kitchen/dining table. I wanted him to be happy and thought it would be nice if Jim would date other women. He didn't agree. Instead, he'd say, "I could never find anyone to match up to you. You have the best qualities of my first wife, and the best qualities of my second wife. It could never get better than that."

[See Postscript 2 for more on Jim.]

Top: Christmas Dance 1984
Bottom: Jim and I in our apartment in 1986.

Our happiest times.

Chapter 21

Someday

O ne day my Dad called me. "Where's Mom?"
"I don't know, isn't she with you?"

"No. She's disappeared. I can't think where she might be."

He called my other siblings too, and we stayed up late worrying about her.

The next day Mom called me.

"Where are you?"

"I don't want to tell you. I don't want to say where. I don't want Dad to find me."

"Mom, you must tell me where you are!"

"I'm in a motel."

"Mom! Where? Why?"

"Elaine, he…he hit me! You know how Dad's car never works—he doesn't have money to maintain it, but my car runs. He came in where I was sitting and wanted me to drive him some long distance. He asks me a lot, and sometimes I drive him around. But this time I didn't want to, and he blew up. He just gets angrier all the time, and I was so scared. Dad slapped me four times, my glasses broke as they flew off my face and when I tried to get up he pushed me back down! Then he kept slamming doors and chairs. I knew the time had come, so I packed my car as full as I could with clothes and left."

She promised me she would keep in touch as to her whereabouts and then we hung up the telephone.

Mom spent a couple of days at the motel and then went to Kansas to stay with friends for a while.

Eventually, she went back home because someone made her feel guilty, as if she were the sick person. Too often I have seen this, that while the truly sick one (Dad) could appear sweet and charming to the general public, the wounded ones (our family) would take the blame and crawl on our knees back home to take more punishment.

Going to pieces, she couldn't take it at home, so a "worldly" friend took her to a hospital in Newton, Kansas where she was admitted.

Around this time my mother wrote the following poem:

A long time ago—when I was innocent and free
I met a stranger who asked to marry me
He promised to nurture and care for me—
Through any kind of storm
Sad to say—it wasn't true.
Although my love for him was strong—
He treated me with much disdain—
And very, very wrong
It seemed no matter what I did—
To try and do his will,
In the field and in the barn,
At his every beck and call—
Leave my work to do his work—
And got scolded through it all
My heart would break,
I'd tried so hard—
To please and satisfy—without regard—
To my feelings and health and oh—so tired

In my blindness and denial—
That things were really so bad,
I used to hope for better days—
Instead, they got more sad.
Forty six years is such a long time—
I can't believe the life was mine,
Of turmoil and stress, anger and rage—
While others thought our life was fine;
No one knew what we were going through—
Till one tragic day on our Anniversary Day
I knew it was time—to go away—
To save my soul and sort things out
My mind was all messed up—no doubt
God granted grace to escape this confusion
And the wrath that condemned and scolded
To his opinion—
And what did I do to create such hate?
Only God knows why it was my fate
To give my life for such a cause—
He had many warnings and hundreds of chances
To make it right to me
But Satan was in control of his soul—
He could not otherwise be—
People looked on—and put judgment on me
Out with her—the leaders said
It crushed my heart, and filled me with dread
So we'll discipline her in front of all to see
Can't they see what's in my heart?
If I can't get support for my shattered nerves
From the people of God—
Then where does one go—
I felt so betrayed and so alone—but
God has promised to see me through—
Because He loves me and I love Him.
Like Job of old, as I was told—

Surely there's something you need to see—
I searched my heart and pled with God—
To grant me grace and liberty,
To serve Him whole-heartedly
My life was in shambles—I need to be free
But no one to care and no one to share,
Seemed to be my destiny—
There was no place of safety—Or peace to be found—
As I sobbed out my heart in pleadings to God
How long will it be—can't anyone see
It's putting me into insanity—
How much can one endure—
Of baffling behavior and so bizarre—
God—where are you—Please rescue me
From this awful hell, of which I'm hardly able to tell
I've always believed You are there and
Someday—
There will be rest for my weary soul.

Mom and Dad's life was spiraling downward. This was the worst of times for them. Dad continued his letter writing to get Mom's attention. *He was desperate, and looking for love.*

One of his notes reads:

My gut hurts this morning. I wonder is there any love for me, as I am sinking down. Will somebody take my hand and help lift me up. How long do I have to suffer? I feel so lonely and lost. Ben

Snippets from a letter:

I was in such deep despair all last night, my spirit groaned under my burden. I am going under and there is no one to rescue me. I am in such a deep depression that I have lost all my appetite to eat. My stomach is always in a turmoil. Every day is a day of grief as there is no hope in my life anymore. I wonder where do I go from here? Ben

Around this time Dad wrote a lengthy letter of confession. Here is a small portion:

Often Ruth would sit and be silent but the tears would roll down her cheeks as I was mean to my dear baby daughter. One time my brother Fred came over to see us where we lived south of town. Elaine was scared of his brace on his leg, and I thought that was so stupid and I took her out and spanked her so hard in my anger. When I brought her in she still was afraid and cried so I spanked her again hard, and threw her in her crib. Then when I came to the crib again she screamed so hard just to see me come as she thought that she would be beaten again. Then my conscience stopped me, then a little later I looked at her body and it was black and blue. To this day I am haunted by this great sin and abuse to my baby girl. And the grief I brought to Ruth. And so it went, on and on in our married life. I began to yell and talk loud to Ruth and abuse her and the children. Elaine suffered the most as she was the oldest. Pearl and Mary Jane suffered from the way I treated their mother. I was good to Earl until he was about 14 years old, then I tried to control him too. One time I spanked him so hard because he wouldn't get his hair cut short enough. I will never forget as I happened to look into his room and he had his back to the mirror and was looking at the blue stripes across his back. I had lashed him so hard. To this day this haunts me. For being so cruel. He worked with me for 26 years. He tried so hard to please me, but I was very abusive to him. My spirit in me was evil.

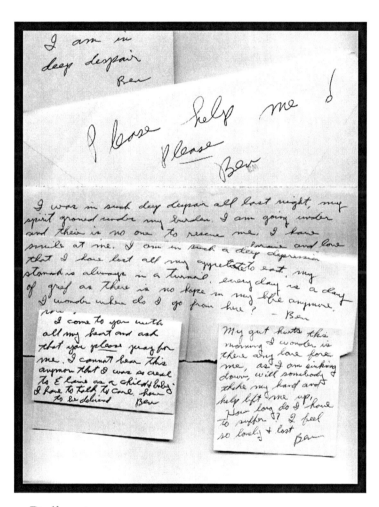

Dad's notes.

Chapter 22

Another Start

I was getting settled into a new routine of being single again, while trying to put my parents' problems aside. This was difficult to do, as I heard from one of them about every day.

The year 1993 was a good one for me personally. I was forty-seven, happy in my job, and I owned my own home. Now, with no obligations to anyone, I had more money at my disposal. Jim took me out to dinner occasionally. I felt pretty content in everything.

After I had been excommunicated from the Mennonite church, I did not attend any denomination of church except for the occasional wedding or funeral.

I thought those people needed to get a life, who went to church on Sunday morning! To me, Sunday meant relaxing, having a cup of coffee and reading the morning newspaper.

God was not a part of my life. I did not read the Bible or any book concerning the Scriptures. Mom had given me a couple of decorative wall plaques that quoted Bible verses but they were put away, not to be displayed.

In this contented stage of my life, something spiritual was tugging at my heart. Was it because there was nothing to hold me back?

Thinking it might be a good time to explore the *possibility* of visiting a church, I took notice of the churches in my surrounding area. There was a Baptist one close by that had just enlarged their facility and it looked inviting.

One Sunday morning I decided it was time to go to church. I was nervous, but felt peaceful as I entered the building. They sang hymns I was familiar with. But most of all I didn't feel the condemnation that I was attending the "wrong church."

At the conclusion of the service, I walked out of the sanctuary and into a foyer full of sunlight. It was like walking into Heaven with such brightness. Sunbeams flooded through large two-story windows and seemed to reach deep into my heart. It felt as though God was showing me the glory of Heaven. I was very moved by the experience.

Even after having such a revelation in my spirit at the Baptist church, I felt led to continue my search. A few blocks south of my condo, I had noticed a small Nazarene church. As I drove by on a Sunday, I noticed how some of the ladies dressed and wore their hair in a plain style. I decided to give it a try.

I found out what time the service started and one Sunday morning I went. The sanctuary was small and inviting. The members were friendly and welcoming, making me feel right at home. I liked the music. They sang the songs I knew.

Each time that I visited an invitation to accept Christ was given at the end of the service. The idea ran through my mind about giving myself up for the Lord. I got sweaty palms and teary eyes, partly out of conviction, and also remembering how many times I had heard the song, *Just As I Am* in my youth.

I imagined myself walking to the front and surrendering my life to God. I thought, "Is this going to be the place where I am actually going to go forward and accept Jesus Christ as my Savior?" But I didn't know anybody there, and I felt too alone. Although there was always a strong urging in my spirit to give my heart to Jesus, I stayed firmly planted in my seat.

Kathy and I got acquainted because she was the new owner-manager of the Lakeshore Club in Wichita. The restaurant had become a favorite spot for our company's business lunches.

One day after I had paid the tab, she mentioned, "I don't know if you're interested, but I'm involved with a multi-level network marketing company, and I'd like to invite you to one of our meetings that we hold downstairs every Tuesday night." She possessed a warm outgoing personality and smile along with an overflowing enthusiasm about her new networking business. I had lots of free time. Indeed, I was immediately intrigued, and ripe for the opportunity to meet new friends!

I went the following Tuesday. She introduced me to Sandy, who also had a sweet, bubbly personality, and I just fell in love with those two ladies. They shared freely the fact they were Christians, and their enthusiasm for Jesus was something that I had not seen before.

The company they introduced me to was called Australian Body Care (we called it ABC). Their number one seller was a dietary supplement called "TG-2000," a capsule promoted to give you energy and help you lose weight.

This group held weekly meetings to bring in new people, and hear testimonials of success stories from others who had used the products. As I listened to them, they seemed so positive and there was such an excitement in the air. This was new territory for me, as I had never done any sort of network marketing before. Oh, I take that back, who hasn't been persuaded to buy into Amway and has a box of Amway supplies in their closet? I was impressed and decided that night to sign up and become a distributor.

As I walked up the open stairway to leave, I glanced down at all the people below and told myself, "F*or whatever reason, my life will never be the same from this point on.*"

Network marketing can be lots of fun and it was. I looked forward to the weekly meetings. I usually worked at the registration table, where I provided brochures, sold books and took in our dues.

Right away Kathy and Sandy were excitedly telling me about the individual who got them started in the business. His name was Carl Mears, and he was single! They told me how he sometimes came to speak at their meetings and was known in the network-marketing circle to be a great motivational speaker.

"He's a Christian, and we just think that you two should meet!"

Then they told Carl about me, and my Mennonite background. He seemed anxious to meet me.

In October, he would be in Wichita to speak at our regional meeting. They made arrangements with Carl for us to be introduced. I was thrilled beyond words to have the privilege of meeting him. I drew the conclusion that he was a pretty important person.

Kathy, Sandy and I discussed what I should wear to the meeting. We decided on a blue fitted dress. They really thought we would be smitten, convinced that we would make a perfect match.

When that evening came, and I walked up to the entrance of the Harvey Hotel, I saw a big gray and white Lincoln parked right in front and said to myself, "I hope that's Carl's car." And it was.

I was a nervous wreck, wringing my hands and hoping my dress looked all right, as I stood in the hallway with Kathy and Sandy in front of the convention ballroom doors waiting for Carl to appear.

He came walking down the hall grinning from ear to ear.

"Well if you aren't the prettiest little Mennonite girl I've ever met!"

I was feeling quite flushed as we were introduced. Carl continued to grin as he immediately attached an ABC pin to my dress collar.

Carl was ten years older than I, about my height, with a nice tan and beautiful silver-gray hair. His brown eyes were expressive behind wire-rimmed glasses and hard for me to ignore. They twinkled like none I had seen before. He talked and joked constantly, moving his open-palmed hands in large smooth gestures.

We hit it off immediately.

As the guest speaker, Carl got the crowd motivated. I listened, waiting impatiently for our time to be together again.

Almost always, after any ABC meeting our group would go to a nearby restaurant, usually the Village Inn Pancake House for coffee. Excited about the product and our friends, we would continue our conversation late into the night.

Of course this night everyone wanted to ogle Carl. Sitting side by side at the table in the restaurant he whispered to me, "Let's get out of here and go where we can have some privacy. I want to get to know you!" It was getting late and we had a time finding another restaurant close by that was still open. We found Applebee's, where we had dinner and talked until they closed and we were forced to leave.

We continued our conversation through the night sitting in his car, back at the hotel. Carl convinced me to go up to his room and spend the remainder of the night in the hotel. I lay on the bed with my clothes on; we visited, slept a little and in the early morning hours watched the movie *Free Willie* on television.

After breakfast in the hotel restaurant, we said our good-byes. Later that day I went to my job in a grocery store where I worked as a part-time checker, in addition to my full-time job. I looked up and there was Carl, grinning as he handed me a greeting card. (I thought he had already left to go home.) I was flattered by the beautiful card that he gave me.

Carl lived in Tulsa, Oklahoma, a three-hour drive southeast of Wichita. He called me that first week and invited me to visit him the coming weekend. My sister Mary Jane also lived in Tulsa, as it turned out only a couple of miles away.

I was anxious for her to meet Carl, so she and I drove over together that first visit. Introductions were made, after which Carl pulled out his guitar. Sitting in the kitchen in front of the fireplace, strumming his guitar, he started singing gospel songs. Mary Jane loves to sing and quickly joined in, as she knew every one of the songs. I was not familiar with them, other than the hymns I grew up with.

She was quite charmed by all of his music and thought he was just fine! Although Carl played guitar in chords quite simply, he had a pleasant tenor voice. We went away impressed with our initial visit, gushing over him and his home.

Very quickly, I fell in love with Carl. He had an incredible sense of humor; he was ornery and liked to pull practical jokes. Fun to be with. But what I really fell in love with was the lifestyle he lived and gave me.

Carl lived in a big house. The kitchen, living room, and master bedroom each had a large red brick gas fireplace. A main foyer staircase and another one off the kitchen led to the second story, and I lost count of the bedrooms, of which there were five or six. There was a mother-in-law apartment over his three-car garage. So much space!

I started driving my car almost every weekend to see Carl. In the beginning of our relationship I stayed with Mary

Jane. But it wasn't long before I was spending most of my time with him.

Tulsa was a beautiful city. The streets were hilly and winding, yielding glimpses of the city lights as I wound through the streets to his house. My breath would catch at the sight. What splendor this was, compared to the flat streets of Wichita. I never tired of sitting in hilltop restaurants and looking over the city. Everything sparkled...apparently I was in love with the city, too.

I would drive down after work on Friday and then get up at four a.m. on Monday morning to get ready for the drive back to Wichita, going directly to the office. He'd get up too and sit in his chair in the master bedroom by the fireplace, strumming his guitar and singing while I put on my makeup. He would frequently beg me to sing with him, so I would sit at his feet and hum the tune, trying to harmonize.

Carl had an easy life, as he did not have a regular eight to five business job or anything close to it. He was a professional network marketer. A usual day for us on Saturday consisted of meeting with some of his ABC associates for coffee at the Village Inn restaurant. Even if we didn't plan on meeting somebody, we still went to the Village Inn. We were always in movement.

We went to ABC meetings, either in Wichita or Tulsa, where he spoke and I soaked it all in. I never got tired of the meetings, and I loved playing the part of his assistant.

We ate the majority of our meals at restaurants. I always noticed his graciousness whenever we were leaving. He would wait for me, and it made me feel like a lady.

When we were home we would sit across from the other, each in our own blue glider, rocking back and forth by the kitchen fireplace. Carl would have instant coffee and snack on his favorite "nutty bars." There was a large Jacuzzi on his patio and he coaxed me out for the occasional midnight soak.

In January, ABC was having a convention in Honolulu, Hawaii and Carl asked me to go with him. I was beyond excited!

To prepare for the trip, Sandy went along with me as I shopped for some new clothes in Wichita. Carl also took me shopping for something glamorous to wear in the evening. We found a jacket covered in green, blue and purple sequins that flashed brilliantly in the light. I had never worn an outfit with so many sequins and I thought it was just beautiful. I wore it with a long black skirt. And he purchased a red slack outfit for me that I loved.

We had a wonderful time in Hawaii. But it was a strange trip. Not once were we invited (that I knew of) to share any meals or down time with his peers. We did everything on our own, and I found that quite odd, and a mystery, as all these people I had earlier been introduced to, were now in their own group and Carl and I were alone. When I mentioned to Carl that it would be nice to spend some time with the others, he said he didn't want to be with them. I began to wonder, "Did these people not like to be with Carl? Was it only the people that he supervised that looked up to him?"

On our return trip, we flew into Los Angeles immediately after the strong earthquake in January of 1994. I was able to take great aerial photographs of the fires. Of course, we had to fly to another city for departure back to Tulsa, as the LA airport was closed.

Carl was not rich by any means. But he had more than I was accustomed to having. He never let me pay for anything. And for once, it didn't bother me. I was totally at ease with it.

One day, I thought, *"Is this what my life will be like?"* I wondered if Carl was the man I was going to marry. My friends helped fuel the "marrying" fire as they thought we made such a cute couple.

It was all fun, living such a carefree life. No responsibility. I didn't have to cook. I traveled back and forth and went to a lot of hotels for meetings. It was like living a dream.

Sadly, I was ignoring the warning signs that said "Hold it. Take a serious look at the red flags you are seeing." Instead of facing reality, I forged ahead. I thought I had too much to lose.

For certain, Carl was all about Carl—one hundred percent. He loved to laugh and talk about himself. He was very proud of who he was, he was *Carl*, and you better know it.

Carl smoked, and I was dead set against smoking. Our first time out, as we sat in that hotel parking lot he promised that he was quitting. I expected that to happen, but Carl could not, or would not, stop. This quickly became a very sore spot in our relationship. He'd hide his cigarettes from me, and then he'd step out to "water the plants" and come back inside smelling of smoke.

And gradually I began to realize: "He lies a lot." At first I wondered, "Is it my imagination, did I hear things the wrong way, am I interpreting things incorrectly? He would lie about what he was doing or where he was, or had been. When I would ask him he always had a puzzling but acceptable explanation. I saw his paychecks, as he'd show me he was making "twenty-five thousand" a month, then tell the neighbors "thirty-seven thousand." Why?

When I would arrive at his house for the weekend, he'd ask me not to park in his driveway, but across the street behind the bushes. He explained that an ABC person might pass by, and if they saw a car parked in front they would assume Carl was home and would knock until he answered the door. I just believed him, said "OK, Carl," and parked where he said to. Eventually he made space in the garage for my car.

Often I'd arrive to find a certain woman hanging around, but he always said it was only business, that she was picking up product or something.

He *never* called me by my given name. The whole time we were together, I was known as "Babe."

I had given him a framed photo of us sitting together in a restaurant booth taken when we were in Hawaii. Initially it was displayed in his home office shelf, but later, whenever I arrived at the house, it was missing. Week after week, I would find it either lying face down or hidden in the drawer below. I would put it out, only to find it gone the next week. He always said, "The housekeeper must have done that!"

Carl owned a beautiful diamond bracelet. The first time that he showed it to me, I thought it was a gift. It was one of the prettiest pieces of jewelry I had ever seen, let alone wear. And I love bracelets. But he said I couldn't keep it, I always had to give it back after I wore it. When we were going out, he would get the bracelet and "give" it to me to wear. When Carl wanted to impress, I was allowed to wear it, including the time we took our trip to Hawaii.

He also confirmed that I was not valuable enough to "really give it to me." How could I be so gullible? The dollar value of the bracelet was not the issue. I can't imagine another girl allowing herself such humiliation in playing the back and forth game!

I realized that I was once again a pawn in a situation with a man where I put up with the bad in order to enjoy the good things. I pretended. I kept quiet instead of demanding explanations, or walking away. I was not honest with myself about my relationship with Carl.

Carl told me he used to be a minister. That's the only story I got. He didn't explain why he wasn't one any longer. He kept a large well-worn Bible in the house, but I never saw him actually open it, although he quoted Bible verses to me every day. He never prayed, and he wouldn't go to church, except for one time I coaxed him into going, but we walked out of the service before it was over.

Even though I had not made a commitment to God, I knew I was moving in that direction. And when they told me about Carl, I was happy when I heard that he was a Christian.

One of the songs Carl sang began to touch a deep spot in my heart; a song by Gary S. Paxton *He Was There All the Time*. This song spoke to me of my life. It was beginning to register in my spirit that Jesus *was* my Savior, and that He had been there beside me all the time. As I looked back, I understood that He had kept me alive for a purpose, a reason. All those years, while I ignored Him, He waited.

At the dawn of Friday, April 8, 1994, I did not know it would be the greatest day of my life! That evening I attended a Women's Aglow meeting (a Christian women's organization) with my friend Sandy. The conference was held in the Airport Hilton Hotel on the west edge of Wichita. Rows of folding chairs quickly filled up with women. Sandy and I went for a front row seat. I was excited to be there, to hear the keynote speaker give her testimony of God's tremendous grace and healing power. My heart simmered with the desire to seek God.

Towards the end of the meeting, the speaker said, "If anyone here wants to receive Jesus Christ as your personal Savior, I invite you to stand." Almost without hesitation I rose to my feet and closed my eyes. As she prayed a prayer of salvation, something began to happen. In my spirit, I felt water coming down on me. Lots of water that seemed to pour over me by the bucket full, splashing onto my shoulders. It felt so good and refreshing.

After a while I realized that it must be time to sit down, that I might be the only one standing. How could I? I didn't want to move! I didn't want to open my eyes and look because then it would end. A wonderful feeling had consumed me, such as I never felt before! I forced myself to come back to the moment, I needed to sit down. Crying softly, I slowly lowered myself into the chair while the meeting came to a close.

Afterward, the speaker came my way and said a few words before she prayed. Then she quoted a scripture verse: *"For God hath not given us a spirit of fear: but of power, and of love, and of a sound mind."* II Timothy 1:7

Weeks before, Sandy had written that exact scripture verse out for me on a three-by-five white index card when she was challenging me to be confident in myself. Only God knew I had that verse taped on my bathroom mirror. Now, I felt it was a personal confirmation that He was right there with me.

As Sandy and I walked out of the room, she turned to me and said, "One day you will be up on that stage telling your story."

To which I replied, "No way."

A couple of days later as I was reading, curled up on the couch in my living room, it was as if a quiet voice interrupted my thoughts, "Do you remember when you felt the water being poured over you?"

Yes!

I felt the presence of God whispering softly to me, "It was then that you were forgiven, and your sins were washed away."

I was exhilarated that I had heard the voice of God. I had such peace, and I was so thankful that Jesus was able to cleanse my soul.

I started to read the Bible every day. Along with receiving daily inspiration in the Word, it seemed that frequently I ran into a scripture verse in reference to lying. At first I didn't understand that was one way God speaks to us. I came to realize how God was trying to show me that Carl's lying was wrong and I needed to break off the relationship.

Our immoral lifestyle bothered me more and more. I thought we should stop sleeping together and I spoke to Carl about it. He listened, then said in a mocking, cynical way, "Oh really? You're seriously thinking this way?" Why did he recite Bible verses to me, yet we were cohabiting and it didn't seem to bother him at all? He had a Bible verse for any and every question I ever asked. I really began to doubt if he was aspiring to live with Christian moral values.

The scripture verse he most often repeated was: *"And we know that all things work together for good to them that love God, to them who are the called according to his purpose."* Romans 8:28

It is a wonderful Bible verse, one that I cherish, but I didn't think it was the answer to every discussion we had. We were not able to resolve our differences.

Summer of 1994. Although I was still traveling to Tulsa every weekend, the relationship was starting to wear thin. I was practically living out of a suitcase. How long could I continue to exist between two worlds? My thoughts fluctuated, "Would I rather have my good times with Carl, or turn to the way that truly pleased God?"

Here I had thought I might marry Carl, he had said I was "a keeper" and we sometimes talked of marriage. I dreamed of living in his big house. I wanted to travel with him. But something was wrong. In my heart I knew I should end the relationship. I just didn't want to face that reality, and let him and his lifestyle go.

I started sharing my confused feelings with Sandy. Night after night she would come over to my condo to visit. We would talk till the wee hours of the morning. With the Bible on her lap, she would quote Scripture verses. She openly, freely, and happily told me the importance of the Bible in her life and how I needed to be open to God's Word. Even, if it meant leaving Carl. That was hard to hear, even though I knew that I should.

She talked about the Bible, and I wanted to talk about Carl and how to resolve our problems. Like the issue of smoking, and being a Christian. *I wanted to change Carl.*

I had accepted Jesus Christ as my Savior and I was beginning to see the impact that God had had on my whole life. But giving up everything for Him—well, that's another story. I wasn't quite ready for that yet.

Exactly one year after our introduction, in October of 1994, Carl was scheduled to come to Wichita for a regional meeting. By now, our relationship was pretty tense.

Carl stopped by on his way to the hotel, and we had a serious conversation that led to our sudden break up. I don't recall the details of our discussion. I only remember him walking out of the door, and me being in shock at what had just taken place.

I went to the ABC meeting by myself. I will never forget it, when afterwards our group did our usual. That evening we went to the Outback restaurant for dinner. Carl sat on one end of the table and I was on the opposite end. But he was entertaining another woman.

Carl occasionally called me, telling me he loved me. He continued to ask Sandy and Kathy about me. Sometimes I called him. But it had to be over. Yet how does a person do that?

Top: Carl and his Rolls Royce. Middle: Our introduction. Bottom left: Me in Hawaii.

Top: Elaine, Sandy and Kathy at ABC meeting. Middle: Sandy and me at dinner after an ABC meeting. Bottom: At parent's home Christmas, 1993.

Top: Carl and me in Hawaii. Bottom: At his home. Inset: My New Year's Eve snacks.

Top: Meeting ice skater Dorothy Hamill at private party.
Bottom: Throughout the years at work.

Chapter 23

Your Way

With a new president at the helm of her company, Sally was confident that she could be a successful business owner. But very gradually the company had gotten off course, and things did not run as smoothly as before. Long time store managers, district and area managers started quitting, which meant we were losing good experience in the field. That made for low employee morale. There was more tension in the air as we tried to improve the bottom line and keep our stores in the black.

After the top management people left or were fired, Sally finally understood that the company was not going to make it if things continued as they were.

After another resignation of an area manager on a particular Friday, Sally was forced to come to a difficult decision. When I came to work early the next Monday morning, I could see something was going on. Sally was already there. She pulled me aside and whispered, "I'm going to have to let Keith go today.

When she went to his office, he took it more calmly than we had anticipated, and just like that, he was gone.

I had worked side by side with Keith for fifteen years and had always liked him, even with our challenges in the work place. He knew all my personal ups and downs, and he was still my friend. I would greatly miss him.

My job was not as fun as it used to be. The busyness was gone, and I was getting bored and complacent.

Because money had been tight the last few years, our Christmas parties were definitely not like the old ones, and a couple of years we didn't even have a big party, but rather had a casual dinner held in our office.

To try and improve morale within the company, Sally decided to go ahead and spend the money for a nice party. Although nobody knew it at the time, this would be the company's last Christmas party. Once again, I was the planner.

For years I had dreamed of having a "top hat and tennis shoes" theme party. This time, I got to make it real. Our party would be at the Harvey Hotel. The invitations read, "You can dress in a tuxedo, or you can dress casual and wear your tennis shoes." It was very entertaining to see some employees decked out in tuxes including a cane, while others depended on their jeans to keep them comfortable!

Cocktails and hors d'oeuvres were served in the lobby, where a magician wandered through and played tricks on the guests.

For our dinner I had reserved a beautiful ballroom decorated with huge chandeliers that twinkled and wall mirrors that reflected the sparkle. One side of the ballroom held round tables with white tablecloths and red and green napkins. I designed the floral centerpieces with an upside down black top hat full of red carnations that was placed on a mirror. On one side of the hat we placed a white Keds sneaker with gold shoestrings trailing.

The waiters wore tuxedo coats and tails, Bermuda shorts, and tennis shoes. Soft piano music accompanied dinner.

Afterwards, we moved to the other side of the ball-room, which had been turned into a casino with all forms of gambling tables and prizes stacked everywhere.

It was quite an evening. The hotel told me they had never had so many employees ask to work a party as they had that one.

But that night I noticed something was amiss. Sally was not her normal self, and it bothered me. I wondered if I had done something wrong....

New Year's Eve, and I was alone. I told myself, "It's going to be OK." I set out my coffee table with a tray of snack foods, vegetables and dip. It would be an evening of watching the festivities on television, and of course the countdown at Times Square in New York.

Secretly, I had hoped that Carl and I might spend the time together. I was always dreaming for a miracle, but why? As the evening progressed, I called his home to wish him a Happy New Year, but he didn't answer. That should have settled it. He was probably out and getting over me. For me, it was a lonely night.

Carl did call a couple of days later, and told me how he had been with his sons on a camping trip. My quiet misgivings: on New Year's Eve, out in the cold rain? I happened to know that he was basically estranged from his sons, and seldom socialized with his family. I was going crazy with his stories.

By January 8th, my head was spinning. Why wouldn't Carl stop calling me and why couldn't I get over him? *Please God, help me!* This contact between us had to stop!

I started to talk to God while I was cleaning the house. I was trying to rationalize everything. And as I was in the shower cleaning, with my hands dripping wet, the still small voice of the Holy Spirit spoke clearly inside me, *"Go pray."*

In my thoughts, I replied, "I'm going to finish what I'm doing, and *then* I'll go pray."

Again He spoke to me, *Stop what you are doing now and go pray.* So I wiped off my hands and went to a chair, knelt down, and began to pray, *"God, will you please give me clarity of mind. I just want to do your will. Please help me in my ability to end this relationship. It isn't right. I can't go on like this day after day. In Jesus Name, Amen."* He spoke very clearly, it seemed almost audibly, *"Carl is on a date."*

After I got up from praying, I went to the telephone and called Carl. No answer. I tried later in the evening. Again, no answer. The third time, around 11:30 p.m., I tried once more. The telephone rang and then I heard it pick up. Very nervous, I waited to hear Carl's voice. I got right to the point.

"Hi, have you been on a date?"

"Well…"

"Is that a yes, or no?"

"Well, yes."

"Is she there with you in the house?"

"Yes, she's studying her Sunday school lesson over there in the other room, and then she'll be going home."

"Well then Carl, this is our final good-bye."

I quickly hung up the telephone, not wanting to hear any more lies or stories from him.

All the while Carl was supposedly "still in love with me," he was only playing games. I was angry that he had a woman in his house, when he was still telling me he loved me. Yet I felt a tremendous peace and freedom. I kept marveling at how the Lord had answered my prayer. In my moment of confusion and despair, I cried out and He had heard me.

That evening I went to bed expecting a restful night's sleep. I felt confident God would give me the strength to keep my farewell words to Carl. Nevertheless, I was anxious about what the future now held for me.

Sometime in the early morning hours, I woke up lying flat on my back (I usually sleep on my side). What happened next was like a vision. First I heard a voice from Heaven very clearly speaking to me: *"I have something so much more wonderful for you, more than you can even imagine. But you will have to give yourself totally to Me."* The presence was so powerful that it consumed the room, and I had no doubt that it was the Holy Spirit of God speaking.

As I lay there in the darkness with my arms unconsciously outstretched, I found that I was in the middle of a battle. I could sense the power of God and the wickedness of Satan. God reached for me, while at the same time I felt an evil weight trying to hold my body down. Each time I strained my arms toward Heaven, "Yes, Lord, I will give everything to you," Satan would pull me back with a thought, "If you go God's way, you won't be able to dance..." Or, "You won't be able to do any of the things you enjoy. You won't have any fun." I didn't *want* to give up earthly things. Up and down I went, tossing back and forth. But—but—oh, what a conflict.

It wasn't easy to release my life to God. Still, over-whelming any thought was God's promise to me! I couldn't let go of that, no matter what. *I wanted everything God had for me.* "Yes, Lord, whatever it takes, I want to go Your way."

Immediately, the pressure subsided and I lay there, silence all around me. It was a complete surrender; there were no doubts left in my mind. Full of peace, I went back to sleep.

Waking up in the morning I could remember it all. The struggle, how my arms had been lifted. The pressure, holding my body down. And what had been spoken to my spirit. Could there truly be something more wonderful for me? Yes, God had said it. I felt relieved and believed that my life with Carl was really over. I looked forward to what lay ahead.

Chapter 24

Perfect Peace

At work, Sally had hired a new president and he came on board in the New Year. At our first staff meeting, he promised us, "You have nothing to worry about—I'm not going to change much—and no one is going to lose their job, who works in the office."

Nevertheless, rumors were abundant that positions were going to be cut. I could sense that changes were in the making. Might I actually lose *my* job?

Several times during my career working at the company, I had imagined how I might react if I were ever let go. Working there was my life! I had my own private office. I was convinced they'd have to drag me out, while I clung to the beautiful oak desk and credenza that I had personally chosen and dearly liked. No matter what else was going on in my world, all of my struggles, I had always counted on the security I had at the office.

One day in the early part of January of 1995, I walked into Larry's office, my supervisor and the controller. He and another coworker were huddled over a calendar turned ahead to the following Christmas season. I quickly realized they were planning on taking the week that had always been reserved for my vacation. And they were going to ask for it now so they'd be sure to get it, because we couldn't all take vacation at the same time.

Inside, I became upset. That was my time! I had it off every year because of my involvement with our Christmas party. Well, I listened to their discussion for a minute, but instead of saying anything, I turned and walked out. As I passed through the door, in my spirit, I heard a small voice say, "W*hat do you care, you won't be here anyhow.*" At the time I paid no attention to those words.

The new president told me he wanted a small round conference table and chairs for his upstairs office. For three days I went to numerous furniture stores searching for just the right pieces. It seemed that no matter what I brought back, he wanted something different. It was becoming a joke, and I was getting quite weary of the process. Yet, I took my duty seriously and tried in vain to find what he was looking for.

About five p.m. on the 18th of January, the third day of this shopping go-around, Larry asked me to come into his office. The owner, Sally, was already seated in a chair, and I could plainly see what this was all about. I knew my time was up.

Without delay, Larry stated the reason I had been called into his office. "As you know, the company has been forced to make many changes. Unfortunately, we must let you go. This hasn't been an easy decision." Sally said very little. There was nothing to say....

That's why I had been sent shopping, to keep me out of the office, because they couldn't face me once the president had determined that I would be laid off! Larry told me he could not look directly at me, and had tried to avoid me, knowing how devastated I would be about leaving.

Collecting my thoughts and without much ado, I went back to my office to pack up all of my belongings. I spent a couple of hours going through stuff. I had a ton of pictures

I had taken of our company activities and had kept every company newsletter and almost every memo since I started back in 1978.

Almost eighteen years of my life had just been terminated! But I was so peaceful, so unaffected by what had just taken place. God was there with me; He would take care of me. Larry even stuck his head in the office, and commented how surprised he was by my calm reaction to the news.

I took box after box out to the car. Soon it was time to say good-bye to a job that had been a *huge* part of my life. There were no other employees there except Larry, and our words were few. He walked me to the car, and then I drove off into the darkness of the night.

Driving down the road with my thoughts going over everything, I remembered that a couple of weeks earlier, God had already prepared me for this event. I was reminded of the Old Testament verse, *"Thou wilt keep him in perfect peace, whose mind is stayed on thee: because he trusteth in thee."* Isaiah 26:3

I went straight to my friend Sandy's. She opened the door to find me in tears. Even though I had been very calm, now it all seemed to be sinking in. I had lost my job, one into which I had poured my heart and soul. We had been a family, and now we were breaking apart!

I told Sandy that I had just been terminated from the company. What was happening to me? I had just ended my relationship with Carl, and now this!

As we sat there talking, Carl called. Sandy told him that I was there and what had happened. Although I was no longer speaking to him, through Sandy he conveyed his concern.

After spending time with my dear girlfriend, I knew I must go back outside and face the next step, whatever that might be. So I got in the car and drove home in serious contemplation.

I walked into my house, alone, no one to comfort me. *Yes*, there was someone. God! I knew I would be OK. I brought all my boxes in from the car, and then just sat in my chair, kind of dazed and thinking over what had transpired that day.

P.S. Over the course of that year, many more employees left, some were laid off, and even the new president was let go. Sally decided to sell or close all of the restaurants. A couple of employees bought the warehouse business. She had remarried by this time, and she went on to have a good life.

January 19th was a new day. As I read the Bible that morning, a verse sang out to me: *"In all thy ways acknowledge him, and he shall direct thy paths."* Proverbs 3:6. Yes, I knew without a doubt that God would watch over me. I would take each step and each minute as He directed.

There were boxes scattered all over my kitchen, on the counters and on the floor. I could not look inside any of them. Too many memories! For now I would just work around the boxes.

Reality began to sink in. I didn't have to go to work that morning! My life would never be the same. That job was now in the past. I couldn't believe it was over, but I would go on somehow....

The boxes of memories of the good times stayed unopened on the floor a number of days.

I decided to take a little time off before I started to look for new employment. And not stress about my unplanned vacation! My meager two weeks' severance pay wasn't going to last long. I had a house payment to make. So the first thing I did was file for unemployment benefits, and learned I could receive unemployment for up to six months. With that, plus money in savings, I felt I would be OK.

I can only describe the next couple of months as wonderful. I did not think about past or future job, but just enjoyed the present time, having lunch with my best friends Sandy and Kathy almost every day. We would stay in the restaurant till three or four in the afternoon. We talked about our multi-networking business, but mostly, we talked about God. We were so in love with Jesus and in awe of the little miracles He brought to our daily lives.

Best of all was the time I had alone with God. Every day I spent hours reading. As a new Christian, I devoured the Bible. It seemed as though God had given me this time just to meditate on His Word.

I started at the very beginning in the book of Genesis, and I underlined in red any and every scripture verse that spoke to me. One of my favorites: *"This book of the law shall not depart out of thy mouth; but thou shall meditate therein day and night, that thou mayest observe to do according to all that is written therein: for then thou shalt make thy way prosperous, and then thou shalt have good success."* Joshua 1:8

Sandy had been asking me to go with her to her church. She really liked the pastor and was anxious for me to hear him. Taking copious notes on his weekly sermons, she felt he had a lot of good things to say. I had been very hesitant about going to her church, as she told me it was charismatic. From our conversations I determined that most of the songs they sang were not the hymns that I grew up with, but a style of more modern praise and worship choruses.

I had lived next door to some people that went to a charismatic church and they got pretty loud in their prayers. And when my sister Mary Jane left the Mennonite church, she got connected with friends that believed in the charismatic faith.

She felt peace and came to know the presence of the Holy Spirit in that religion. But it made my parents angry, as they didn't believe in that kind of Christianity at all.

Finally, one day, I said I would go. After she picked me up, we arrived at the church in plenty of time before the service began.

The first thing I noticed was the size of the church building. It was very impressive, although not nearly full. Up front was a band comprised of piano, drums, guitars, saxophones, and horns. When they opened the service I was astounded at how loud they played in worship. But the congregation's faces were indeed joyful, exuberant as unto the Lord. A majority of them lifted their hands and swayed or clapped in time to the music. This was so foreign compared to the solemn church that I had grown up in, which would never allow such a gleeful expression of praise. I liked this, but it was just so *different.*

I was thankful and I certainly wanted to praise God, so why shouldn't I join in? Torn between my childhood remembrances of church, but also taken in with the enthusiasm of the audience, I wasn't quite sure what to do.

After church, Sandy and her husband invited me to lunch, but I declined. My head was hurting, and it felt like I was getting a migraine. I needed to go home and absorb everything I had witnessed that morning.

Well, I went back, and then again. It wasn't long before I joined in with this new style of praise and worship. Once I surrendered my pride, it became easy to lift my hands in adoration to God.

Although I now attended every week, I had no desire to become a member. During praise and worship I felt a real closeness with God. Yet when the pastor spoke, I felt an uneasiness that I couldn't explain. His "sermons" were enjoyable, but mostly contained motivational sayings that kept the audience laughing. It wasn't really preaching like I was used to, that is, teaching from the Bible. While he spoke, he paced back and forth across the stage, constantly. I sensed uneasiness in the pastor, but I couldn't put my finger on it. Right after the service, he did not hang around as pastors sometimes do; he'd quickly disappear. Frequently, we were "treated" to a guest speaker, or even a videotape of a guest speaker, instead of our pastor ministering to his flock.

The morning of April 19th, I was volunteering my services at the church when the church secretary got the horrible news about the Oklahoma City Bombing via a telephone call. It was almost too hard to fathom what all we were being told. I continued with my cleaning, and didn't fully comprehend the horrible destruction until later, when I got home and turned on the television.

I kept going to church. I was more comfortable in worship, but still felt quite tentative about the pastor.

Then one day my friend Kathy (who also attended the same church) and I were having lunch. She said she had some shocking news to tell me, but it was news that mustn't get out! "Pastor will not be preaching in church tomorrow." She didn't know a whole lot of details, "but something about him being arrested down in Texas."

Still, the news broke fast, and the newspaper articles revealed that our pastor had been arrested in San Antonio and charged with three counts of money laundering and one count of conspiring to launder money. The story went on to say that between 1989 and 1995, he had built a new church, bought several radio stations, and run up more than ten million dollars in debt through the sale of bonds and promissory notes.

So there was a problem! Our pastor had been laundering money right in our church! He had been trying to make money to pay off the church debt. I was sorry he became involved in such a scheme, that he had allowed himself to be so misguided.

The pastor was convicted of the above charges and in April of the following year he was sentenced to fourteen years in prison. I do believe he got out after serving a short time.

Through all of that experience I kept my faith strong. Even though mankind fails, God is always on the throne, and I would continue to look to Him for guidance, knowing that we all fall short of the kingdom of God.

Chapter 25

A New Day

I began looking for a job, with no success. I thought I could bring positive and professional qualities to a position, but that didn't seem to be the case. Nobody was hiring me. An attorney interviewed me for a secretarial opening. He told me, "I really can't see you sitting at a typewriter all day." For a position at a large bank, the manager queried, "Can you tell me this is *really* what you want to do?" Even when I went to an employment agency and took some computer tests, strange things happened. I spent a couple of hours testing on a PC and at the finish, just when the score would show, the computer crashed! The next day, I tried it again. Same thing! The lady in charge said, "We've never seen anything like this."

So it went. I just kept on spending my days reading the Bible.

As the summer progressed and I was having no success at landing a job, I thought about moving to Texas.

God kept stirring in my heart, and I really started praying about it. It is so amazing how God will put the right books in our hands at the time we need them. A friend gave me some books by Benny Hinn and Kenneth Hagin.

First I read about knowing the Holy Spirit, the presence of God who helps us in our daily lives. Next, I read about growing our faith in God and knowing His will. I really was seeking information and simply devoured it.

I had mixed feelings about leaving my condo. I loved certain things about it; the ceramic tile I had installed in the kitchen, the tile and the floor-to-ceiling mirrors in the entry, the sun room addition, and the huge garage with all of its storage cabinets that my brother-in-law had built. But I didn't like the cathedral ceiling in the living room. In the winter it seemed that all the heat went up there and I stayed cold. Still this was my home, my security. In a few more years, I would own it free and clear. Could I give all this up?

In May, I felt even more strongly that God was speaking to me and I needed to seriously consider making the move. I kept praying. I still couldn't find a job, and my unemployment benefits would be running out in a couple of months so it was time to do something.

After all that I had been through in my lifetime, I was still working on comprehending the goodness of God. I remembered how He had saved me, how He had been directing my steps. Now I had complete confidence in Him, that He *would* direct my steps.

One night I specifically asked God for an answer as to what He wanted me to do. I remember so vividly walking around the path in the back area amidst the trees, in meditation with God. All I wanted to do was to be in His will. His will, that's all that mattered.

I slept peacefully that night. The next morning I awoke refreshed, and my mind was clear. I was moving to Texas.

I felt strongly that I could sell my home without going through a real estate agency. I bought a "For Sale by Owner" sign and stuck it in my front yard. Then I prayed about the price I should be asking for it. In my spirit I felt an urging to ask a certain price and I stuck with it. Calls came in for a while, but then slowed down for quite some time.

Finally one night I got on my knees and asked God to help me. You might say I confronted Him: "OK God, what *is* it? What do you want me to do?" The next morning I received a call from some neighbors, asking to see the property. They were interested in it for their mother. They looked, liked what they saw, and we made the deal.

Things started moving really fast, and what an exciting time it was. I cannot tell you the happiness I felt during this time. Things moved so quickly and flowed smoothly. The people that were buying my home said it was unreal. Their mortgage officer said they had never seen anything like it. There were just no complications.

During this time I drove to Dallas, Texas for a conference and to find a place to live. On my return trip I stopped in Denton, just outside of Dallas on Interstate 35, and decided to check it out. I rented an apartment that very afternoon, drove around town, and then got a motel for the night. The next morning I drove back to Wichita.

My family came to help me have a garage sale and get rid of things I knew I wouldn't have room for, going from a house to an apartment.

Moving to a new place was always an adventure; it appealed to my gypsy nature. I had so much fun packing and stacking boxes, labeling every one. It was easy, with no job and no pressure.

Now, everything was set!

Even my last unemployment check paid for my last house payment.

My closing date appointment was set for a Friday, but I got to thinking, it might be better to close on Wednesday so we wouldn't be driving on the weekend. I called the buyer and she didn't have any objections. When I got ready to call the title company, I heard that still small voice in my spirit,

"Don't change the date." Still, I went ahead and changed the dates.

I had already arranged for movers to unload the U-Haul truck when I arrived in Texas, so I called them and changed move-in day to Thursday instead of Saturday.

Wednesday morning arrived and I paced with excitement. We were going to close at one in the afternoon, and then I would be on my way to Texas. The telephone rang. The person on the other end told me we could not close because the buyer's loan had fallen through! How could that be? Everything had been done and we were hours away from signing papers!

But it was true. Apparently, her mortgage company had not realized she was buying a condo and the loan they were giving her was for a house. They would not finance a condo. We didn't know how they could have overlooked such an important detail, but somehow it had happened and nothing could change that fact now.

What had promised to be an incredibly easy and smooth transition all of a sudden became a very complicated process.

The truck was loaded with all my belongings and I sat in an empty house pondering what to do next. First I called the escrow company and set up new appointments for Thursday morning and afternoon in case we could close that day.

This now caused a number of people to be inconvenienced with moving plans. The buyer could not move into my place yet, and that meant the people who had purchased her home could not move into her house yet, and the people who were moving into that couple's home could not move in.

I sat down on the floor with a sinking feeling that I had caused this upheaval. If I had just listened to that still small voice!

I questioned myself, "What difference did it make what day we closed? Why would God care what day it was?" Yet I knew in my spirit, in the depths of my being, that I had not obeyed, and that was all that mattered. We don't have to know His reasoning.

Thursday morning I received calls telling me there was no way we could plan on closing in such a short time. The buyer was going to have to completely start over and find new financing. This could take up to a couple of weeks!

No, I thought to myself, I will not accept this. I remained calm and put all my faith and trust in God, remembering a passage from the Bible: *"But Jesus beheld them, and said unto them, With men this is impossible: but with God all things are possible."* Matthew 19:26

I called and canceled the appointments and rescheduled them for Friday.

Not much else to do but wait…. I also had to reschedule for the movers in Texas. That posed a problem for them, not knowing when I would be arriving. They would do the best they could but I would have to be worked in at their convenience. Thursday evening, my buyer did move some things into the garage.

Friday was a new day, and I woke up feeling confident that everything would work out. My next-door neighbor showed up and could not understand why I wasn't extremely angry about what had happened. "After all," he reasoned, "the mortgage company made a mistake and they should have to pay for it somehow." I just said with assurance, "We will close today and it will be OK."

The hour was fast approaching for my scheduled one p.m. appointment. As my phone had by now been disconnected, I had to go to the neighbor to call and say I would not be able to make the appointment. But when I called, they had just received a call from the mortgage company to say all was a go and I should come in immediately to sign the papers! We might not be able to get our money yet, but it was guaranteed to come and we could go ahead with our closing.

We all arrived at the escrow company, and in the middle of our signing there was a knock on the door. The secretary entered with check in hand! Even the escrow officers were amazed at how quickly that came in. And it only cost me a total of one hundred and twenty-four dollars to sell my condo. I gave thanks to God.

Chapter 26

Hopeless

It was late and dark when I arrived at my apartment in Denton. I could not see spending money for a motel room when I had my own place, even if it didn't have any furniture! So I borrowed a lounge chair from the swimming pool and used it for my bed.

Another day dawned, and I wondered how I would ever find space for everything in my new apartment. It seemed hopeless. Boxes and furniture filled every room, piled to the ceiling with only a path in the middle. I was fast learning that when you become a Christian, you put your trust in God for everything to work out and you stay calm. Well, I did, but it took me three weeks to get everything unpacked.

When I rented the unit, I had asked for new carpeting and new wallpaper, as it was worn and dated, but the manager told me I could not have new unless there was something wrong with it.

Two days after everything was in its place, I came home from church one night to find the carpet covered with water. There had been a leak in a third floor unit above me and it all came down to my apartment! Some maintenance men came with a water vacuum and we moved things around as best we could. Because the kitchen was dry, we placed the furniture in there.

Now all the things I had worked so hard to put in order had to be moved again. Every dish had to be taken out of the china buffet and curio cabinet, which only a few days before had been arranged ever so carefully. My apartment was a total mess.

I did not like having to do so much work over again, but I did get new carpeting and wallpaper!

We were having beautiful fall weather. Every day was flawlessly sunny with pleasant temperatures in the seventies. Accustomed to colder temperatures by this time of year, I was shocked to see people playing tennis in shorts!

Denton, like a lot of Texas towns, was built around a courthouse square bordered with one-way streets. Restaurants, antique stores, and old buildings lined these streets. I loved going down there to wander around, go through the courthouse, and sit under the huge trees in the courtyard. I lived five minutes away from the square on one side and a shopping mall five minutes the opposite direction.

Mom and I spoke often on the telephone, and sometimes Dad listened on the other line while I shared my joy of living in Texas. I was anxious for my parents to visit and they agreed to come down in October. It would be the first trip they had taken together in a long time.

I was happy to have them both in my home, and tried to make everything perfect...catering to their every whim. For whatever reason, Dad had let his appearance and hygiene suffer and he was quite unkempt. Preparing to go on an outing, I finally had to tell him I would not get in the car with him unless he showered, because of the odor. I was so embarrassed to have to say that and waited as long as I could...hoping he would take it upon himself to bathe.

One day we drove to the town of Granbury, to see where Mary Jane had lived for a short time. I was very surprised that Dad was not interested in most of the tourist sites that he normally would have been anxious to visit. He had no desire to go into Dallas to see Dealey Plaza where John F. Kennedy was assassinated. This was not my father.

After making the trip to Texas, in November Mom and Dad decided to spend Thanksgiving in Tulsa with Mary Jane, and I would drive up. I reserved a room for all of us at the Embassy Suites Hotel.

We checked into the hotel the night before Thanksgiving, crowding into one room. Even Mary Jane checked in, although she lived not far away, as we all shared the same love for hotels and travel, enamored by it all.

We experienced the best ever evening at dinner with our Dad and Mom. Dad was relaxed and happy. *We laughed!* (Seldom did we ever laugh together with Dad.) He seemed to be his true inner self. The humorous nature that he was born with came out. It was a most precious evening, one of a kind, and never to be duplicated again.

The next day was happy as well, as we celebrated Thanksgiving dinner together. My dad loved being in that hotel. He liked watching television and reading the latest newspaper, and being around all of the people. Most of all it took him out of his own troubled environment. But as we prepared to leave, Mom and Dad went to their separate corners of the couch in the lobby as the melancholy returned.

Winding path in Derby behind my condo.
Insert: In Denton, 1995.

Top: Mary Jane, Elaine and Pearl in Tulsa.
Bottom: Mom, Earl, Elaine and Mary Jane in parent's house, 1994.

Snapshots of my mother: Traveling on Amtrak. Touring an old hotel in WA.

In her kitchen at home. Her favorite place to read the Bible.

Well, just a few weeks later it was Christmas, 1995. As usual, we kids went home. Mary Jane came from Tulsa, Pearl and her family was there, and Earl and his wife Michelle flew in from Seattle.

Family gatherings were the best times for us in our lives because we loved to be together. And yet, they were also the most stressful of times.

This Christmas Day, Dad wanted to be the center of attention and almost acted like a child in order to get that attention. When he was left out of the conversation, he went to the bedroom and proceeded to sing songs out of their church hymnal in a very loud voice. To us, it seemed highly disruptive, and it put such a conflict in our hearts. We loved Dad and yet we didn't want him in the room.

It was a cycle that had no beginning and no end. It was continuous. Because of his selfish attitude, we paid no attention to him. But because we paid no attention, he became even *more* desperate for our love and affection.

Anyway, here we were, at another holiday dinner. Dad, with his head down, shuffled back and forth from the kitchen counter where the food was, to the dining room table, just listening to all the happiness and joyful talk around him.

As the afternoon wore on, the play continued. If Dad occupied one room, the rest of us would migrate into another room. What was so strange about our relationship is we would move from him, and yet, he would also move away from us. We maintained our separateness in our togetherness.

We opened our presents on Christmas Day. We would wait as long as we could stand it! Finally, maybe as late as four or five in the afternoon, someone would say "It's time!" and we would proceed. Wanting the celebration to last as long as possible, we opened our gifts one at a time while everyone else watched.

Dad would sit off to the side, in his rocking chair, squeaking with each move. Observing the annual tradition, he sat there stroking his beard. Each year we scraped together enough money to get a big pile of presents (although inexpensive presents) for each other, but Dad usually got a box of chocolates and small incidental gifts. I could sense his disappointment and it made me feel terrible. Without fail, after a while he would lose interest and walk away. *The turmoil was always in the pit of my stomach as to his state of being or happiness.*

Of course, we were aware of his every move. If he talked, it might turn into an argument. So as the rest of the family heartily bantered back and forth, we still felt the anxiety of what might happen next.

Overall, our Christmases were still the best. We did our best to push away the sadness of not being able to be a *complete* family, and instead focused on the fact we were together.

Late that afternoon, as I walked through the doorway into the living room, I heard a still soft voice in my spirit say, *"This is the last Christmas you will all spend together."* I couldn't believe it, and thought surely it had to be my imagination!

Whether it was Christmas or any other time I visited home, the rituals were always the same, the tension always thick, and my stomach always sick.

In the morning while Mom and I and/or any of my sisters were having our coffee, Dad would come into the house from his shop, and see what was going on. It was an irritating source of interruption. How very sad it was, but we were aware that our conversation would in all probability be repeated by Dad on his trips to the café in town. This made him feel important, as sometimes we talked about interesting things, but things everybody did not need to know. For the most part he was ignored, and then he would just return to his shop.

A little while later I would stand at the front door looking out towards his shop, feeling guilty and thinking I should spend some time with him.

In June of 1996 our family was home for Earl and Mary Jane's high school reunion. One day Dad came into the house while we were sitting around in the living room. As he crossed the room he said, "I am a very sick man." He told us how tired he was. He had been complaining of severe headaches, but that was nothing new to our family. Dad had suffered from headaches for years. Stomach ulcers had put him in the hospital a number of times. We were used to him not feeling well. With that in mind, I didn't think much of his comment.

Looking back, those were strong words and I am sure he meant every one.

I went home again. Mom was doing better, but she was quite determined to move out of the house. In fact she had secretly looked at a couple of places in town, and showed them to me with mixed feelings, knowing she would be going against every grain in her body if she actually left.

I visited with Dad about Mom's situation in her presence. I remember sitting on the floor in the living room, and speaking gently to him.

"Dad, *please* make an effort toward reconciliation. This means compromise on your part also. But please do not expect her to change bedrooms at this time...if she is forced back she might possibly leave the house."

He blustered back, "Over my dead body, that'll never happen! I won't allow it. She is my wife and she will stay under my roof."

At some point, I quoted a Bible verse to him. He replied sourly, "There you go, quoting scripture verses again!" This was indeed a shocking puzzle to me. Why didn't he welcome the words of the Bible?

This was typical of any religious conversation we might have together. He could not accept the fact that I had become a Christian, because, I was no longer a Mennonite. To him, the only way to come back to God was through their church.

In fact, when I had expressed my interest in becoming baptized again in my newfound faith, Dad went to great lengths to obtain my original baptism certificate to prove that I had already been baptized. He was adamant that his thinking was right, and was very against me getting baptized "again."

Our conversation quickly went downhill and there were no conciliatory remarks to make Mom feel any better, only anger at my preposterous suggestion that she leave the house. So once again, everything stayed the same.

Pearl's children had been living in South Dakota a couple of years at this point, really liking it after making numerous visits to the area where Pearl grew up. In 1996, Pearl and her husband made the difficult decision to join them, in part to separate themselves from the stress that Dad caused to those around him. Mom was heartbroken, as she had survived much, by holding on to us kids.

By Fall, Mom was calling me daily with her pleas. She sounded desperate. "Elaine, what should I do? I have to leave home but I don't know how to go about it with Dad." Over and over I told her, "Mom, you are the one to decide whether you will leave or stay."

"But what would he do to you kids if I broke up the home?"

I assured her, "Whatever choice you make, we will accept your decision. But you have to be the one to choose. Stop looking at others to make your decisions." She was almost incapable of making such choices. I thought it was amazing how a person could be married for over fifty years, and then the time comes when she can take no more.

She continued to worry: How should she go about leaving, she didn't have any money as she wasn't employed, and her social security income was small.

I don't know how she did it, but the day came when she gave me the news that she had found an apartment and was going to move.

Mom was able to get into a government-subsidized apartment. It was such a timely provision; I was convinced that God had intervened. As I helped her move, I was very impressed by her tenacity to carry it out. She was so fed up in remembering how she had purchased everything in the house that she took both of their beds with her when she moved. That left Dad with only the sleeper sofa to sleep on.

It was a terrible, horribly stressful time. Dad stayed in his shop. We avoided all contact.

Mom had suffered back problems for years. At times I even had to push her around in a wheelchair because she just couldn't walk. The church people didn't believe her, though. Sometimes they had suggested to her to have company over for Sunday dinner to make Dad happy. She would protest how much she hurt, but they only criticized her.

Before she moved into her apartment, she got her strength up and drove to Kansas to see some doctors. They diagnosed the problem and scheduled back surgery. Because they lived on a highway, she became determined to find an apartment quickly, so she would have a place to walk for exercise, which the doctor had said was very important to aid in her recovery.

While she was in the hospital, my brother Earl planned to go to South Dakota for pheasant hunting. As Mom lay in her hospital bed, I was on the phone trying to be a mediator. Dad wanted to come up to South Dakota also, but we didn't think it would work. So I had to ask Earl to ask Dad not to come. This was very hard on Earl and I regret that choice, but at the time it seemed the only solution. Dad begged to come see her and did make one trip up.

Mom's recovery was speedy, except for a staph infection, which kept her in the hospital an extra seventeen days. But one day after surgery, she was in little pain. I am convinced our prayers were answered and she had a healing touch from God. I was able to take off work and be with her most of the time. Wonderful friends who owned a van brought her back to Fairview, as she had to travel lying down.

Pearl had been taking care of Mom, and then Mary Jane and I went home for Thanksgiving to take over. We took Mom to the local restaurant for Thanksgiving dinner. I called and invited Dad to join us but he declined, so I purchased a gift certificate for him to eat a meal at the restaurant. I felt sorry for him. None of us girls saw him on that trip.

Dad stayed his distance, though he must have felt sad. But all of a sudden, my Mom was happy. The apartment she moved into was very nice, and she purchased a new couch and recliner. She was settling in and seemed to be at peace.

By now Mom was able to drive her car again. She came down to my place to complete her healing. We were having a beautiful warm winter in Texas and she was able to walk every day per her doctor's orders.

In December, we became a disintegrated family. My siblings stayed with their own families or friends in distant cities. Pearl was in South Dakota, Mary Jane in Tulsa, Earl in Seattle, and I in Texas.

For Christmas Day, Mom and I enjoyed dinner at a local restaurant. Dad would call now and then on the phone. As Mom did not want to visit with him all that much, I kept him updated on her progress.

While Mom was in Texas with me, Dad got really sick. He had a terrible cold that wasn't getting better, and it seemed like he had the flu too. He said he was very tired and weak. He was still having bad headaches, and now he reported high fevers as well. We just accepted the situation and went on to do our own things.

There was still the sleeper sofa in the house, but for whatever reason, Dad told me he spent a lot of time sleeping on the couch in his office.

Chapter 27

Reconciliation

It had been about four weeks, Dad still had his cold and he wasn't getting any better. Mom was making such good progress in her recovery that she determined that she needed to go home to see about Dad.

In early January 1997, Mom took off for home. She was very apprehensive about the future; what could happen now? A couple of times Dad had gone to the doctor, but the doctor thought the symptoms indicated the flu.

Arriving back in Fairview, she quickly realized how bad the situation was. My dad's sister, Mabel, had been staying with him most of the time. Now Mom helped take over. Eventually, she insisted that they go to the doctor again, and this time they drew blood for testing.

A few days later, on February 14th, Valentine's Day, Mom called me with the horrible test results. Dad had been diagnosed with Myelodysplasia, which is a rare disease of the blood.

After conversing with Mom, I then called the doctor and learned more about the disease. The doctor did not know how long Dad had been sick; neither could he determine the long term prognosis. It is a mysterious disease in which the blood cells become abnormal. The patient can become very anemic, with headaches, fatigue, and weakened immunity. *One thing was certain, he would not get better; he would die.*

My heart and head were spinning. How could this be? My dad was supposed to live to be a hundred. His dad had lived to old age. Our whole family expected the same thing. Even though I had often wondered how I would deal with my father in his old age, I was not ready for this!

The doctor said there would be up and down days, and we would never know from one minute to the next how long he would live. He could be fine and five minutes later be gone.

Because of this uncertainty, the doctor told us never to leave him alone, so Mabel and Mom took turns staying by his side. Mom would usually stay at the house during the day and then go home to her apartment at night. It all seemed so strange.

I went home the first weekend after hearing the news. Dad was sleeping on the floor. I immediately pulled out the sleeper sofa and made it into a nice bed, but the next day when I came back to the house, it had been closed up and he was on the floor again. My heart broke. My dad was sick and he was sleeping on the floor! I called the deacons at church and they helped me purchase a bed for Dad. It was delivered to the house in a couple of hours.

I went home every weekend after that, just to be there. Dad and I did not talk much. His health was never mentioned.

Mom was totally confused as to why Dad would not communicate with her. She wanted to know what he was thinking. But as he lay there on his bed and she sat in a chair beside him in the bedroom, he did not talk about the things she hoped he would. He did not bring up their past life together, good or bad, nor did he talk about the future. He remained silent.

Dad recovered from the flu and cold. The doctor explained that his immunity was down from the disease and therefore it took a long time to get over something.

When visitors came to see Dad, they would comment, "He looks well enough." When you looked at him, he didn't necessary look like a sick person, as he was of a large stature and a little on the heavy side. They didn't see, how after they left, that Dad was exhausted and he would immediately go to his bed and lie down.

The doctor decided to put Dad on some drugs that had to be given by an injection. One time I drove him to the doctor's office to get his dosage. He was surprisingly cooperative with everything, even polite. But it was so awkward as we rode in the car together, side by side. My strong father was weak. He was big, and I felt so small, yet I was the one in charge. It bothered me being in such close proximity, when I was used to keeping him at a distance. I was more comfortable being in the presence of a threatening man, the only father I had ever known. Now I felt exposed, naked and scared, seeing him so vulnerable. Everything was backwards.

Sometimes Dad got raging fevers. The doctor had instructed Mom to take him directly to the hospital when his temperature got too high. This happened twice in the next couple of weeks. On one such trip she had a car accident on the way to the hospital. Her nerves were frayed. She was months from having back surgery, had made a major change in moving to her own apartment and now she was dealing with something none of us could have imagined.

Dad was in the hospital for the second time the weekend of March 23rd. I called Earl and highly suggested that he plan a trip to come see Dad. It didn't look good. As I prepared to leave, Dad sat up in bed and we hugged. He told me in a quivering voice, "Times are uncertain now, please come home as often as you can." That was the first and only time my father acknowledged his illness to me.

The next weekend was my birthday, March 30th and also Easter. I remember leaving the hospital on Sunday for a couple hours and going shopping with Mom. I collect Delph ceramic and I hurriedly ran into a couple of antique shops to see if I could find something from the town of Enid. I spotted a Delph couple about five inches high and I really liked the coloring on them. But they seemed to be priced a little high, so I left them in the cabinet. (Exactly one year later I was in Enid again. I was still hoping to find the pieces. While my family waited in the car, I quickly walked into the antique store and went directly to the cabinet where I had seen them. Thrilled they were still there, I purchased the two pieces at a reduced price. The pieces are a constant reminder of my last days with my father.)

The next week I left for Oklahoma on Friday, April 4th. I grabbed a few clothes as usual, but this time I wished I had taken more. Mom, Mary Jane and Earl were at the hospital when I arrived. Pearl arrived shortly.

At this point it seemed as though God was walking every step of the way with our family, because we all grouped together at once. Pearl had planned on coming a week later, but changed plans at the last minute. Earl had arrived on Thursday. Dad had had a good day and as Earl approached his room, Dad walked out to greet him. That was quite a surprise to Earl, because just a few days earlier I had told him that Dad was very sick and almost bedridden. This was the nature of the illness; the patient could appear healthy.

I believe Dad was determined to live until he saw Earl. For days he had been asking, "When will Earl be here?" As soon as Earl arrived, Dad's condition went downhill fast.

Friday night he was plainly getting worse, losing the strength even to get out of bed. Our family decided to keep someone with Dad continuously and we took turns standing watch by his side. Mom came in and out of the room. She has been on anti-depressant medicine for years, and they seemed to dull her emotions. She acted numb, not once crying or acting distressed. Nonchalantly, she would sit at the foot of his bed. (Her demeanor was nothing new. I had watched my mother through the years go from the extreme of almost a death cry in heartbreak, to not being able to shed a tear.)

Before our eyes, Dad was becoming a quiet and gentle person. *He was so nice to us.* We had never known our father as we were observing him now. He took everything in stride and never got upset. The "old Dad" used to get angry at nurses and at anything when things didn't go as he thought they should. I had seen his behavior in hospitals in previous years. Now as he lay there in bed with an oxygen mask on and tubes in his arms, he did not complain. His mouth would get so very dry and we gave him water through a straw. If it spilled, he would say, "That's OK."

We fixed up beds in an activity room on the same floor. Mom, Mary Jane and Earl each had a single bed, and Pearl made up a bed on the floor. I stayed with Dad all night in a recliner right beside the bed. Around four or five in the morning Pearl came in and I left to get a little nap.

On Saturday, we realized Dad was not going to leave the hospital this time. We made arrangements for a friend to come in and have Dad sign a living will. That was hard to do, as we were acknowledging to our father that we knew he was dying.

Dad told the visiting ministers that he was at peace and was ready to die.

Saturday night the hospital staff would not allow us to sleep in the activity room, so we rented a motel room that was close by. I don't remember whether any of us even slept there; I think it was just used for taking showers. Our family was knitted together and we could not be apart.

I spent the night in the recliner. Pearl wanted to be close by too, so she put two chairs together and made a bed. The other family members wandered in and out all night. For some reason, the hospital staff constantly took blood samples from Dad for testing. They'd wake him up in the wee hours of morning, put him in a wheelchair and haul him off. It seemed to cause him distress and pain every time. Even though we knew there had to be a medical reason for this, it hurt and puzzled us to see him put through it. When a person is dying, why does the staff have to cause any more anguish? Eventually, they had taken so much blood from him, that they began having trouble drawing any more. Sometimes they would have a different nurse come in to help, and other times they just gave up.

Dad's fever raged, and he sweat so heavily that his gown and sheets got soaking wet. The staff had to change his sheets every forty-five minutes. We could see that he was miserable. Pearl gently wiped his face and arms. One time he told her softly, "That's so soothing."

Can you imagine what we kids went through as we heard Dad's kind words to us? It was the best and worst time that a person could endure in life. Here was our father showing so much love to us. It just flowed. But this wonderful new man was dying right before our eyes.

Sunday morning, Dad said he felt good; for lunch he had a liquid meal. I will always remember feeding him red jello and gazing at the peaceful expression on his face. Some of the deep lines had relaxed, and his green eyes had lost their wild glare.

In the afternoon, Mom and I left to get something to eat. Mary Jane was resting outside the room. Then Dad suddenly got sicker; his temperature spiked in another fever. Earl and Pearl sat by him holding his hand and wiping the sweat from his body. The staff wheeled him away for an EKG, and then returned him to the room.

Things started happening fast. A nurse came in and quickly took the blood from his IV tree. Another nurse came in, and then another. They seemed to swarm over him. They tilted his bed head down and brought in a heart monitor. Pearl told Earl, "It looks serious—you'd better get the others." Mom and I had returned and were hovering outside the room. We hurried in to squeeze between the nurses and stand by his bed. One nurse kept trying to get his blood pressure…nothing…another nurse tried...nothing. A nurse told Pearl, "Here, hold the oxygen mask on tight to his face," which she did, also wiping his head. Another nurse injected shots into his IV…it didn't work.

"I'm sorry," she said. "I'll try again, but this is the last thing we can do. If you have anything to say to him, you better say it now."

Then the nurses left the room.

Pearl took her place at the head of the bed, wiping his brow, and Earl stood at the foot with Mary Jane, with Mom on one side and Mabel and me on the other. Seeing all of us crying and telling him good-bye, Dad asked "Why are you all so serious? Do you know something I don't know?"

Pearl said, "Dad, it is serious"

"And am I forgiven?" he asked. We replied, "Yes, yes, a million times over." Pearl told him, "Remember what you told me yesterday? 'If I can live, Praise be to God, but if not, I have that anchor in Jesus.'"

Dad said, "There'll be no sorrows there."

Mom took his hand and said, "I'm going to miss you." Dad then raised himself up, still hooked up to all of his tubes, and gave her a hug, patting her shoulder and saying, "Oh, sweetheart."

I rubbed his arm. "Dad, thank you for teaching me about books and sharing with me your love of books and travel." He smiled at me and then turned to his beloved son. "Earl, carry on with what I have taught you."

Our cousin Judy and her husband Steve came in. They were on their way to church, but turned to come to the hospital instead. They said a beautiful prayer. At that moment, their prayer seemed like a gift from God himself. I glanced out the window and noticed the sun was setting.

God had just given us an incredible miracle, to have us all there, encircling his bed and speaking our love for him while he was still conscious. Our family was witness to a reconciliation that we could not have imagined.

But it was not yet his time to go. His heart rate and blood pressure rallied. The nurses came in to check him, and then informed us, "He has a strong heart!"

Soon it was 7:00, then 8:00 and then 9:30 p.m., and he kept getting stronger.

We traded off spending the night with Dad.

I went almost totally without sleep the last few days at the hospital. Nothing but God's strength and grace could have gotten me through with so little sleep. We talked about it. It was another miracle.

Chapter 28

I Need Thee

Monday, we had new decisions to make. Earl, Pearl and Mary Jane were all scheduled to leave. I was supposed to have gone the previous day. Earl canceled his airline flight, Mary Jane left at ten a.m. and Pearl around noon.

The staff had decided to put a stent under his collarbone at 5:30 p.m. At 4:30 he asked me what time it was—he seemed ready to do the surgery. I think he thought it would help him get better.

As they took him away, he seemed cheerful, and we called out, "We'll see you when you get back!"

What was to be a short procedure turned into a lengthy wait, and we became anxious and concerned and asked where Dad was. We then found out they had put him in another room and hadn't told us.

As Mom, Earl and I hurried to his room we were reminded sharply of what the doctor had stated a few days ago: "He could rally and live for quite a while. Or he could die, just like that." Now it was obvious, we were losing Dad. He was very sick again, lying flat and sweating profusely. The nurses were constantly changing his IV. He was going through them so fast the nurse would bring in six bottles at a time. She filled the wastebasket with boxes and bottles and I got her another wastebasket.

By ten p.m. Dad was really suffering. He kept trying to take off his oxygen mask, which looked like it cut into his face. His lips were bleeding from the dry oxygen. He seemed to fight for each breath he took. We learned that he'd had no painkiller since 2:00 p.m., and we asked for more and more morphine, until the nurse said, "That's too much!" But our family discussed it, and agreed, we didn't want to see our father suffer anymore.

At some point I said, "I want his hand to be held every minute," and so it was. If I couldn't be holding it, another family member or friend did.

Between 10:30 p.m. and 3:30 a.m. Tuesday, Dad talked constantly. Some things we could understand but most words we could not. The mask made it very difficult. I wish I could have understood every last word that he spoke to us. At one point we heard him say, "I want to go to the hills and lie down and rest."

Oh, Dad, you suffered so in your life. I can understand your desire to rest!

At 3:30 a.m. Earl and I asked for more pain relief and then by 4:00 a.m. Dad became silent except for a groan with each breath he took.

Sometime between 4 a.m. and 8 a.m. as I was lying in the recliner beside his bed, I heard a familiar voice, a voice that I had heard a hundred times, humming a tune in a way that only my dad did. Sometimes, instead of saying the words to a song, he would sing, "Da, da, da, da, da, da." Now I heard those syllables sung to the tune of the song, *I Need Thee Every Hour.*

I need Thee every hour, Most gracious Lord;
No tender voice like Thine Can peace afford.

(chorus) I need Thee, oh, I need Thee;
Every hour I need Thee;
O bless me now, my Saviour!
I come to Thee.

I need Thee every hour, Stay Thou near by;
Temptations lose their pow'r When Thou art nigh.

(chorus)

I need Thee every hour, In joy or pain;
Come quickly and abide, Or life is vain.

(chorus)

I need Thee every hour, Teach me Thy will;
And Thy rich promises In me fulfill

(chorus)

I need Thee every hour, Most Holy One;
Oh, make me Thine indeed, thou blessed Son.

(chorus) I need Thee, oh, I need Thee;
Every hour I need Thee;
O bless me now, my Saviour!
I come to Thee.

Then immediately, Dad became totally and completely silent.

Oh, Dad, how God was comforting you at this very moment in your life. All your heart was at peace, and God was calling you ever so gently to come home. A place where you had questioned so many times in your life: If you would go to Heaven. A place you wanted to go so badly. Now the time was drawing near when He would take you in His arms and give you the Love you so craved.

Earl and I made calls to the family to return. We sat at his bedside all day while relatives and friends drifted in and out of the room.

In the evening God once again allowed Earl to be at the right place at the right time. He had planned to eat dinner at a certain sit-down restaurant, but it was closed when it was supposed to be open. Earl grabbed a fast bite to eat somewhere, and then quickly returned.

Just as he walked in the door, he looked at the heart monitor and said, "It's changing rapidly." I rushed to get Mom, who had been resting in a waiting room nearby. The three of us encircled the bed. Earl on one side, Mom sitting at the foot of the bed and me on the other side. With no one else around, there we were, quietly surrounding each other, but with our own thoughts. With no sound except the beeping of the monitor, there seemed to be a sacred stillness to the night.

With pride, I watched the tremendous strength of my brother. Side by side, the oldest child and the youngest child, as God had planned it to be. It would have been too difficult for Pearl and Mary Jane.

I didn't want my dad to leave us, but I also had not asked God to let him stay. And now as his pulse was slowing down with every minute that passed, I kept saying, "*No, no, no.*"

I loved my dad and I knew from this moment on I would not be able to tell him again until we meet in Heaven. Slowly,

slowly, we watched, touching him...until finally, he took his last breath, and the sound of the monitor told us his life was over. The time was 11:05 p.m. on the 8th day of April, 1997.

Earl and I went to the pay phone in the waiting room and called our sisters. Pearl had just gotten home to South Dakota. She jotted down a little poem that went in Dad's obituary.

Dearest Daddy.
You have left us
For the mansions
In the blest
We will miss you.
Oh! We'll miss you
But to Jesus,
We'll let you go
...to rest.
Although life for you
Had its many struggles
Yet to the Lord
You wanted to remain true
Your last days were
Special days
Of love and gentleness...
We will remember you.

In the span of less than one year Pearl lost her father, her father-in-law and her mother-in-law. She made many trips back and forth from South Dakota to Oklahoma that year. Now, she got a couple of hours sleep, and then she and Frank set out again for Oklahoma.

The typical funeral arrangements had to be made. Earl, Pearl and I met with church cemetery people to pick out a plot. When we got to the place we had selected on paper, I said it was perfect. It was beside a tree, and looking to the east we saw cattle grazing, and to the south we saw the rolling hills. We cried as we remembered his last words. After a lifetime of strife, our father got to "lie down in those green hills and rest."

A difficult and sad task was to pick out a headstone. Our family came to an agreement as to what should go on the headstone quite quickly. On the front we had stalks of wheat engraved on each side of an open book. His name and dates were written on the pages of the book. On the other side was the song title, *I Need Thee Every Hour* and the names of family members.

We took Mom to pick out flowers for the casket spray. She picked yellow daises and purple Japanese iris. Those would be the only flowers allowed in the church sanctuary. A few arrangements stood in the entrance hall of the church.

I had to go buy clothes for the funeral service. Fairview was a small town so my choices were limited, but I was able to find a black dress with a white collar and black shoes.

Friday morning we went to the funeral home. I have never seen my dad look so handsome, as he did lying in the casket. His beard had been trimmed neatly, and his hair combed. Maybe it was the tranquility in him.

Mary Jane approached the casket, looked at her dad and then walked back to where our family was huddled. She turned to me and spoke the saddest words a child could utter, "I have never felt peace like I do now." For the first time in her life, she was able to go to her father, and not feel any of the condemnation that had consumed their relationship.

It is traditional in the church to have a "remembrance" the evening before the funeral service. Our family, including all relatives and friends, were served dinner in the church fellowship hall and then different people spoke of their memories of Dad.

The funeral was on Saturday afternoon at 2:00 p.m. on the 12th of April. It was a very cold and windy day.

The family and relatives all gathered downstairs at church, and then we walked upstairs and into the sanctuary while the congregation sang *Rock of Ages*, one of Dad's favorite songs.

During the service the minister told the audience the miracle of our special song, the song that confirmed to us that Dad had relinquished his soul and spirit to the God above.

The choir sang the song, *I Need Thee Every Hour.*

On a return trip home a few weeks later, as I drove by the house I was crying and talking to God. I whispered, "God, it *must* have been a miracle when Dad sang that song." In my spirit I felt an immediate reply, "It *was* a miracle."

To my family, the song is like a gift that we can cling to whenever we think of Dad. After such a tormented life, when it was all over, Dad said, "I come to Thee."

Top: Mom middle left surrounded by Michelle, Earl, Pearl, Mary Jane and other family members in SD. Dad, alone, on right side, 1995.

Bottom: Dad in his bedroom with his beloved books.

Top: Dad's headstone.

Bottom: Mary Jane, Earl, Elaine and Pearl at home preparing for estate sale.

Postscript 1

In August of 1998, I received a call from Jim that Bob had passed away. He had just read the obituary in the newspaper. Immediately I called his daughter Tiffany to give her my regards, and asked if I could get together with her. We arranged to meet at Bob's house in Wichita sometime shortly after the funeral.

On a Saturday morning I drove up to the house where I used to live. *What a strange feeling*, I thought, as so many memories flooded my mind. I got out of the car, and walked hesitantly to the door. How would Tiffany receive me? She was still a child when I divorced her father.

Going up the steps, I paused and lingered, while noticing everything in the front yard. I wanted to see if there were any plants in the flower bed that I might have planted, or any similarities. I wanted to latch onto any evidence of my life.

With my heart pounding, I knocked on the door. Too soon, the door opened and I stepped inside the small entry room with the beige tiled floor that I had picked out. I greeted Tiffany, but froze right inside the door. *I could not move.* I had a difficult time concentrating on a proper greeting, as my eyes shifted from one side of the room to the other. Nothing had changed! A time capsule, that's what it was! Everything looked exactly as it had when I moved out more than seventeen years ago. I could not believe it. As I deliberately proceeded throughout the house I entered a state of shock.

In the living room, *Life* magazines from 1979 to 1981 sat on the coffee table. The same curtains were still on the windows, the same pictures on the wall. The same green and white striped towels hung on the rack in the bathroom. The same silk fern plant dangled over the sink.

The items of furniture I had taken, and one large picture, had been replaced with almost identical pieces.

I opened a closet door in the hallway. The same puzzles, games, and books, still sat in place on the shelves, just as I had stored them.

In the kitchen everything was the same, rugs on the floor, hand towels, and my antique dishes on the corner shelf. My decorating touches, candles and vases, were still where I had left them! I shuddered, absolutely stunned.

I wondered to myself, "What was Bob's purpose in leaving everything the same?" I had always assumed that another woman would move into the house. Apparently that had never happened.

After getting my mind back to the present, and trying to calm down the intense emotions I was feeling, I was able to sit down with Tiffany at the heavy oak dining room table, and get re-acquainted. She sat on one end with me on the side.

Tiffany shared how she'd thought I would be angry for the way she had treated me when she was a child. She told me she was concerned enough about our meeting, that she brought a friend along. As we visited, the friend wandered in and out of the room.

Growing up, Tiffany had been told that I was a bad person. "You had taken my Daddy away from my Mommy," she mused. We talked and she soon realized, listening to me, that the stories she had heard as a child were not true.

Later in the conversation she said, "I know you are telling the truth." She had not asked particular details, I was just providing some of the pieces of the puzzle she had never been able to put together. For instance, her parents were already divorced when Bob and I met. I had not taken her father away from her mother! And she was so glad to know that.

She spoke of her childhood memories, and revealed that she had really liked me, but she couldn't show me that love, because that would mean she was being disloyal to her mother. She had never had a relationship with her dad until he became ill.

The last few years he refused to take care of himself where his health was concerned. He wouldn't take diet instructions or medications as prescribed. It was like he was trying to die. He became a virtual recluse, closing out even his best friend Herb who had stood beside him so often, no matter how Bob treated him. To the end, Bob was angry and bitter.

Tiffany asked me, "Did you ever see my dad read a Bible?" No, I hadn't. "Well, let me show you, there are a dozen Bibles here." I sat down on the living room floor and scrutinized each one. Bookmarks and sales receipts showed that some had been purchased right after I filed for divorce.

She also wanted to know, "Did my father drink?" She showed me the dozens of unopened wine and liquor bottles in the house, shocked at how much a person could accumulate. Now we both wondered what the reason was for all of the alcohol. I had seen him with a drink only on rare occasions, with other people present in a social setting. Mostly this was with his sister Norma Jean, when she'd fix him a "whiskey sour."

The house was full of other items. He became not only a recluse but continued to hoard so many things that a person could not walk through the basement. I was not surprised. During our marriage he rebuffed my suggestion to throw anything away. I finally refused to clean the basement because of the empty boxes and bottles of every sort that he collected.

I told Tiffany how I would like to have the photographs that I had taken during our marriage, and she gave me permission to look for them. As I went through box after box I became concerned; I couldn't find even one of the family photos I sought. They had to be someplace! We started searching through the house. In the bedroom, hidden in the back of a chest of drawers, we found a small brown paper sack, neatly folded at the top with my name on it. Inside were the pictures of my family! We will never know why they were separated from the rest. Had he intended to give them to me some day?

My next question, "Have you ever seen a crocheted white bedspread with yellow flowers on it? It was made especially for me. When I left Bob, it was on the bed in the guest room." She hadn't seen it. We looked, but it seemed nowhere to be found. Finally, in the back of a closet, we discovered a box with my name written on it. Inside, wrapped in a garbage bag, was the beautiful bedspread. We discussed what Bob might have intended. Apparently he planned on me having it someday. But had I not been there, Tiffany might just have figured that I left it.

She also said I could take the big shiny oak dining room table and six upholstered chairs that I had wished for all so many years! Bob listed only two items in his will. One was the dining room table that he had willed to his grand-daughter, but she was too young to want it, and it was too large to store. The other was his clown collection that he had acquired during our marriage and which I loved; it was to go to his grandson.

To prepare for selling the house, Tiffany was going to have an estate sale. Cautiously I asked, "Can I come back for that?"

"Certainly," she replied. I heaved a sigh of relief that she would allow me once more to intrude.

As the day drew to a close and I prepared to leave, she asked me to forgive her for being so mean to me. There was no need to apologize. She had been placed in difficult situations, and I had always understood her behavior. Our day became one of tears, laughter and hugs.

Just before walking out the door, she let me in on one last shocker. In the nursing home where Bob was at the last, the nurses asked Tiffany, *"Who is Elaine?"* Bob was always calling for Elaine. "The nurses assumed he was calling for Tiffany's mother. They didn't know her name was Susan."

I wonder why he called my name—did he want to see me, did he have something to say, after all those many years?

I made an appointment with Tiffany to return a few weeks later, one week before the estate sale. That day, Tiffany let me in and then she left the house. I was alone and free to browse as long as I wanted. The tables were spread out with many keepsakes from when I resided there. As I picked up each item, the memories of our times together came flooding back. A glass dish with the Continental Trailways bus logo. Our vacation souvenirs. Shirts and matching neckties that I had purchased for Bob. My record albums! I spent all day amongst his (our) stuff, reminiscing, touching everything.

After a while I called Jim and invited him over. It was very strange, and I did not think he would come. But he did, and we made a stack of the things each of us wanted. Can you imagine the humor of buying things that you had already purchased? I bought a couple of wall pictures, the mirror that hung over the mantel, my old albums and some dishes. I found a red Christmas stocking with my name written in colorful sequins, but I refused to pay for that.

So it went and then it was time for a final good-bye to the house. We carried out the dining room set. I thought, "God gives back what has been taken from us, and in ways we never thought possible."

I had not intended ever to step inside that house again and had given up hope on getting back any of my photographs.

As I walked to my car I realized I was completing one chapter of my life.

Postscript 2

Jim and I continued to see each other on a regular basis for about a year after our divorce.

Later, after I moved away and I was not dating anyone, with the agreement that it be a platonic friendship, he came to see me, and I traveled to Wichita to visit him. We remained good friends.

We'd put on the country song that went something like this: "I want to dance with you, and I want to twirl you around the floor."

The song continued: "I just want to dance, and hold you in my arms once more." We felt the song was for us. And we would dance in the apartment, better than we ever danced married. The tension was gone, and the memories of our good days filled our heads. We had come full circle—dancing, as the sounds of good old country music filled the air.

Jim was planning to come see me in a month in Seattle, where I had recently moved from Texas a few months earlier. He was looking forward to visiting an old Navy base where he had shipped out while in the Navy. I was excited, as I knew that would make him happy, to reminisce about those days.

But on May 1st, 2002, I received a message to call one of Jim's daughters. In my heart I *knew* the reason. There could be no other, and I had known that dreaded call would come some day. But I wasn't ready for it yet.

She told me the sad news that Jim had died in his sleep in the early morning hours after celebrating a family birthday the previous evening and apparently feeling good. He had left the party a little early as he told them he wanted to get home to watch some special movie on television. It happened to have a Christian theme, but I don't remember the name of the program.

When she went to his apartment to check on him after a missed lunch date, she knew what she would find when she saw the newspaper still waiting to be picked up at the front door.

Still in bed, he had died peacefully, as his hands were folded under his head and the covers were pulled neatly up to his face. Jim had gotten his wish; he had always said that when it was his time, he wanted to go fast.

An open Bible lay on his coffee table.

His daughter sent me the tee shirt he was wearing. It was one I had purchased for him years ago on one of our cruises and he really liked it and wore it often.

With a move and a new job I wasn't able to attend his funeral. I had always imagined it to be a sad but joyous occasion, as that would have been his desire. Sure enough, they played his favorite secular songs, *King of the Road*, *Alley Cat* and *Milk Cow Blues*. I later listened to the service on tape.

I had sent a bouquet of seven red roses. It was placed right next to his casket. The card read: "A rose for each year we were together. I will miss you."

Epilogue

M y father obviously was aware of the traits that can be passed down from one generation to the next. In one of his notes he states:

> *Our fathers become a role model to us. Right or wrong we take from them traits etc., without being aware of it, only to wake up somewhere down the road, if we ever do. To break this seems impossible, but with God it is possible for no one can turn the course of nature but Jesus Christ.*

I know that his utmost desire was to live a Christ-driven life, and I feel certain that I do not know the half of the pain he suffered. For that, my heart aches. If only (as we always say), *somehow,* my dad could have conquered the demons that tormented him. I wanted to love him, and I did, but my love wasn't enough. I am thankful to God that I will have another chance to put my arms around my father when I see him in Heaven.

As you have read in my story, Bob hated his father, as did Bill. Jim did not use the word hate, as Bob and Bill did, but he definitely was hurt by the pain of his father's alcoholism. Each one of these men developed anger in them because of what they witnessed in their fathers.

My mother in her innocence married my dad, but could do nothing to ease his pain and suffering. I followed in her footsteps, only to realize that my desperate need to love, and be loved, caused me to fall in love with the wrong men. Sub-consciously, I was searching *for what I was familiar with.* I felt I had to fight to get approval and love, and that I had to sacrifice my happiness, in order to prove my love for others—the cycle never ended until Jesus came into my life. *He* made me whole, and made me realize what a true loving relationship really was.

Lyle eventually married again. As a result of that marriage, he was excommunicated from the Mennonite church. The church still considers me as his lawful wife. So as long as I am alive, he cannot be a member of the church.

I might also add that both my father and mother were excommunicated from the Mennonite church for a time. Both of them were later re-accepted. That means that out of my six immediate family members, five have gone through the process of church excommunication. My brother Earl and my sister Mary Jane have been expelled since their youth, but both lead solid Christian lives. Pearl and Mom remain true to their Christian Mennonite faith.

Carl passed away in November of 1995. In the summer of 1994, he started telling me how tired he was feeling. Sitting out in his patio, he would often comment that he was an ambitious person; that he had always been strong in his body, yet now he couldn't understand why he didn't have any energy. Determined to hold his marketing meetings as long as possible, he had to be driven back and forth as he got weaker in his body. Per my request for no communication between us, we never spoke. A request I regret. I would have liked to say good-bye. He continued to smoke to the last, suffering more because of it. He died while in the hospital. In an ironic twist, he died of the same rare blood disease my father did: myelodysplasia.

It was difficult to select pictures for the book of my time with Bob and Jim. You might take note of the sadness in my face during my marriage to Bob. I could find very few pictures of either of us smiling. And even less, of us taken together.... On the other hand, I had hundreds of Jim and myself smiling and happy. It was hard to whittle down the number of pictures of him. I wanted to fill the book with our happy times....

I pray that some woman will read this book and see herself. And that you will have the courage to change what you need to. *Never give up hope.* I was a victim, now I take responsibility and don't hold myself hostage because of my upbringing.

Don't let your past dictate who you are,
but let it be a part of who you become.

My desire is that the reader will find encouragement in my story to break unhealthy cycles, and to realize the joy that comes when you have an intimate relationship with Jesus Christ. He will ease your burden. He will bring you strength. Only God can keep you in complete peace and contentment.

I have accomplished much in writing this book, if my story will help someone that is reading it. God has been so good to me, and I feel truly blessed. I pray the same for you.

Early on, God gave me the following scripture verse, and I have held tight to it:

For the vision is yet for an appointed time, but at the end it shall speak, and not lie: though it tarry, wait for it; because it will surely come, it will not tarry. Habakkuk 2:3.

With this thought in mind, I now close another chapter of my life. May God bless you.

Appendix

Mennonite History

W anting to write a short article on the Mennonites, I was nonetheless stumped when it came to writing about where I came from. As I have stated, history is not my forte. *But then,* weeks before I planned to submit the manuscript for publishing, I found the following paper written by my father. Stunned at my find, it was just what I needed. I felt God's blessing on including this article, as it had always been my dad's lifelong desire to teach. (Some errors in verbiage, spelling and punctuation have been corrected.)

This is almost certainly a compilation of his lifelong studies of Mennonite history and genealogies. My father would be proud:

Mennonites, Mennonites, where do they all come from anyway. There are Mennonite Brethren, General Conference Mennonites, Church of God in Christ Mennonite, Old Mennonite, Old Order Mennonite, Reformed Mennonites, Old Colony Mennonites, Amish Mennonites, Evangelical Mennonite Brethren, Beachy Amish Mennonites, Krimmer Mennonite Brethren. There are also the related groups such as the Church of the Brethren, Brethren in Christ and the Hutterites, whose leader was Jacob Hutter. There are two distinct lines of Mennonites, the Swiss who come from

Switzerland, and the Alsac Loraine, and the Dutch, which come from Holland and Belgium. Some also come from Germany.

To understand the Mennonite faith one must go back to the faith in Jesus Christ, who died on the cross to atone for our sins and thus became our Saviour. When Jesus went to heaven he commanded his twelve apostles to go into all the world and teach and preach the gospel. So the faith of Jesus Christ was established by the apostles' teachings. In time these teachings became a written confession of faith. This confession consisted of twelve articles of faith, which became known as the apostles' creed. The early Christian Church used this creed as teaching of fundamental truth, and became known as the Apostolic Faith. Upon this faith Jesus Christ built his church, and the gates of hell shall not prevail against it. The faith that was once delivered to the saints (Jude 3). The first and only Christian church which was the universal (Catholic) church was the New Testament Church. History tells us that some in the years following the death of the apostles ceased to teach the whole truth and became worldly and took on new doctrines and lost the true faith. When infant baptism became a teaching and was practiced, those that followed the apostles faith rejected this form of baptism and were re-baptized. These people then were called Anabaptist, meaning re-baptized. Theliman J. Vanbracht who compiled the Martyrs Mirror in the year 1660, states that those who lived the apostles' faith through the centuries were at different times called by various names until the time of the Waldenses and the Anabaptists during the reformation of the fifteen hundreds.

It must be noted here that there were different groups of Anabaptists, almost anyone who rejected infant baptism was called Anabaptist. It must also be noted here that only those Anabaptists who had embraced the true faith are the ones referred to here in this article. Space does not permit to record the turmoil and confusion of these different groups. Anabaptists who were called heretics by the Roman Catholic (state church) were persecuted, and many died for the faith. Menno Simon joined the Anabaptists at this time in the year 1536, and was baptized. Menno Simon then became a faithful follower of Jesus Christ. He then taught from the scriptures with all diligence. He was ordained to the ministry in 1537 by Obbe Phillips. Menno was not the founder of the Mennonite Church. He accepted what he believed to be the true faith. He did much writing and teaching to help his fellow brethren to be delivered from the untruth. In time his followers became known as Mennonites, because of his outstanding leadership. Not all was victory, though. Even before he died in 1561 the church had divided into three distinct groups, known as the Flemish, Friesians, and the Waterlander. The distinctions were according to the area where they lived. The Flemish were of Flanders, Belgium, the Friesians were of Friesland, Holland, and the Waterlanders of Amsterdam, Holland. The Waterlanders were the group which John Smyth belonged to, who later founded the Baptist Church in England in 1611.

From this point forward the Mennonites in this article will refer only to the Dutch Mennonites. The Swiss and south German Mennonites are another history. The Swiss and south German Mennonites came to America as early as 1683 settling at Germantown, Pennsylvania. The Dutch Mennonites moved eastward into north Germany and Danzig, known as West Prussia. The Vistula River area between Danzing and Warsaw was home to many Mennonite people for 400 years from 1545 to 1945. Some Mennonites moved to what was then known as Poland-Russia around 1765. About the same year Catherine the Great issued the manifesto offering freedom of religion and exemption from military conscription. Many Germans moved from Germany to the Volga area and also to the Black Sea area, these Germans were not Mennonites, but were mostly Lutheran and

Catholic. The first groups of Mennonites left West Prussia around 1789 settling along the Deniper River just north of the Black Sea. The first settlement was Chortitzia. Later some moved along the Molotshna River. These Mennonites then became known as the Molotshna people. The others that moved to Poland-Russia near the city of Ostrog in the year 1802, which is Russia today, were known as Ostrogers. They had such common names as Schmidt, Nightengale, Unruh, Koehn, Wedel, Becker, Vogth, Boeths, Jantz etc. While the common names among the Molotshna were Penner, Toews, Wiens, Wichert, Ensz, Kliewer, Lowen, Goosen, Barkman, Cornelsen, Wohlgemuth, etc.

The Mennonites that moved from West Prussia and Brandenburg were the Friesians, the Flemish and Alt Flemish. Perhaps all of the Mennonites who now live in Major County, Oklahoma are of Flemish or Alt Flemish decent. The many different groups as we know them today did not exist in Russia before 1814. In those years most all Mennonites were identified very much alike with the same fundamental beliefs.

The first major split or division occurred under the leadership of Class Reimer in the year 1814. He believed the Mennonites had lost out, or decayed to where he could not fellowship with the old church called Grosse Gemiende (the big church). Class Reimer's followers were then called the Kline Gemiende (small church). Then in 1860 another break came with the Big or Old Church. The leaders of this group were namely Classen, Cornelson, Reimer, and others. This movement came about through the Baptists' influence and also a Lutheran Minister, Eduard Wust. They also felt the Old Church had become decayed and had left the teachings of Menno Simon and the true faith. Through the strong Baptist influence immersion baptism was accepted.

The Mennonite people lived in what was called the Mennonite Commonwealth. They were not subject to

Russian law or military service. They had total religious freedom, however, under the watchful eye of the Russian government. So when the Mennonite Brethren withdrew from the Old or Big Church, they considered themselves to be Mennonite-Baptists, as they related so closely to the Baptists. The Russians had questions about being Baptists or Mennonites, saying that the Baptists were under Russian law. Only the Mennonites had total exemption from military service, and religious freedom. In time the Russian government reorganized them as Mennonites, regardless of their Baptist connections. So instead of being called Mennonite-Baptist they called themselves Mennonite Brethren. After 1874 when 18,000 Mennonites came to America the Old or Big Church organized into what is known as the General Conference of Mennonites. The Krimmen Mennonite Brethren, under the leadership of Jacob Wiebe separated from the Kleine Gemiende in Russia, but has later merged with the Mennonite Brethren Church.

Coming back to the Mennonites the forgoing groups were the Molotschna Mennonites. The others that came to America in 1874 came from the villages of Karswalde and Antanafka. These were the Ostrog Mennonites. They were called Ostrogers, because they lived near the Russian town of Ostrog. Some of this group joined the Church of God. These were the Unruhs, Koens, Schmidts, Beckers, Nightengales, Vogths, Jantzs, Boehs etc. John Holdeman was the leader of this church. He came to Kansas from Wayne County, Ohio. John had withdrawn himself from the Old Mennonites there because he felt they were too lax in teaching the true faith. John Holdeman was of the Swiss Mennonite lineage. His ancestors came to Pennsylvania in 1727 from Bern, Switzerland. It might be noted here that of the Old or Big Church in Russia had not separated or withdrawn themselves as was the case with the Mennonite Brethren, Kliene, Gremde, and Krimmer Mennonite Brethren. When many of the Ostrog Mennonites joined themselves to John Holdeman, it was the only group that linked themselves to the Swiss Mennonite faith. This was known as the Old Mennonite Church of America, having settled at Germantown, Pennsylvania, in the year 1683.

The Mennonites of Major County, Oklahoma, The General Conference Mennonite, Mennonite Brethren, and The Church of God in Christ Mennonite are all of Flemish decent and at one time or another all embodied the Mennonite Confession of Faith as it was affirmed at Dortrecht, Holland on April 21, 1632, consisting of eighteen articles of faith. Today some Mennonites no longer teach or practice the Mennonite faith, but have aligned themselves to mainstream American denominations, therefore having lost their identity. However, there are still those that believe in Menno Simon's interpretation of the word of God and live and teach the apostolic faith as taught by the apostles.

In 1760 these people were all one in faith, all being of the Groninger Old Flemish Mennonite Church. They lived at a place called Wintersdorf on the west side of the Vistula River in West Prussia, and surrounding villages. In 1763 around thirty-five families moved 125 miles west to the Newmark area along the Netz River under the rule of Frederick the Great. Forming the village of Brenkenshofwalde, Frantzel in the state of Brandenburg. After the year of 1802 a number of these families moved to Ostrog and formed the villages of Karlswolde, and Antonafka. Some of these later became Holdemans and General Conference Mennonites. Large numbers moved to the Molotshna and formed the village of Gnadenfeld under the leadership of Minister Lange. This is where the Mennonite Brethren Church began in 1860. After the immigration of 1874 the name Flemish was dropped. The people settled around Hillsboro, Kansas forming the Ebenfelt Mennonite Brethren Church. The Ostrog people formed the Canton Church. John also preached at the Gnadenaw Church, (Krimmen Mennonite Brethren) and others at Hillsboro, but very few if any joined up with him of this group. This is a very short history of our Mennonite heritage. The Holdemans are still the Old Flemish, while the Mennonite Brethren are the Mennonite-Baptists.

To those who have often asked me "where did you all come from and what is the difference," I have explained it the best I could in a very condensed form. If I have misrepresented anything I am open for correction.

Ben Schmidt